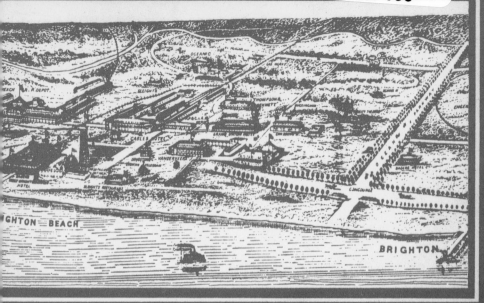

Coney Island in 1879

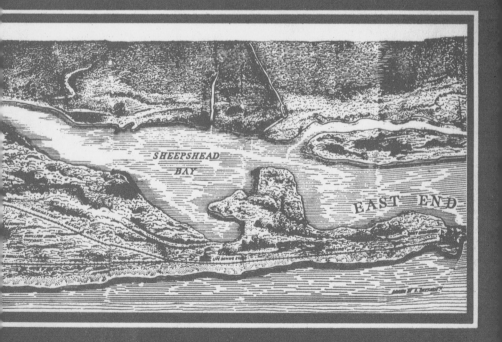

GOOD OLD CONEY ISLAND

EDO McCULLOUGH

GOOD OLD
CONEY ISLAND

A Sentimental Journey Into The Past

THE MOST

RAMBUNCTIOUS •	SCANDALOUS •	RAPSCALLION
SPLENDIFEROUS •	PUGNACIOUS •	SPECTACULAR
ILLUSTRIOUS •	PRODIGIOUS •	FROLICSOME
		ISLAND
		ON EARTH

CHARLES SCRIBNER'S SONS NEW YORK

ACKNOWLEDGMENTS

I have to thank the following for copyright material quoted:

Doubleday and Company, Inc., and Don Marquis for the lines from "the song of mehitabel."

The Scott Meredith Literary Agency, Inc., and P. G. Wodehouse, for the quotation from Mr. Wodehouse.

I should like also to acknowledge the following sources:

Coney Island, an Illustrated Guide to the Sea, Season of 1883, Containing an Account of a Ramble on the Beach by a Pleasure Party, besides Local Information (Truax & Co., 253 Fulton Street, Brooklyn, New York) for the account of the incident reported on page 34.

Autobiography of a Thief, recorded by Hutchins Hapgood (Fox, Duffield and Company, 1903) for the quotation on page 63.

"How Salvator Won, and Other Recitations" by Ella Wheeler Wilcox (W. B. Conkey Co., 1895) for the lines quoted on page 136.

Munsey's Magazine (September, 1901) and Guy Wetmore Carryl for the two stanzas of Mr. Carryl's poem on page 315.

The Independent (August 8, 1907) for the paragraph reprinted from Maxim Gorky's article "Boredom," on page 315.

Affectionately dedicated to
the memory of my mother, the former
KATHRYN A. TILYOU,
a daughter of Coney Island pioneers

A PREFATORY NOTE

SOME men collect match-book covers, others go around the world in amphibious jeeps. I collect material about Coney Island. It is a harmless vice, but habit-forming. I have been doing it now for upwards of twenty years, and I suppose that by now I could be certified as a monomaniac.

I can, however, claim a certain logic for my foolishness. I come by my affection for Coney naturally enough: it is in the marrow of my bones. One of Coney's earliest settlers, Peter Tilyou, was my grandfather; one of Coney's greatest showmen, George C. Tilyou, was my uncle; my father owned and operated a dozen shooting galleries at Coney and was the first to introduce moving targets as a greater challenge for his customers; today my brothers and cousins are still hip-deep in Coney entertainments. On top of all this, one winter's day in 1935 I went up to the attic to get a sled for one of my nephews, and I came upon an old scrapbook that had been started by my grandfather in 1876. It was pasted fat with clippings from newspapers long since dead and forgotten, but every clipping fascinated me. That book is the cornerstone of my collection.

Every collector has, I suppose, his own ground-rules. I have only one. The item must in some fashion, however tenuous, relate to Coney. If it is something about Ethel Barrymore or Buster Keaton or Fatty Arbuckle or Clark & McCullough or Nora Bayes and Jack Norworth, I collect it, for I recall that these and many others played the New Brighton Theatre at Coney in the days when vaudeville made powerful magic. If it has to do with Sophie Tucker or Al Jolson or Bert Williams or the Avon Comedy Four, into my ragbag it goes, for they were among the favorites who played Fred Henderson's Music Hall on Surf Avenue. I imagine Phil Silvers was gratified, in March, 1956, to be thrice honored by the Academy of Television Arts and Sciences; lost in my gentle madness, I, when I read about his achievement in the newspapers, was only reminded that he got his start in show business at thirteen, when Gus Edwards heard him singing on the beach at Coney and booked him for his Kiddie Revue, then playing at Henderson's. (Henderson himself, as I had long since noted in my collection, went west to found the Orpheum Theatre in San Francisco, launch a vaudeville circuit, combine with the Keith-Albee interests, and lay the groundwork for what is today the RKO motion-picture business.) In any event, the item about Phil Silvers went into my collection.

And so did any item about George Burns who, when *he* was thirteen, was the star performer of the Peewee Quartet, four youngsters who sang on the beach of Coney, and on the trolley cars to and from Coney, and anywhere else where they could find an audience.

But after a time, while some men were still fitting together their jig-saw puzzles and others were polishing their classic sports cars, I grew dissatisfied with my collection of clippings. There were, I came to realize, gaps, riddles, unanswered questions about Coney's past; and I wanted to fill them, solve them, get them answered. I had to go back to the beginning.

Now when you go to a Hall of Records, for example, and ask to look at yellowing documents, you are likely to be met, in your turn, with another, entirely reasonable question: "Why are you bothering me? What do you want this information for?" I was obliged to manufacture an excuse. I said that I was writing a book.

It is amazing how many doors will open, how many courtesies will be extended, how many skeletons will be eagerly hustled out of closets in response to this magic formula. As a technique for adding to my collection, it had only one flaw. Sooner or later, the word got around that I was writing a book and presently, to my chagrin, I had to face the further question: "How's your book coming along?" The only way I found out of *that* dilemma was to write this book.

I have enjoyed it. I have also tried to make it as accurate as I know how. This has entailed going to original sources whenever possible. It has meant further that I have had the considerable satisfaction of turning up material that no one—so far as I know—has ever come up with before. For making available the town records of Gravesend (which until 1894 included Coney Island), I am obliged to James Kelly, Brooklyn's Deputy County Clerk and Borough Historian, and to James Waters, his assistant; Miss Marion D. Koenen, assistant librarian of the New York State Library, found for me the transcripts of two investigations; without this material the second and third chapters could not have been written. For most of the other chapters I have had recourse to contemporary newspapers and magazines, and principally the *Brooklyn Argus* and *Eagle;* the *New York Times, World, Tribune, Herald,* and *Sun; McClure's, Munsey's, Everybody's, Scribner's, The Century,* and *Harper's Weekly.* Stiles's *History of Brooklyn* was invaluable. The other sources, since mine is not a work that pretends to scholarship, I shall say simply are too numerous to mention. I must express my gratitude to the staffs of the New York and Brooklyn Libraries, and especially to the staff of the Newspaper Division of the New York Public Library; my thanks are also due Miss Helen Ruskell of the New York Society Library.

There are, fortunately, many pictures to enliven the pages that follow. I want to express my special gratitude to Francis K. Moore for so graciously making his unique collection of early Coney Island photographs available to me. I am immeasurably indebted to him.

Readers will notice that, on occasion, the names of some of my near relatives crop up during the course of my story. In order to save myself embarrassment, I have maintained the studied pretense that these people were not in fact related to me.

Brooklyn, N. Y., 1957   Edo McCullough

We live for those who love us,
For those whose hearts are true,
For the God that reigns above us,
And the good that we may do.

VERSE CARVED ON THE BELLS OF THE
SHRINE CHURCH OF OUR LADY OF SOLACE,
CONEY ISLAND.
THE BELLS RANG FROM THE CHIMES TOWER
OF STEEPLECHASE PARK PRIOR TO THE FIRE
THAT DESTROYED THE PARK IN 1907.

At first there was only the wind and the waves, endlessly rocking, and Coney Island was a wild tangle of scrub and great shifting dunes.

The Most--

FOR three-quarters of a century Coney Island has been the most famous seaside resort in the world. In that time, like anything living, growing, and changing, it has passed through several different stages; but at Coney, where the abiding talent is for the exaggerated and the superlative, the changes have been so violent and complete as to obliterate, each time, the memory of what was there before. On one shorefront lot at Coney, for example, there has been in succession an untidy tangle of bathhouses, a vast casino, an arena in which were fought three world's championship heavyweight prizefights, the most beautiful outdoor amusement park in the world, a freak show, a parking lot, and—today—New York City's brand-new aquarium. Yet while all these changes have been encompassed in the span of a man's lifetime, nothing is remembered of this stretch of real estate save that yesterday it was a parking lot and today it is an aquarium. Coney's day-before-yesterday is incredible today.

Coney has been by turns a slow-measured, sea-tossed, delightful wilderness; a raffish and raucous boom-town; a popular hang-out for criminals; a fashionable watering place for the

3

rich and well-born; a gay and rollicking playground for the
well-to-do middle class; and a gaudy, tinselled nickel empire
for the masses; and it is still undergoing change. Its complete
obliteration as a seaside resort has been freely predicted, increasingly often of late, but the prudent gambler would do
well not to bet on that possibility. For Coney today is rather
like Don Marquis's sterling cat Mehitabel, whose memorable
song runs:

> *i have had my ups and downs*
> *but wotthehell wotthehell*
> *yesterday sceptres and crowns*
> *fried oysters and velvet gowns*
> *and today i heard with bums*
> *but wotthehell wotthehell*

> *my youth i shall never forget*
> *but there s nothing i really regret*
> *there s a dance in the old dame yet*
> *toujours gai toujours gai* *

Unlike Mehitabel, Coney is no snob, but there is no doubt that,
like Mehitabel, Coney is still very gay.

In the course of its fabulous history, something like two
billion people—if repeaters are included—have paid a visit to
Coney, and something like two hundred imitations have sprung
up all over the world, some of them such slavish copy-cats that
they have even stolen the name. Coney's influence on our
national tastes in entertainment has been pervasive. Indeed,
it would not be too much to say that at Coney America learned
how to play. During the first seventy-five years of the nineteenth century the American emphasis was on toil; when the

---

* From: *the lives and times of archy and mehitabel,* by Don Marquis. Copyright 1927 by Doubleday and Company, Inc.

work-week was six days of ten hours each a man had little left to bring to his leisure time; the Sabbath was devoted to pious reflection. Rest, relaxation, play, fun: this was all Satan's mischief for idle hands: labor was a moral, almost a tyrannical master. Even when, in 1874, the Chautauqua movement was launched, with its innocent entertainments, its limited success was achieved in virtue of its close ties with religon. Moreover, the country was largely immobile. People planned for weeks ahead before taking off on a one-day jaunt and, having gotten wherever, were more often than not at a loss as to how to amuse themselves. Exchange of social experience was limited. The rise of Coney coincided with the developing network of railroads and the shifting emphasis from production to consumption, from work to play. But how to take advantage of this new freedom? Those who came to Coney around 1880 not only did not know how to swim, they were not even confident about what sort of clothes they should wear into the ocean. And if they were not to bathe, what then were they to do on a holiday?

Coney undertook to teach them. At Coney the business of providing outdoor amusements was pioneered and its authority has ever since been absolute: here in 1884 the first roller coaster was built, here the most successful rides have been invented and tried out, here the first outdoor amusement parks were developed and perfected. At one time, Coney's cabarets and vaudeville theatres were the proving grounds for the nation's songs, and the list of entertainers who learned their craft in Coney's seaside honky-tonks includes men and women who are still today's most brilliant stars on Broadway and on television. At Coney, America first learned how to spend a holiday weekend.

As, in the course of its spasmodic mutations, Coney changed from wild and bonny seacoast to densely thronged and blaring

midway, a remarkable number of parasites fastened themselves on the community and sucked its blood as greedily as
possible. Political bosses, grifters, con men, concessionaires
with gimmicked games, thugs, rowdies, and gangsters have
strutted, at various times, along Coney's seaside walks, men
of malign consequence, and over the years they have managed
to hang a luxuriant shiner on the island's eye. Coney's reputation is today a very mixed quantity. Over the years the preachers have preached and the reformers have complained, and
the newspaper editorial writers have inveighed and, more
often than not, with excellent reason. There is no doubt that
Coney has harbored its share of the iniquitous and the evil.
And anybody poking about among the bones can find it. A man
who spends his life listening to the history of a town as it is
recounted in its police-courts or its saloons will come up with
one kind of a tale and very likely, if he is a careful reporter,

The early farmers regarded the beach only as a place where they could
pot snipe or rabbits, or rake up a basketful of clams.   COURTESY THE
FRANCIS K. MOORE COLLECTION

it will be an accurate tale so far as it goes. At Coney, the advantage of such a report is manifest: where the peccadilloes have been so empurpled, the copy can afford lurid reading. But two stubborn, if less sensational, facts emerge from the entirety of Coney's history:

The natural distinction of the beach has in every period of its history overridden the mean and sorry efforts of men to cheat, to gull.

The two billion visitors to Coney came to have a good time and, mostly, they had it.

Nature has been uncommonly kind to Coney Island.* She contrived that the five miles of beach should lie along an east-west axis in such fashion that the sun would shine down the entire length of the strand from dawn to dusk. Ten miles south into the Atlantic she threw up the Atlantic Highlands and the long curving spit of sand called Sandy Hook so as to create a sheltered basin and gentle the waves of the sea before they should lap on Coney. And, at least until around the turn of the last century, industriously she kept piling up more sand on Coney's beach. It was as if an intelligence had decreed that just here, convenient to what would become the world's largest city, there should be a splendid place for bathing. "There is a dream, a picture," wrote Walt Whitman, who in the years before the Civil War knew this beach as well as any man, "that for years has come noiselessly up before me. It is nothing more or less than a stretch of interminable white-brown sand, hard

* The name has been, for rather more than a century, inaccurate. There was a time when Gravesend Bay and Sheepshead Bay were connected by a thin ribbon of water that ran through marshland and was called Coney Island Creek. But equinoctial storms, aided by man, filled the creek; so many roads, bridges, culverts, highways and footpaths were laid across the marshland that even the creek's course has been blotted out; Coney Island is indissolubly part of Long Island; it is still, however, as Islanders are cheered to point out, not part of the mainland.

and smooth and broad, with the ocean perpetually, grandly, rolling in upon it, with slow-measured sweep, with rustle and hiss and foam, and many a thump as of low bass drums." It was Whitman's pleasure, on his lonely jaunts, to swim naked off Coney's beach, but when the first great throngs of pleasure-seekers reached their timid toes into the sea they were uncomfortably prim.

The idea of bathing in an ocean was so strange and unlikely to the first tourists that they sought advice as to how they should behave and what they should wear not from a swimming instructor or an expert on etiquette or fashions in beachwear but from a physician. They were apprehensive, for there were those who warned that sea bathing might "leach away the essential salts of the body." A Dr. Durant undertook to

A hundred years ago, about the only thing that could get sunburned was the tip of your nose, and that only if your hat blew off. *Leslie's Illustrated, 1856*

Twenty-five years later bathers were more daring, and swam off Manhattan Beach in the weak glare of a primitive, naked electric light.
Scribner's Magazine, 1880

reassure them. "The bathing dress should be made of a woollen fabric," he announced. "We particularly insist upon woollen as the material to be worn, as it retains the heat of the body, and therefore prevents a too rapid evaporation. Maroon and blue are the proper colors," he proceeded, pontifical where there were none who dared gainsay him, "as they resist the corrosive and bleaching effects of the salt-water. The dress should consist essentially of two parts—a pair of pantaloons and a blouse . . . The pantaloons . . . should not be buttoned too tightly to the ankles, as circulation would thereby be impeded . . . Enter the water resolutely and briskly, until the water reaches the waist . . . If you can swim three strokes without going under, it is a fair start."

In the face of this bleak counsel the ocean nevertheless be-

"The glass of fashion and the mould of form the observed of all observers"—at least, in 1897. COURTESY THE FRANCIS K. MOORE COLLECTION

came Coney's most popular feature and so it was to remain down through the years. When Manhattan Beach was developed, Austin Corbin took "Swept by Ocean Breezes" for its slogan, and for years this phrase, shouted from a vast advertising placard, dominated Madison Square. Even during the worst period of John Y. McKane's misrule of the resort, when visitors to Coney were liable to arrest and imprisonment on any pretext the Pooh-Bah might choose to trump up, still the lure of the ocean and the beach kept the crowds growing. The Islanders, early sniffing a good thing, by 1883 began to stake off riparian rights in the sand, stringing barbed-wire fences out into the water, checkerboarding the beach into so many private enclaves. The practice was, to say the least, unpopular; and it was in any event doomed to failure, for in time, as bathing suits shrank to practical size, so many tons of humanity funneled out onto the beach that all barriers—whether of barbed wire or of racial discrimination—were perforce wiped away. By 1940 so dense were the crowds that Robert Moses, New York City's park commissioner, observed with distaste that the beach afforded its bathers less each than the sixteen square feet required for a coffin. "It would seem," he said, with his customary sprightly mordancy, "that a community which calls itself civilized might do a little more by way of recreation for its citizens between the tight spaces of the cradle and the grave. Certainly there is no reason to perpetuate out-of-doors the overcrowding of our tenements." But the cramped bathers have never seemed to care. They have always departed for Coney determined to have fun, and it is a frame of mind that works wonders.

Coney's visitors have always arrived in the mood for laughter. Down through the years it has been the resort's surest resource.

The day is sunny, and the year (1906) is benign. Ahead lie Luna, and Dreamland, and Steeplechase. Anyone for the Shoot-the-Chutes? COURTESY THE FRANCIS K. MOORE COLLECTION

An actor, the late William Collier, once remarked that if he made a stage entrance in perfect seriousness and gravity and said in a hushed voice, "Father's dead," his audience would dissolve in laughter. Coney has traditionally worked the same magic on its millions. They will do at Coney what they would never dream of doing elsewhere—and enjoy it. They will suffer indignities, even physical punishment, at Coney—and roar with mirth. Observe the dignified littérateur, Albert Bigelow Paine, sliding on the helter-skelter: "Suddenly childhood returned, and we slid and kept on sliding until we were altogether certain that we had lost the respect of any friend or relative who might happen to be in the crowd of spectators below." The gentle William Mangels, inventor of many amusement park devices, in 1906 contrived a fiendish ride deceptively called the Tickler. Presently P. G. Wodehouse happened along and climbed in. The next day, when he was somewhat improved, he sat up in bed to write:

> The principle at the bottom of Coney Island's success is the eminently sound one that what would be a brutal assault, if administered gratis, becomes a rollicking pleasure when charged for at the rate of fifteen cents per assault. Suppose one laid hand upon you and put you in a large tub; suppose he then proceeded to send the tub spinning down an incline so arranged that at intervals of a few feet it spun around and violently bumped into something. Next day he would hear from your lawyer. But in Coney Island you jump into the Tickler and enjoy it; you have to enjoy it because you have paid good money to do so. Being in America, Coney Island is thought a little vulgar; if it were in France we would have written how essentially refined the Tickler and the Human Roulette Wheel were, and with what abundance and polish the French people took its pleasure.*

* Reprinted by permission of the author, and the author's agents, Scott Meredith Literary Agency, Inc.

The anatomists of laughter, such men as Henri Bergson and Sigmund Freud, agree that one of the principal sources of the comic is our anticipation, our expectation that, by God, we are going to be amused whether or not a given situation is in all circumstances truly funny. And herein lies Coney's great strength. Bergson was never afforded the opportunity of testing his theories by being confronted with Coney, but Freud was. The greatest psychologist of his era paid one visit to America; he arrived on the evening of August 29, 1909; two days later, a Tuesday, he was taken down the bay on a steamboat to be introduced to what was, at the time, as well known to Europeans as Niagara Falls. The circumstance is provocative: one wishes that he might have set down his reactions in detail: what might he have thought of a ride in the Tickler? But his only comment was a phrase in a letter to his wife. For various reasons, his visit to America was not a happy one; later he was to say, "America is a mistake, a gigantic mistake, it is true, but none the less a mistake," and one only partially mitigated by the fact of tobacco having been discovered here. But Coney impressed him. It was, he wrote, "ein grossartiger Wurstelprater," as who would say, a magnificent amusement park. He saw it at its best.

Once upon a time, in 1830, some seamen aboard the brig *Vineyard* mutinied, murdered the captain, and put off in two boats, laden with $54,000 in Mexican silver dollars. One boat was lost at sea; all but $5,000 was tossed overside of the other to lighten its load. The four survivors buried their treasure in the sands of Coney Island, fell out among themselves, and landed in the hands of the authorities. Eight years later a storm washed much of the cache up and into sight. When word of it reached the nearby village of Gravesend, it was the first hint that there were fortunes to be found on Coney Island, and it was a portent. Once upon another time, in 1877, a schooner was swamped off Coney Island Point and its cargo, $20,000 worth of pineapples, was scattered all over the seascape. The pineapple was, in those days, a rare and exotic fruit. Once again the villagers of Gravesend gathered greedily around, for here was another fortune, of sorts. The pineapples were, as well, a portent. For a few years ago, when the pollution by city garbage of the waters off Coney Island was at its most outrageous, *The New Yorker* printed a cartoon that pictured two plump women in the surf, one delightedly exclaiming to the other, "Look, Mrs. Koppel, pineapples!" Just as everything from refuse to riches has been washed up on Coney's beaches, so Coney itself has in the course of its history been a little of everything, marvelous, bizarre, bawdy, cockeyed, and incredibly vulgar.

But always there has been the salt sea and the sand, and always there has been the fun.

Harper's Weekly, 1887
N. Y. PUBLIC LIBRARY PICTURE COLLECTION

~*Rambunctious*~

In 1867 the citizens of Gravesend, a small farming community south of Brooklyn, N.Y., gathered in annual town meeting, as was their custom, on the first Tuesday after the first Monday in April. Their agenda was routine, not to say dull. There were a handful of trifling reports to approve; there was the election of a slate of town officials for the coming year. Of these, the least important were the three town constables. So casual, so offhand were the freeholders of Gravesend on this score that in the minutes of their town meeting they erred in recording the name of the third constable elected, the man with the smallest number of winning votes. They called him John Y. Kane.

Thus trivially, amid botched proceedings, accompanied by the sound of offstage slapsticks, an authentic character swaggered his way onto the stage of American politics. He was no original; he was rather a travesty, a burlesque carbon-copy of the nineteenth-century political boss; but there could be no blinking his vivid and colorful figure. He would never amount to more than a footnote on the pages of American history, but he would be a footnote printed, so to say, in bold-faced type.

15

This was John Y. McKane, Grand Pooh-Bah of Coney Island, leader of a motley assortment of barkeeps, sports, gamblers, pugilists, thieves, and bawds. For the moralist, his career was to offer a matchless example of Lord Acton's dictum that "Power tends to corrupt; absolute power corrupts absolutely." Moreover, his life course was to conform, in offbeat, raffish fashion, to the rigid rules of classical tragedy: he would ever be flanked by his dissolute *chorus;* he would be caught up in an *agon,* a fateful conflict; he would fall victim to his own *hubris,* his overweening arrogance; his clash with his fates would be featured by *peripeteia,* the swift reversal; and his life would end in *pathos.* It would all be there; and before his career had run its unbridled course through a quarter century he would have had a controlling hand in the creation of the nation's most glittering seaside resort, would have played a decisive role in changing the climate of public opinion as to prizefighting and horseracing, would have assisted in the founding of a half-dozen substantial fortunes, and would even have twice seen his influence extend to the White House itself.

The farmers and freeholders of Gravesend, however, their vision limited to the humdrum present, perceived nothing remarkable about their newly elected third constable. They saw a sturdy man of about twenty-five, with a curly, light-brown beard and mustache, and a rough-and-ready air about him. But they were not likely to give him a second glance, for he was a man of little standing in their community. Those who troubled to inquire could learn that McKane had been born in County Antrim, in Ireland; that he had been brought to this country while still an infant; that during his boyhood he had been a clam-digger around Sheepshead Bay; that he had dodged the draft in the recent Civil War on the grounds that he was an alien; that he had learned the carpenter's trade and only the year before had launched his own building business; that he had recently been named superintendent of the Methodist Episcopal Sunday School. To the Gravesenders, a commonplace sort.

McKane, for his part, as he surveyed them with, it may be presumed, some small impatience, saw gentry. Many of the well-to-do freeholders of Gravesend were the direct descendants of those who had originally settled the town more than two centuries before. The first settlers had disposed of the land granted them by patent in unusual fashion, and, because that disposition was of crucial importance in the subsequent exploitation of Coney Island, it must be described.

Gravesend's colonists were led by an extraordinary woman, Lady Deborah Moody, widow of an English baronet, a woman of wealth, education, and character. It happened that, in 1635, Lady Moody ran afoul of Charles I's iniquitous Star Chamber (her ostensible offense was that she had chosen to leave her country residence and live for a time in London, but clearly the real issue was one of religious conscience), and so in 1640 she sailed for Massachusetts. Here she presently came under the influence of Roger Williams. She subscribed to his ideas on infant baptism; for this she was first admonished by the Salem elders, next disfellowshipped, and finally excommunicated. In consequence, she removed with her son and a party of like-thinking friends to New Amsterdam, still searching for a place where she might enjoy freedom of conscience. If she had feared that she would fetch up among Dutch foreigners, with strange speech and strange customs, she was agreeably surprised, for there was quite a settlement of English residents living on Manhattan's east side, at approximately where Sixtieth Street and York Avenue now meet. Their spokesman was Nicholas Stillwell, a planter who had come there for much the same reasons as those of Lady Moody. The two groups joined and, when the Dutch Director-General invited them to choose from the unassigned lands of the West India Company, decided upon Gravesend as their site. They were granted a patent in 1643. There was a confirmatory patent issued by the Dutch in 1645, another by the English in 1670, and still another in 1686; moreover, at Lady Moody's behest, the colonists had undertaken to clear their title with the Canarsie Indians for various considerations, including "one blanket, one gun, one kettle," and fifteen fathoms of seawant (a kind of wampum), two guns, and three pounds of gunpowder. These steps were necessary; at nearly every stage there were efforts to contest the title; as late as 1789 the town was obliged to retain Aaron Burr to defend the title in Supreme Court at Flatbush (he won the case and charged the town £35).

Meanwhile, the original patentees had laid out their town. It was a square comprising about sixteen acres and enclosed, for protection against the Indians, by a palisade fence. Radiating outward from the square for a few rods were forty triangular lots, the apexes resting on the town fence. Thus each could leave his home and farm his land without trespassing even a step on his neighbor's land; thus each might swiftly retire within the palisade to take up common defense.

But while there were surely forty original patentees (there is a map on file in the Hall of Records in Brooklyn, testifying to the original plan), something happened to one of them. As to this fortieth, the tradition varies. Some say he simply died without heir, some that he forfeited all his title in the original patent by profligacy or worse. In any event, whenever thereafter the land granted by the original patent was divided, it was cut up amongst only thirty-nine patentees. In such fashion they divided their grant several times, carving up meadowland, slicing up woodland, not methodically, but only when, at town meeting, the pressures to cut up another stretch of land were strong enough. At length, as they considered, whatever land was of

Gravesend May the seven 1654, certain Indians (viz) Mattinoh Sachemacho of Niocke, being demanded concerning a certain parcel of lande (viz) a Neck of Land, from Antonie Johnson's house southward, and an Island called Conyne Island, to whom it did belong, unto; they did all declare that it was to their knowledge the right and true proper Land of one Guttaquoh, and called by them Narriockh that is to say the Island, and the Neck of Land is called by them Manahanung, and in testimony of the premises have hereunto set their hands.

Signum: Matt [mark] Nauoh

Signum: Vtta [mark] chin

The abovesaid quantity of Land being within the Bounds and lymits of the Land Granted by Patent to certain pattentees and Inhabitants of Gravesend by the late Governor Kieft the abovesaid Guttaquoh doth hereby acknowledge & declare to have sold all his Right title Interest & Claim to the abovesaid quantity of Land called Narriockh & Manahanung unto the Honourable the Lords Bewinthabbers of the west India Company of the Chamber of Amsterdam, for the use right & property of the abovesaid pattentees & Inhabitants of Gravesend, as having received fifteen fathoms of sewan two guns three pounds of Powder for & in consideration of the said land of the said pattentees & Inhabitants, and do therefore by virtue hereof assign, sell and make over all my Right, Title, & Interest unto the said Land, unto them their Heirs, Executors, Administrators and Assigns, to enjoy as their own proper land together with all the Meddow land & Marsh Land thereunto appertaining, in confirmation whereof I have hereunto put my hand this seventh of may 1654

Signum: Gutta [mark] quoh

Subscribed & acknowledged in the presence of us

Signū Geo Right

Jnꝰ R Randall

Huet interpreter

Signū Jo. W Wilson

A true Copy of the Original remaining in the Town Clerk's office in Gravesend

Test Stephen Voorhees Town Clerk

On the seventh of May, 1654, an Indian named Guttaquoh, declared to be the owner of "Conyne Island"—he called it Narrioch—formally put his mark on a deed conveying the Island to the 40 patentees. FROM KINGS COUNTY CLERK'S OFFICE. PHOTO COURTESY ABRAHAM AND STRAUS

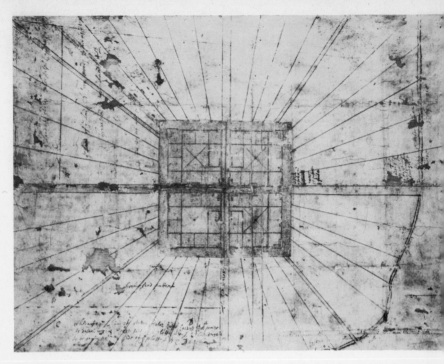

Those curious enough to count the slices in this pie—the original town plan of Gravesend—will find 41 slices for the 40 patentees. The reason is that Lady Moody, as chief of the party, got two slices. COURTESY THE KINGS COUNTY CLERK'S OFFICE

value had been allotted. All that was left lay to the south—marshland, some sandy beaches, worthless for cultivation. So far as they were concerned, the marshes were a good place to hunt snipe, but nothing more; as for the beaches, the sea-scrubbed white sand was useful to scatter on the floors of their farmhouses, but nothing more. They were content to let the sea have its pleasure of the five-mile stretch to their south. This would be Coney Island.

It would take a while to become Coney Island. The island was compounded out of a slow and gradual process. The sea worked its eternal changes. Storms and erosion cut inlets deep back through the sandy soil; at times there were as many as four islands, separate and distinct; the names bear witness to

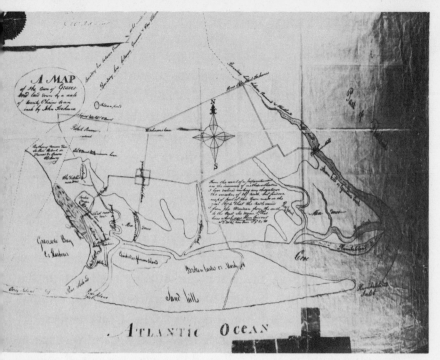

When this map was drawn (1827), Coney was three separate islands, mostly marshes and sand dunes. Clams and snipe abounded. The original plan of Gravesend is the small square below and left of center.

the shifting of the sands: Narrioch (which is Canarsie Indian for "the place without shadows"), Pine Island, Guisbert's Island, Plumb (or Plum) Island, Pelican Beach, Barren Island; at least once, in the great storm of New Year's Day, 1839, the raging sea boiled up and submerged much of the stretch of beach. Since that fearsome blow, however, Coney has maintained substantially the same shape: a hammerhead of land presenting to the ocean a magnificent five-mile sweep of sand, with Gravesend Bay cutting back to the west and Sheepshead Bay cutting back to the east.

Who owned this wild and weedy paradise? There was no question about that part of the island that had been formally divided—roughly two-fifths had been cut into long, narrow, ribbon-shaped parcels of land running from Coney Island Creek to the ocean, the lots numbered one to thirty-nine, and from Sheepshead Bay to the ocean, the lots numbered one to thirty-nine once again—but what of that part that lay undivided? Was it the property of the heirs of the thirty-nine patentees? Or, in the absence of any formal division agreed upon in town meeting, did it belong to the town of Gravesend? What gave this question explosive impact was the enormous potential value of the property involved. Before the Civil War the value was less apparent, but within less than a decade after the war was over, this swatch of scrubby real estate was to become as bitterly contested as any along the Atlantic seaboard. If the town could establish its rights to the undivided land, to what the townspeople called "the common lands," Gravesend would certainly become the wealthiest town in the state, perhaps in the entire country. And it followed that whoever gained control of the town would grasp an unprecedented opportunity for political and financial skulduggery. But these issues were not immediately apparent. In fact, the question as to ownership of the common lands was never to be settled by law or by judicial proceeding, but only by a combination of inertia and the force of circumstances. Like some delectably ripening fruit, the matter was left dangling, awaiting the propitious moment, ready to the hand of the first shrewd and unscrupulous man who might happen along.

Pending his advent, however, rather than chicanery there was only apathy. The Gravesend freeholders were advised by their town supervisor that the beaches had value. They shrugged; they were content with their farms. As an extreme example, there is the case of Rutgert Stillwell, a Gravesender who, from the time he was thirty-seven until his death at seventy-eight, never stirred off his farm. He was no recluse; he delighted in having company; he loved conversation and sociability, but on his terms; he was at home and at home he stayed. In consequence of a community frame of mind akin to this, it required private capital to bridge the Coney Island Creek, lay down a shell road to the island, and build the comfortable inn called the Coney Island House. The inn stood on land that had never been apportioned; the town required of the innkeeper that he pay a rent that was turned over to the town treasurer; this procedure became a precedent.

The inn's very loneliness, perched as it was amidst the dunes, and boasting an unexampled view of the harbor, gave it fame. In time its register was signed by some illustrious names. Washington Irving brought his nieces down from Tarrytown for a visit in 1848. The next year, there was Herman Melville, with four popular successes under his belt, then hard at work on *Moby Dick* and down, presumably, to look again on the fathomless sea that he loved and dreaded. In July of 1850, here came Henry Clay and Daniel Webster, stealing away together that they might discuss undisturbed the tricky manoeuvering necessary to guide the Missouri Compromise through Congress. Here, too, came Sam Houston and William Macready, the English actor, and Fitz-Greene Halleck, the poet, and the elder James Gordon Bennett, publisher of the *New York Herald*, who sniffed censoriously, wrinkled his nose, and declared he found the place "an objectionable resort . . . sandy, clammy and fishy." Jenny Lind, the Swedish Nightingale, was not so captious: Phineas T. Barnum escorted her to the Coney Island House for dinner on the day of her arrival in 1850; she was back again in a fortnight, after her first Castle Garden recital. And Walt Whitman, after he quit his job on the *Brooklyn Eagle*, rejoiced in the "long, bare, unfrequented shore, which I had all to myself, and where I loved, after bathing, to race up and down the hard sand, and declaim Homer or Shakespeare to the surf and seagulls by the hour."

The first road across Coney Island Creek was built of shells, the second of planks. This is the toll gate on the Plank Road, in 1857. COURTESY THE FRANCIS K. MOORE COLLECTION

The trouble was, from the Gravesenders' point of view, their beach was becoming entirely too frequented. Dan Morrell, the toll-collector on the shell road, counted more than three hundred vehicles on one warm Fourth of July, a Sunday, and the townsfolk "cried out that it was a shameful breach of the Sabbath peace." Moreover, down at Coney Island Point, the western tip of the island, two New Yorkers named Eddy and Hart had built a large circular wooden platform and reared above it an enormous tent; this was the Pavilion; they surrounded it with bathing-houses and flanked it with a jetty at which a small side-wheeler from New York could dock and disgorge happy picnickers. But the Gravesenders chose not to complain about the Pavilion, for they were receiving $400 annual rent for the western point, and this sum went a good way toward paying all the expenses of the town's school. It constituted still another precedent: money from rental of the common lands was going to the use of the whole town; no one even considered dividing it among the heirs of the thirty-nine patentees. More rent was paid by John Wyckoff, himself a former Gravesend schoolmaster, who built a second hotel on the island as soon as the success of the Coney Island House had become apparent.

Even the Civil War did not stop the further development of the beach. In 1863 a Brooklyn harness-maker, Peter Ravenhall, leased some shore front from the town and built a restaurant. In 1865 Peter Tilyou built a hotel and restaurant, the Surf House, on the beach hard by the terminus of the first railroad to reach the island. This was properly known as the Brooklyn, Bath and Coney Island Railroad, but everybody called it the Dummy Road in friendly derision of its slowpoke behavior. Until its engine had crossed the Brooklyn city line on its journey

In the summertime there were always crowds around Tilyou's Surf House; his chowder was famous. This shot was taken November, 1874.
COURTESY THE FRANCIS K. MOORE COLLECTION

south to the island it was preceded by a man on horseback, waving a red signal flag; since at best it never went much faster than a jogtrot, people sniggered and claimed the horse was needed to pull it. Nevertheless, the Dummy Road gave impetus to the erection of more hotels and restaurants, as did the extension to Coney of the horse-car line. There were a handful of celebrated summer residents, too; pioneer exurbanites; William Wheatley was one. Wheatley was a most popular actor-manager of the period; he had performed with Macready and John Drew and Edwin Forrest, and as a manager he had presented Edwin Booth; yet today he is remembered, if at all, because he produced *The Black Crook* for the first time on an American stage, and thereby introduced that hardy perennial, the chorus girl. (*The Black Crook* ran for sixteen months in New York and, despite the wails of contemporary preachers, grossed more than $1,000,000.) The theatrical folk who came down to weekend at his summer home on the beach went back

Peter Tilyou

to New York to spread the word. By the summer of 1866 Coney was beginning to attract attention in the New York newspapers. "The long, wide, winding, smooth, gently shelving beach," wrote a reporter for the *New York Times,* made it "one of the most convenient as well as pleasant resorts" available to the city's hot and harassed crowds. On one sultry Sunday afternoon, he noted, there were "more on the island than there had ever been before at one time"—surely one of the earliest examples of the journalistic need to people Coney with record-breaking crowds—and "they were as happy as the clams they later ate at the Pavilion or the Tivoli or any one of a dozen or more hotels" scattered along the shore. At one hotel, he reported, more than 10,000 clams were consumed in a single day. "Go," he urged, "go, bathe, and be cool."

None of this gratifying growth was lost on John Y. McKane, at his home in the village of Sheepshead Bay. As a young man newly launched in the building business, growth was what he was for. The Gravesend gentry might be dismayed by the bustle and the throngs, by the excursions and the alarums being sounded at their back door, but not McKane, and not the coterie he had already gathered around him—fishermen, blacksmiths, barkeeps, carpenters, clam-diggers—the young and hard-muscled of the town, the men chiefly responsible for his election as third constable. McKane saw not only a welcome opportunity for an expanding construction business—and indeed he had his hands as full as could be, tossing together the ramshackle bathing establishments and the hasty shelters for lager-beer saloons that were already crowding each other, shoulder to shoulder, along the beach—McKane perceived something else as well. Almost alone of the Gravesenders, he recognized that the town's common lands had been underestimated. As an honest and upright citizen, he considered that these lands should yield a better income to the town's treasury than they had. As a tough-minded businessman, he smelled something fishy.

The leasing of the common lands was the responsibility of three town commissioners. They were bound by only two restrictions: they could not draw a lease for a longer period than ten years, and a lease could be renewed only in the last year of its life. Nothing else restrained them, not even the dictates of common sense. They had been known to lease ocean-front lots for as little as three dollars a year. Moreover, when the word "lot" is used, it should not summon up a picture of the pipsqueak lot of present-day realty; most of the Coney Island common lands lots were three hundred feet wide, and some of them ran all the way from the ocean to the Coney Island Creek, a matter of anywhere from a quarter-mile to a half-mile. It was jumbo lots like these that had been leased for three or five or ten or twelve dollars a year. Nor, typically, had this been done dishonestly, to oblige a pal, but only because the commissioners honestly did not believe the land should fetch more. The commissioners were not knaves, they were genteel farmers: to them such land, being useless for plow or seed, had no value. They were slow to learn. McKane, concerned and conscientious, engaged to teach them.

In 1868 the rental of the common land netted the town of Gravesend $728.50. At the annual meeting of April, 1869, McKane was elected one of the three commissioners. He became, by any standard, the most scrupulous and punctilious commissioner ever elected to office in the township. Personally, he collected the rents. Personally, he attended to the renewals. Personally, he leased lands that had theretofore lain idle. Everywhere he went he made friends. At every door along the beach he found the right word to say. He admired Cap MacPherson's hotel lobby, fitted out like a ship's cabin, and approved his technique of permitting his customers to sign their I.O.U.'s on clamshells. He complimented Mary Ravenhall on the border of flowers in front of her restaurant; who else could grow pansies and nasturtiums in such sandy soil? He chuckled at Peter Tilyou's conceit of firing off a toy howitzer, nicknamed Molly, at every notable occasion such as the passing of a ship offshore, the arrival of a crowd of customers on the Dummy Road, or a stranger's standing all a drink on the house. McKane was, moreover, exceptionally well behaved. When he came collecting rents, he refused the customary segar, he smiled and declined the customary drink. Apparently his only vice was a game of dominoes. Along the beach they loved him.

They loved him, too, when at the next annual meeting he reported that the rental of the common lands had netted $1,511.50, a one hundred per cent increase. In addition—and here was the best testimonial to McKane's conscientiousness— this sum was only two dollars less than the gross receipts. In his second year as commissioner he did even better: he cut his expenses to one dollar and turned over $1,527.50 to the town treasurer. His reports became the high point of the town's annual meetings. Here were numbers to warm the hearts of the Gravesend gentry. They looked at their ex-constable with new respect. They would not get his name wrong again. His head, they agreed, was screwed on the right way; they could only wish there were more men like him in the town.

McKane acknowledged their kind words with circumspection. He was thinking, as they spoke, of something else. He was thinking of his building contracts and of the many friends he was making among the cribs and cabins down along the beach. He was thinking, too, of how some of those new friends were making a handsome profit by subleasing fractions of their generous lots; he was wondering about the ethics of such transactions: could the town not profit from such subleases? Or, if the town could not, was it not at least possible for some individual to profit—somehow? Three or four of those whom he had met along the beach had given him here a wink, offered him there an outright bribe; all of McKane's acquisitive Scottish-Irish instincts were stirred; if others were getting theirs, as the town's commissioner of common lands he meant to get some for the town—or for himself.

For now the beach was booming. The rush came first to Coney Island Point, at the western tip of the long sweep of sand. The reason for this was simple: a boat trip down the bay was cooler, much shorter, and infinitely more pleasant than the dusty, jouncing ride in a horse-car past the flat farmlands and cemeteries that lay south of Brooklyn. And a boat trip meant the Point, since here—at least at first—was the only pier for a steamboat. Competition among the steamboat lines grew lively. A party of would-be bathers hurrying to catch the packet at Pier One in the North River might be met by a barker, dolefully announcing that there had been a breakdown and any desirous of getting to Coney Island Point had better scurry to Pier Two; at Pier Two would be another barker, bent on the same dark work, seeking to tout the trippers back to Pier One. The fare for the round-trip was two dollars (later reduced to one dollar), bathing-suits could be rented for twenty-five cents, the restaurant on the Point was cool and clean, clams were plentiful and so was clam chowder, the beach was superb. But there arose one slight difficulty. As always seems to happen once Eden is ready to hand, a serpent appeared. In naughty New York City, William Marcy Tweed was elected Grand Sachem of Tammany Hall, and the lid came off.

There might seem to be little connection between the access to power of a New York boss and the popularity and clientele of a seaside watering-place some distance off. The relationship, however, was direct and immediate. When the Tweed Ring took over New York there was launched an era remarkable for

To this pier came the steamboats from New York. This was Coney Island Point in 1874: ramshackle portal to a scapegrace playground. COURTESY THE FRANCIS K. MOORE COLLECTION

its lawlessness, and generous dollops of it spilled over onto Coney Island Point. Boat trips down the bay became adventures into a perilous unknown. The roughs of New York and their doxies, the pickpockets, confidence men, strong-arm guys, gamblers, till-tappers, moll-buzzers and rowdies, had discovered the joys of the more abundant life; they too wanted to sport in the waves and sprawl in the sun. They brought their manners with them, and these included free and often pointed comment on the physical charms of ladies to whom they had not always been introduced, underwater pranks and games involving the same ladies without their consent, and a certain truculence (as like as not backed up by knuckledusters) directed toward any who might gainsay them.

Nor were matters appreciably improved when, having quit the beach, the ladies retired to their bathhouses. Walls, as they knew, sometimes have ears, but they began to suspect uneasily that these flimsy bathhouse walls had eyes as well. Indeed, one

New York newspaper flatly insisted that the eyes were not accidental knot-holes but holes bored on purpose. Moreover, it became increasingly clear that the Point was regularly attracting some ladies, light of heart and loose of scruple, who, so far from deprecating the holes bored in the walls, positively gloried in them as opportunities for advertising the enticements of their ancient profession.

If all this were not enough to give Coney Island Point a gaudy reputation, there were the picnics and excursions. Picnics (in Grandfather's day they were called pic-nics) and excursions were essentially similar, except that the pic-nic might be a trifle smaller and a trifle more exclusive. In any event, Coney Island Point was a magnet for pic-nic and excursion alike. Alike they were tendered by social organizations and political associations. Some of these groups, man being occasionally wicked, were of the sort that called for police scrutiny. According to one anxious writer, there were in New York City alone nearly three hundred different societies "according to police estimation" that "indulge

As a cartoonist for *Puck* saw Coney Island's belles in 1878.   N. Y. PUBLIC LIBRARY

in at least one pic-nic during the summer." "The object of such pic-nics," wrote another, equally troubled contemporary commentator, "is either to increase the business at the bar of the place where it is held, or to make money for those who conduct it." Lest these innocent aims were not enough to scarify his readers, he hastily added, "It is a well-known fact to the authorities that pic-nics are often arranged for the sole benefit of pickpockets, prostitutes, and rowdies . . . panel-girls, swindlers, and other wolves in sheepskin . . . The history of many prostitutes has begun with seduction at a pic-nic."

As for the excursions ("they are like immense pic-nics in which scarcely anyone knows the person sitting next to him"), they were organized by political clubs run for the benefit of one Tweed boodler or another and were in consequence even more likely to erupt in colorful violence. "It even happened once," wrote Lening, in *The Dark Side of New York Life,* "that a band of rowdies got the vessel under their control, and then proceeded to rob the passengers, to knock down the men, insult the ladies, and even committed a dastardly outrage on one lady. To avoid arrest, the band forced the pilot to steer towards a deserted landing-place and to set them on shore there."

No matter how little truth there was to this or any other of the lurid reports that trickled back from Coney Island Point, unquestionably interest was quickened. Across the vasty seven-mile deep of harbor water from Coney to Manhattan, id called to id, and by the thousands more came down every weekend to see what all the shouting was about.

Whenever two or three thousand are gathered together in the name of profane amusement, in all likelihood there will be on hand to minister to them the dedicated fraternity of sharpers, and so it turned out this time. The game was three-card monte and, since this hoary swindle had traditionally been employed against hayseeds in small country fairs, New

Swimming is not the only way to get cleaned, by the seashore. Here a pair of three-card monte men are busy at their genial tasks. *Valentine's Manual, 1869.* N. Y. PUBLIC LIBRARY PICTURE COLLECTION

Yorkers were quite cross to find it operating so successfully in a playground they regarded as the big city's own. Monte dealers, using small one-legged tables, could be found trying to gather a push of gullible people all the way from the Point to the center of the Island. Some years later a respectable New Yorker, reflecting on how the Island had changed, would recall his encounter with one of these grifters. He had been strolling along the beach when he came upon a tinhorn "plying his trade with considerable success."

"A capper exclaimed: 'I can beat that game,' and turning to me, said: 'Be kind enough to hold my umbrella, please. Me and you can win some money.'

"Looking with profound contempt and disgust at the speaker, I said: 'Look at me well, do I look like a person you can rope into a skin game?'

"Humiliated and keenly cut that my appearance did not command more respect, I avoided the island for some years afterward."

Three-card monte, in common with all confidence games, requires to insure successful operation fundamental dishonesty on the part of the victim. If all the visitors to Coney had been as upright as this man, the swindle would have died a-borning. There were, however, plenty of men around with money in their pants and larceny in their hearts—professional bounty-jumpers, fly-by-night entrepreneurs grown fat on fraudulent army contracts, land speculators loaded with loot from the Pennsylvania oil boom—and these gravitated naturally to bare-faced swindling, were parted from minor sums, and moved on, sadder but not notably wiser. The swindlers themselves came to be an accepted part of the landscape. They were a bore and a nuisance; they gave the Island a bad name; but still they were suffered, for a time, rather as is the puppy that has not yet been housebroken. A reporter for the *Brooklyn Argus* has handed down to us a picture of the most celebrated of these swindlers:

A large group was gathered about one man, whose move-ments and utterances seemed to create profound respect and deep regret—respect that the man should offer to his audience so fair and square a way of making money and regret that they had not sufficient means to engage in the game. He was a short, stout-built person, who manipulated the three cards on the one-legged table before him, and he wore a pair of green glasses. His suit was plain and neat, and nothing ex-travagant was apparent in his dress or person, except his nose —but that unusual redness must have been caused by the sun beating down and under his hat brim, which was somewhat less in width than that of a Quaker's. His face and neck were sadly tanned, almost redly tanned, and each individual hair of his moustache stood out like a bristle. For an instant he paused in his game and removed his glasses. [Here the re-porter's tone becomes the clarion of a fanfare.] He was Valen-tine, the "Chow Chow Man," the King of the Monte Players.

A modest appearing young man, prettily framed in a suit
of blue with brass buttons, here came rapidly along the
beach, and as he whisked past the Chow Chow Man he said
in a saddened tone of voice, "You'll have to stop this." The
monte man pocketed his pack, picked up his one-legged table,
and proceeded at a painfully slow gait about forty feet up the
beach, where he resumed business, "thankful for past patron-
age and hopeful for a continuance of the same."

But after a time the top-flight New York gamblers who came
to the Point for relaxation tired of the monte players. They took
up their challenge and beat them at their own game, driving
them east down the beach, away from the Point and, eventually, all the way to Rockaway. Not, however, before the damage
had been done: the west end had become a hissing and a by-
word, and respectable folk would shun it for years.

And what of John Y. McKane, Commissioner of Common
Lands for the Town of Gravesend? Did he care? Did he object
to goings-on calculated to depreciate the rental value of those
lands? Did he, the superintendent of Sabbath School in the
Methodist Episcopal Church, harken to the philippics from the
pulpits of half-a-hundred Brooklyn churches? Not he; not John
McKane. He was grinding to become letter-perfect in a bland,
self-serving protestation that was to stand him in adequate stead

Mike Norton took over the west end of Coney in 1875; from then on it
was called Norton's Point. This is his Point Comfort House. FROM HOTEL
BRIGHTON SOUVENIR BOOKLET c. 1880. N. Y. PUBLIC LIBRARY

in later years. What I don't see, John McKane would say, doesn't hurt anybody, and on Sunday I'm home in Sheepshead Bay, far from Coney Island, and I don't see anything. McKane was to become one of the finest latter-day disciples of Bishop Berkeley: the sins, crimes, misfeasances and malfeasances that he did not see simply did not exist. (But he was learning from what he had not seen; it was part of his continuing education.)

Moreover, the attitude of laissez-faire toward Coney Island Point seems to have been justified. Those who don't like what goes on there, we can imagine him saying, can stay away. The sports, the big gamblers, the politicians, and their ladies continued to come, and in droves. Indeed, in 1873 McKane authorized a new lease for the Coney Island Point, and at a whopping increase. It had rented before at $400 a year; now it went for $6,100 a year. The lessee was a man from whom McKane could gain a great deal: important friends, lessons in cutting corners, techniques in figuring angles, methods of reducing percentages. This was Robert Furey, a close friend of Hugh McLaughlin, Brooklyn's Democratic boss. Furey was, at forty, already an extremely rich man by virtue of having been Brooklyn's Street Commissioner at, fortuitously, the same time he was principal stockholder in an asphalt contracting firm. Furey was also a generous man: he chose to share his good fortune in leasing Coney Island Point with three other Brooklyn politicians. One of them was Francis Swift. It is unlikely that the New Yorkers who sailed down the bay to Coney had ever heard of Francis Swift but they had, many of them, at least a sniffing acquaintance with his line of work. For Francis Swift had the contract for removing dead animals from the city of Brooklyn; his scow, the *Argo*, referred to by the knowledgeable as Frank Swift's steam yacht, used often, but often, to precede the steamboats from New York down the bay. Laden as it was with carcasses headed for the rendering plant on Barren Island, the *Argo* could, under a hot summer sun and assisted by a gentle harbor breeze, contrive to make its presence felt. New Yorkers, cursing his stink, never realized that presently they would be drinking lager at his hotel to his profit.

Eighteen seventy-three, the year McKane leased the Point to Furey, was an important year in his career. It was the year when he cemented himself in solid with the conservative town elders of Gravesend. The town's income from rental of the common lands soared up five hundred per cent, to well over $9,000. The bulk of this increase, of course, was attributable to McKane's successful flirtation with the Brooklyn politicians, but there was, as well, another important new name on the rent roll. This was William A. Engeman.

When Engeman first came to Coney he was only twenty-eight years old, but he had crammed several careers and uncounted ergs of derring-do into that span. He had been a shipwright in Camden, a river-rat along the Mississippi, a hobo throughout the middle west, a deckhand and galley-chef on a schooner in the Gulf of Mexico, a smuggler of contraband into Mexico, a bus-driver in New Orleans, a mule-skinner on the western frontier, and a sutler in Indian territory. After narrowly escaping a lynching by Union sympathizers in Washington (they thought he was a Confederate saboteur), a capture by Confederates near St. Louis (they thought he was a Union spy), and an attack by rubeola germs in Leavenworth (*they* thought he was an ordinary mortal), he settled down to the sedentary task of inspecting, purchasing, and shipping to the Union Army upwards of one million horses and mules. In 1865 he pocketed the considerable proceeds of this contract and, returning east, found his way to Coney Island. He desired to relax, to lie on the sands and breathe through his mouth for a time. He arrived in 1868, looked about, saw the possibilities, and promptly set to work.

The possibilities did not include the common lands, for these were not for sale and were in any event already for the most part tied up by lease. But what of those tracts of the Island that were privately owned? There had been, Engeman learned, two divisions among the heirs of the thirty-nine original patentees. One, called the Middle Division, lay just east of the center of the Island, and consisted of several hundred acres of sandy, scrubby wilderness; the other, called the Sedge Bank, was about the same size but lay further to the east and was even sandier and scrubbier. The Middle Division looked like his cup of tea. But how to buy it? The heirs of the original patentees were, by then, in the seventh and eighth generation; they numbered in the hundreds; they were scattered all over the map. Simply to find out who they were, much more to track them down, would be a labor of Sisyphus. Moreover, so soon as word got out of his intention, surely others would compete with him to establish title and send the market soaring. Only a man who had bought and sold a million mules could have found the solution. What he did was simplicity itself. He wangled an introduction to the official surveyor of Gravesend, the man charged with drawing the town's authorized maps, the cicerone to all the complexities of local real estate, and he charmed him out of his boots. This man was William H. Stillwell, himself an eighth generation descendant of a founding father and in consequence an invaluable advocate in dealing with heirs who might otherwise get aggrandized notions about the value of their equity. To win Stillwell's simple heart, one called him "Judge," for he had been a justice of the peace in Gravesend for two or three years. "Judge," said Engeman to Stillwell, in effect, "what can you do to help me?" And indeed there was much that Judge Stillwell could do to oblige. He obliged by placing on file in the town clerk's office a map that declared all the

Middle Division to be the property of William A. Engeman. He thereafter obliged by acting as Engeman's purchasing agent, in order that Engeman's name be kept privy until long after the essential lots had been bought. He even obliged by including some of the town's common lands in his map of what Engeman allegedly owned, enabling his principal to secure leases on these lands at trifling sums. Thanks to Judge Stillwell, Engeman took possession of several hundred acres of choicest ocean-front real estate some time before he had actually purchased any part of it.

With these piratical acts accomplished, Engeman bided his time, Johnny-at-the-rathole, to see how best he could capitalize on them. He had spent perhaps $20,000 to acquire title to the Middle Division; he had dubbed it Brighton Beach; on a sudden whim he had in four days caused a pier to be built out into the ocean from it; now he was content to stand aside and wait to see its value increase. He would not have long to wait.

In the summer of 1873 a wealthy New York banker named Austin Corbin came with his wife and infant son to stay at the Oceanic Hotel. He came not by choice but because a doctor had told him his child needed sea air. Corbin was a big, rawboned, brusque man, impetuous, insatiably curious, unable to stay in one place. He got his wife settled in a rocker on the verandah of the Oceanic, their son in her lap; himself, he was the kind of man who, even on a holiday, was always driving under the goad of his own restless energy. He plunged off east along the beach.

At the Middle Division Corbin was confronted by a deep creek. He took off his boots and stockings, waded across, and kept on going. He walked to the farthest eastern point and back, entranced. How could such a wonder of nature exist so near New York and still be wild? Was it possible no man owned it? Back at the hotel, he asked questions and presently, like a genie out of a bottle, up bobbed the obliging Judge Stillwell. He told Corbin about the Sedge Bank, wagged his head despondently over the complexities of title, but, on a note of optimism, concluded that the job could be done if the right agent were employed. Corbin wondered whether an agent could be enticed to work in return for shares in the development company. Judge Stillwell, with a fortune being tendered him on a silver salver, chose the wrong moment to get canny. He thought the agent would insist on a weekly salary. In this way, he went off Engeman's payroll and on Corbin's. Manhattan Beach had been born.

John Y. McKane, the Commissioner of Common Lands, was not concerned with these two great transactions. They were out of his bailiwick.

John Y. McKane, the builder, was a sensible man and knew there was small chance that he would be able to gaff any construction contracts out of the development of these two great tracts. Perhaps one day he might work for Engeman, who seemed a nice, cooperative young chap; but he knew that to a banker like Corbin he was very small beer.

John Y. McKane, the ambitious politician, on the other hand, found these two developments a matter for thoughtful concern. It was now clear—indeed the island was awhirl with rumors—that important capital was about to pour into Coney. McKane was well enough connected to be able to disregard the fanciful rumors and pin his attention on the facts—and the facts were fanciful enough.

Item: A railroad man named Andrew Culver created the Prospect Park and Coney Island Railroad by consolidating a number of smaller lines; he was in operation for the season of 1875; he brought with him a Cockney restaurant man, Thomas Cable, who made enough money within a year to build a 150-room hotel; on his railroad he brought to Coney one million passengers in his first year and two million in his second; lest the ocean be not enough to amuse them, he imported from the Philadelphia Exposition of 1876 an Iron Tower, three hundred feet tall, two steam elevators in its innards and at its top a telescopic eye that reached for forty miles out to sea or back to land; he brought as well the camera obscura, a giant toy of lenses and mirrors housed in a round hut and offering not quite so good a view of the beach and plaza outside as could be seen by the human eye.

Item: The Ocean Parkway, a magnificent avenue reaching from Brooklyn's Prospect Park to the ocean, almost as straight as a plumb-line, unencumbered by anything but "fountains and statuary . . . trees and shrubbery," seventy feet wide and flanked by two gravel roads each twenty-five feet wide that afforded a splendid opportunity for racing surreys, was completed in 1876; it was an elegant route from Brooklyn to Coney for any who could handle a pair of reins.

Item: Corbin, moving fast, had laid some railroad lines and leased others so that he might bring patrons with a minimum of discomfort right to the portal of the enormous wooden temple he was preparing for their worship of sun and sea. This would be the Manhattan Beach Hotel, bristling with towers and turrets and dormers, boasting a front on the ocean no less than one-eighth of a mile; in 1876, still unfinished, it crouched on the dunes like some monstrous remnant of a savage civilization; it was advertised as ready for the season of 1877.

Item: With Manhattan Beach as leverage, Engeman sold two parcels of his Brighton Beach real estate to a syndicate of New York investors—one on which to build another great hotel, the other sufficient to permit a railroad access to the hotel; the price he got was greater than what he had spent for the entire Middle Division; with some of the profit he was planning to construct a showy bathing pavilion; already, to the west, he had built a more modest hotel; moreover, there was talk in the saloons that he was toying with the idea of a race track.

Item: Yet another syndicate of capitalists was mousing around, talking about a Sea Beach Palace and yet another railroad leading to its door.

In 1876 McKane, summing them up, subtracting all the rumors, was able to count no less than six separate railways to Coney, actual or chartered, in operation or tangibly planned. Moreover, to compete with the pier down at the western tip of the island there were, as he knew, plans afoot to build two modern iron piers into the ocean, one off the beach at Brighton and the other just to the west. (Indeed, armed with this information, McKane had himself taken a flyer into real estate: he

How they built a railroad station at Coney in 1879. The drawing cheats a trifle: the Sea Beach Palace was a block from the beach. COURTESY THE FRANCIS K. MOORE COLLECTION

The Old Iron Pier. In the background, at the left are the Elephant Hotel and Feltman's; at right, Bauer's Casino and the Iron Tower. COURTESY THE FRANCIS K. MOORE COLLECTION

had taken the lease on the half-lot adjoining the one rented to the Iron Pier Company; it would yield him a handsome profit.)

This ferment of investment activity whetted McKane's political instincts. The ambitious politician must be quite as much concerned with imaginary enemies as with actual friends, for he needs the one to gain the other. McKane conjured up enemies in two directions. Because one was in the extreme east and the other in the extreme west, this gave him a spurious moral advantage: he could contrive for his supporters the myth that he was himself a good liberal, conservative middle-of-the-roader, beset on the right hand by Bourbons and on the left by rascals.

On the right, there were the two spanking new developments, Brighton Beach and Manhattan Beach, smart, elegant, and, especially in the case of Manhattan Beach, snobbish. They were to cater to the "best" people from New York. But, as McKane knew, the best people from New York had just gone through the uproarious process of giving the boot to William Marcy Tweed, the political boss; New York was in the hands of thin-blooded reform elements; might there not be an attempt to import these reactionary, blue-stocking notions to Coney Island? And might this not, in turn, blight what gave every sign of becoming a bona fide bonanza?

On the left, the rascal was a jovial, hard-fisted New York politician, Michael Norton, and all things considered McKane was justified in regarding him as the greater potential threat. Norton—his nickname was Thunderbolt Mike because of his reputed ability to knock out a man with one punch, the kind of reputation that had saved him from many a fight—had gotten a toehold on Coney Island through his political connections. The Brooklyn politicians, Bob Furey, Frank Swift, and the others, who had leased Coney Island Point from McKane for $6,100, had sub-leased to a prominent New York gambler, Mike Murray, for $12,500. Murray was a dummy for his brother Jim and for Mike Norton. In 1875, Mike Norton and Jim Murray had taken over the Point and had promptly incarnadined its already fairly crimson reputation. The Point was tailor-made for a man like Mike Norton; it was entirely logical that the area should become known as Norton's Point. He had a wide circle of friends among the sort of people ("pickpockets, prostitutes, and rowdies . . . panel-girls, swindlers, and other wolves in sheepskin") by whom and for whose benefit pic-nics and excursions were organized; Mike saw no reason why he should not own the hotels, saloons, and pavilions that stood to profit from such excursions. He had come by his large circle of friends just as any red-blooded, Irish-born, New York politician might have done. Mike had been a captain in the Twenty-fifth (New York) Regiment in the Civil War, he had been elected an alderman in 1864 and, when he was twenty-eight, a State Senator in 1867. He had early learned the nice techniques necessary to win elections: the Federal Commissioner of Elections for the Southern District of New York reported that, in the presidential election of 1868, there were thirty persons registered from Mike's home at 116 Varick Street and of these twenty-two cast votes, although there were only three who actually lived at the address. For services like these, Mike was admitted to the bar. He matriculated, swotted, was examined, and graduated from law school all in the space of about five minutes. His faculty was a Tweed Ring judge named George C. Barnard, who asked him only one question: "What would be the procedure in case a bill against the city was placed in your hands for collection?" Mike's answer delighted his law-school classmate, Boss Tweed. "I'd go and see the Boss," said Mike. That same year, Mike made a sensible investment: he gave Tweed a clarence and team of horses, complete down through livery for the driver to a whip with a silver handle: it had cost him $6,000. In return, Tweed awarded him twelve sinecures; among other things Mike became Corporation Livery Stable Keeper, Baggage Agent at Castle Garden, Commissioner of Tweed's new Courthouse and of the Jefferson Market Courthouse, and Contractor for the Sprinkling of Harlem-lane. This last position alone netted Mike $25,000 a year. Moreover, Tweed gave Mike $67,250 in cash for his assistance, as State Senator, in securing the passage of Tweed's charter for the city of New York. But every dream must end. Mike had been indicted along with Tweed in 1872, had been arrested in 1873, had jumped his bail, had turned state's evidence in 1874, and, after surrendering to the authorities and getting bailed again, had employed some of his loot to buy the lease on the Coney Island Point and refurbish the tacky old Pavilion and bathhouses.

McKane knew enough of this story to be wary of Norton. McKane knew, too, just how close a relationship Norton had with Tweed. In the course of building up his own personal political machine, McKane had made friends with the only two men who lived, with their families, year-round on Coney Island Point. These were Joseph Kowski, who was in charge of the pier, and James Sangunitto, who tended the harbor light just off the Point. Both men had told McKane a story, the same story, guardedly, out of the corner of their mouths, and McKane, listening, had pursed his lips.

In December, 1875, Tweed had been in the Ludlow Street Jail in Manhattan pending his second trial on a whole battery of charges. His incarceration was an offhand, casual affair: nearly every day, in the company of a pair of wardens, he would drive uptown in a closed carriage and go for a drive through Central Park; once in the open country north of the Park he would climb out of the carriage and take a stroll; on his way back downtown, as like as not he would stop off at his mansion to visit with his wife. This was the routine procedure on December 4, up to a point. On that day Tweed, in the custody of a warden and a keeper, and accompanied by his son, stopped at his home and went up to the second floor to see his wife. The warden and keeper sat in the darkening drawing room. A few minutes after six, the warden instructed young Tweed to call his father. Another minute or two passed before young Tweed tumbled downstairs, apparently consternated, to report that his father was not to be found. There followed the predictable brouhaha, the keeper rushing upstairs, the warden rushing to the front door. Two days later a reward of $10,000 was offered for information that would lead to Tweed's capture.

Where had he gone? In the next few weeks the newspapers were to say that he was in Savannah, Ga., in Dallas, Tex., in

It was this cartoon by Thomas Nast which, having found its way to Spain, led to Boss Tweed's capture there. The Spanish officials thought he must be wanted for kidnapping.
Harper's Weekly, 1876

Havana, Cuba, in Hamilton, Ontario, and in London, England. But for nearly six months Tweed was very nearly within shouting distance of Manhattan. He had been taken first across the Hudson and hidden in the woods back of the Jersey palisades. After a time he was removed to a shack on Staten Island. Then, by boat, he was transported to Coney Island Point—to Norton's Point. Norton was paying off his old debts. On the Point, Tweed lived in relative squalor, but Kowski's family cared for him. At length he received the signal he had been waiting for. On May 29, 1876, Tweed, his beard shaved off and his head incongruously bewigged, clambered aboard a sand barge. There he lay quiet while he was hidden under some of the sand. Thus cowering and comic, the former boss of city and empire state was wafted unmajestically down the lower bay to the schooner *Frank Atwood,* lying at anchor, waiting for the rendezvous. Off he sailed, a furtive figure of fun, to his peculiar destiny: to Florida, to Cuba, to Spain; to recapture and extradition; and back to death in jail.

McKane shared the secret of Tweed's whereabouts from early in March until late in May. He told no one, for no one asked him, and McKane had early learned the inadvisability of volunteering unsolicited information. Nonetheless, the secret lay uncomfortably inside him, like baby's little bubble, nor did he care to share his island with the man—Mike Norton—who had insured Tweed's temporary escape. His reluctance stemmed not so much from his disapproval of Norton's complicities as from his respect for them. McKane's education had carried him beyond the point where he might cavil at moral distinctions, but he was beginning to take an enthusiastic interest in power and its perquisites. Norton made him nervous, because Norton stood in the way of control of Coney. Norton's sublease on the Point was to run until 1883. Long before that time, McKane vowed, Gravesend's political control would be locked up in a vault. It would have to be.

Political control, in Gravesend, was vested in the supervisor. Whoever held that position was also, ex officio, chairman of the Town Board, the Board of Health, the Water Board, the Improvement Board, and the Board of Audit; he also nominated the justices of the peace who, in their frequent spare time, sat as members of these various boards. If the supervisor could make a fist he could hold the town in it. McKane considered that he was supremely capable of making such a fist. Moreover, as commissioner of common lands, he had been in a splendid position to select lessees who, as taxpayers and therefore voters, would appreciate his friendship. And what is wrong with making friends?

Charles Feltman, the inventor of the hot dog, arrived in 1871. He took a sublease of a small shanty on an ocean lot leased by Martin Hook; he paid Hook $500 the first year (Hook, for his whole lot, was paying only $70); when next year Hook rejected his offer of $2,100, Feltman looked around. Whom should he see but McKane? For $15 a year, Feltman got the big lot right next to McKane's own, right next to the lot on which was to be built the New Iron Pier; here he (or, rather, McKane) built his huge Ocean Pavilion. Having thus played tit for tat, Feltman became McKane's friend.

William Vanderveer arrived in 1873. He was a plasterer and bricklayer who, finding his level in Brooklyn politics, became a sewer inspector and made some money. Turning to Coney Island before, as he was later to testify, he had "cut his eye-teeth," he paid $2,196 rent on two of the smaller ocean lots. Then he met McKane and cut his eyeteeth. Subsequently, McKane built bathhouses for him: twelve the first season, seventy-five the next, two hundred the next, a three-story hotel and a three-story bathing pavilion the next. During those years and thereafter, Vanderveer paid only $46 annual rent on one lot, only $15 on the other. Vanderveer became McKane's friend.

Garry Katen arrived in 1876. He had been a barkeep and a gambler in New York, he wanted some more of the same on Coney. Katen took no detours. He went straight to McKane and made him an offer. Presently McKane built for him his Beach House on an ocean lot next to Ravenhall's. Katen paid the town $5 a year rent. Katen became McKane's friend.

Paul Bauer also arrived in 1876. Bauer, an Austrian-born New York maître-d'hôtel, had married the daughter of John J. O'Brien, Republican leader of the teeming area east of the Bowery. He came with his wife, on a visit, and their carriage nearly overturned in the soft sand at the foot of Ocean Park-

way. "This," said his wife bitingly, "is the worst place I ever
saw." "It can be made the best," he answered and, because
he was the son-in-law of a politician, asked questions of the
right people. The lot he hit upon, twelve acres big, just off
the Parkway and close to the Culver Plaza, was already leased
by a knowing Gravesender, James Voorhies, for $75 a year,
and Voorhies insisted on retaining a strip of shorefront to
nourish his clutch of bathhouses. Bauer was agreeable: he
paid Voorhies $1,000 a year for the rights to his lease and
accepted $1 a year as rental for the strip of sand. He also sub-
leased a fraction of his lot to other tenants for $13,000 a year.
Then he looked up McKane and engaged him as contractor to
build the biggest hotel in West Brighton. McKane had it
ready by early May, 1876—complete with rooms for two hundred and fifty guests, a dining-room big enough to serve one
thousand at a time, and four tower rooms for private banquets.
Bauer became McKane's very good friend. He even became his
in-law: McKane's brother James was to marry Bauer's daughter
Katie.

Friendship is a beautiful thing. And it is better to give than
to receive. Nevertheless, the Gravesend town treasurer was
justified in fixing these and many other similar transactions
with a chilly eye. In 1878 the town's income from rental of the
common lands was close to $17,500, an all-time high. Yet, if
the lots had been leased at honest, convenient, and well-
advertised public auction the town's income would have
amounted to no less than $200,000. The Gravesend gentry
were belatedly aware of this, and it vexed them. But irritation,
however passionate, does not count as much at the polls as
votes. When election time came in 1876, the Coney Island
lessees, McKane's rod and his staff, swept him into office.

Well might the Gravesend gentry be dismayed: for the first
time since, in 1714, there had been such an officer as supervisor,

one of theirs was not in the chair. But they had yet to gauge McKane's vast capacity for generous friendship.

There was some land lying east of Austin Corbin's Manhattan Beach and, despite the fact that it was part of the town's common lands, Corbin coveted it. The freeholders, alert to the soaring land values, were reluctant to sell. But McKane, ever zealous to show how friendly he could be, tipped Corbin off that a sale could be authorized by a voice vote at the annual town meeting. It was all Corbin needed to know. With McKane's active consent, Corbin packed the town meeting with a swarm of two hundred toughs, many of them swinging clubs in a thoughtful way. Amid wild confusion, a resolution was whooped through, bidding the town to sell and Corbin to buy at a price to be agreed upon by two appraisers, one appointed by the town, the other named by Corbin. Just to make sure, Corbin's bhoyos stayed in the meeting long enough to elect the chairman, Stephen Voorhies, as the town's appraiser, for Voorhies had been added to Corbin's payroll the day before.

How much was this land worth? In a subsequent investigation conducted by the State Senate's Committee on Villages, witnesses would testify it was worth $100,000. Corbin's own opinion was to be set forth in a prospectus issued by the Manhattan Beach Development Company. To be sure, he may have exaggerated slightly, for after all the purpose of a prospectus is to sell stock. In any event, he stated the worth of the land to be $500,000.

Voorhies, the town's appraiser, examined nothing, looked at no maps, sought advice from no lawyer or real estate expert, in fact talked to no one about the appraisal save only James Armstrong, Corbin's appraiser. Armstrong asked him to put a value on the land. Voorhies, a carpenter, gulped and mentioned a very big number. "How about $2,000?" he suggested. Arm-

The Manhattan Beach Hotel, "swept by ocean breezes." This was for thirty years the most fashionable resort hotel in the U. S.   COURTESY THE FRANCIS K. MOORE COLLECTION

strong seemed staggered. He offered it as his opinion that the land wasn't worth more than $500. The two men agreed to compromise at $1,500.

The magnitude of the theft left the Gravesend gentry numb. Feebly they struggled to avert the inevitable. Thrice they called special town meetings to protest, to repudiate, to reverse; thrice Corbin's ringers trooped back in to pack their meeting and obstruct their will. The last meeting was incredibly raucous and violent. The town's respectability, in its death-throes, lashed about furiously. Fist fights broke out all over the hall. The chairman was a ruffian elected as justice of the peace on the McKane ticket; his gavel was a three-foot bludgeon; he splintered the table in his efforts to maintain order. A New York lawyer, retained by the old guard, at one point sought vainly to make himself heard. He was thrown out. At length

McKane, exasperated and thoroughly out of patience with these genteel farmers who would not take their licking gracefully, sprang up on a chair. His words filtered fitfully through the tumult. He was reading a resolution. "Whereas this meeting is not competent . . . it is not expedient . . . opposed to squandering the money of the town . . . useless litigation . . . gratify private spite . . . Resolved . . . refuse to interfere with the action of the last special meeting . . . refuse to appropriate any money for litigation or expenses of any kind." Bang! went the chairman's bludgeon. "All in favor?" The Ayes were a thunder. Gravesend's freeholders glumly departed.

Power had shifted. Gone from the gently rolling, prosperous farmlands, gone from the hands of the respectable farmers, gone from the hearths and homes of the heirs of the land's pioneers. Coney Island had taken over. The rogues and the rascals had come roistering into control, and McKane was their leader. His teeth showed in an exultant grin. How much had it cost to buy him? Who cared? Who, indeed, would ever know? The town was in his fist. Coney Island was his; his, the nation's newest and gaudiest playground. His toy!

N. Y. PUBLIC LIBRARY
PICTURE COLLECTION

~Scandalous~

THERE was something in the air at Coney, back in the 1880's, that led men to devise queer and monstrous notions. Of these surely the most singular was hatched by James V. Lafferty, a man who must have been gifted either with a spectacular sense of humor or with none at all. He built the Elephant.

The Elephant (it was also billed as The Colossus of Architecture) was a tin-skinned structure 122 feet high, housing a shopping bazaar and several hotel rooms, and built, by an odd coincidence, in the shape of an elephant. It faced the ocean across Surf Avenue, not far from the Sea Beach Palace. Its legs were sixty feet in circumference; in one front leg was a cigar store, in the other a diorama; patrons walked up circular steps in one hind leg and down the other, and those with a thirst for notoriety could engage rooms for the night in thigh, shoulder, hip, cheek, or trunk (this last was a room eleven feet high and eleven feet in diameter); the brute's four-foot glass eyes glittered insanely at night; its howdah was an observatory outfitted with telescopes fore and aft.

When first this jumbo conceit was unveiled, it caused an understandable stir. People went down to Coney just to see the

55

The improbable structure at right, above, is the Elephant Hotel, hedged in behind a scenic railway. Unblinking, it stares upon the casinos, saloons, and dance pavilions of West Brighton; upon a few merry-go-rounds and

Elephant. Indeed, the phrase "seeing the elephant" passed into the language, but in the process it acquired an additional level of meaning. When the vaudeville comic threw the phrase away, when the soubrette winked saucily as she interpolated the words into her song, the sports in their audience howled and smacked thighs. And the others in the audience, harkening to the unmistakable note of lubricity in the laughter, caught wise soon enough. For the phrase was a euphemism: the bucko who arose, stretched, and announced that he was off to see the elephant was understood to say that he was up to no good and looking for a complaisant young lady who would second his motion. This new level of meaning derived exclusively from the loose and easy ways that prevailed on John

other whirligigs; upon Surf Avenue, as yet unpaved, dwindling away to
nothing as it wanders west toward Norton's Point; and upon the beach,
the magnificent wide beach. COURTESY THE FRANCIS K. MOORE COLLECTION

Y. McKane's Coney Island. The Elephant stood spang in the
middle of a neighborhood expressly designed for those who
were up to no good, and thereabouts, too, complaisant young
ladies abounded.

There was a fateful predictability about this state of affairs.
A certain time-lag, while the phrase and all its connotations
seeped into the mind of the community; a few clangorous
incidents to keep the connotations fresh and vivid; a smoking
onslaught from two or three pulpits; a gathering of interested
reformers, like turkey-buzzards wheeling menacingly overhead; and thereafter, in a gentle rain from Albany, down
fluttered the subpoenas, foreboding an investigation. These
were, as usual, twice cursed: by the men on whom they had

been served and, quite as heartily, by the gamblers, con men, mackerels, and bawds who feared for their profits while the heat should be on. McKane, as befitted his role as superintendent of the Methodist Sabbath School, did not curse. But he scowled blackly and summoned his cronies into conference.

Nine years as supervisor of Gravesend had altered McKane. In 1887 he moved with an air of authority, shoulders back and belly forward. Diamonds twinkled discreetly on his shirt front, at his cuffs, on his finger. He had become a man of importance. As president of the county board of supervisors, he was to be reckoned with in county and state politics. He had become one of Brooklyn Boss Hugh McLaughlin's intimates, a circumstance comparable to admission into a course in Advanced Chicane. He had come by this exalted status by doing what comes naturally to any politician: delivering the vote. He had found that it was easier to control Gravesend's votes in a national election than to win them in a local election, and was accorded more respect in county and state. Since all voting was done in the Town Hall, McKane could sit like a spider in a web, eyeing the voters as they filed in. It was not often necessary for him to eye their ballots after they had gone out. The boom on the beach had brought a bulge in the town's population; simultaneously McKane had learned the revealed truth of nineteenth century bosses, that the more votes there are the more votes can be stolen. In 1884 he had delivered a very satisfactory Democratic majority for Grover Cleveland. Then one of his henchmen had pointed out a striking presumption: without McKane, Cleveland could not have made it to the White House. The reasoning ran (and responsible Republicans concurred) that Cleveland had needed New York's electoral vote, that New York had slipped into the Democratic column by less than 1,200 votes, that this would never have occurred without McKane's sharp practice with Gravesend's ballots.

McKane had admired this logic. Reflecting on it, he became a man of self-importance, exacting subservience, intolerant of opposition. Indeed, he believed he had wiped out all opposition. Yet here were these subpoenas. They came from a special investigating committee of the State Assembly, and they seemed to have been plastered with deadly accuracy right on the men who best knew where the bodies were buried. It suggested connivance by someone inside his own fief and it made McKane uneasy. Whence this unknown opposition? Was his adversary one man or a coalition? And exactly how much did the committee's investigators already know, about affairs on Coney? There was plenty to find, if they really knew where to look. And if they found enough, he feared for his control of the resort.

McKane was confident that the committee would not be concerned with the eastern half of his domain. East of Ocean Parkway, where the mammoth wooden hotels and bathing pavilions crowded the prospect, all was gay and fashionable and all was quite decent. The Brighton Beach Hotel drew the bulk

The Brighton Beach Hotel had champagne on draft, at ten cents a glass. But it was never so fashionable as its eastern neighbors. COURTESY THE FRANCIS K. MOORE COLLECTION

This is no French château, but the Oriental Hotel, closed for winter. In the foreground, a boardwalk is under construction. COURTESY THE FRANCIS K. MOORE COLLECTION

of its clientele from the ranks of successful businessmen, theatrical folk, and the more respectable politicians; the Manhattan Beach Hotel was given over to society; and the Oriental Hotel, open since the season of 1880, farthest removed from the hub-bub, was filled with wealthy and sedate families who came down not merely for weekends but for the whole summer season. In the east end, entertainment was restricted to displays of fireworks, seemly band concerts, and strolls along the seashore. Two or three policemen were all that ever patrolled these beaches, and they were rarely called on to lift a nightstick in righteous wrath.

Nor, by 1887, was Norton's Point much shakes any more as a sink of sin. As soon as the two ocean piers were built from the middle of the island, the crowds had forsaken the west end. The pic-nic fell into disrepute, Thunderbolt Mike Norton's

Pavilion lost its glamor, he fell behind in his rent to the Brooklyn politicians who had sold him the lease, they wrangled and squabbled and went to law, Mike himself moved disconsolately through bankruptcy proceedings, the bathhouses sagged into the sand, and the timid sandpipers returned to the beach.

The middle of the Island, however, the section that had come to be known as West Brighton, was apple pie for even the most incompetent of investigators. From the time McKane took over as town supervisor this part of Coney had been wide open. There were, to be sure, a few islands of respectability in West Brighton. Lucy Vanderveer had assumed from her husband the operation of their bathing pavilion, Peter Ravenhall's restaurant was already popular with parties that came down to Coney after the races, Peter Tilyou filled his Surf House with a family trade, Charles Feltman's ever-growing Ocean Pavilion was a center for the substantial German-American middle class whose tastes ran to choral singing and vast schooners of beer, Tom Cable could rightfully claim for his hotel the finest wine-cellar on the Island, and there were a few others. But there was an unmistakable febrile glow that lighted up the whole area. After 1878 the word got around: the fix was in. Coney—which was to say West Brighton —became one of the roughest spots on earth.

A shrewd investigator might relate this change to the day McKane got control of Coney's police force. Previously the beach had been patrolled by Brooklyn cops, but they were not answerable to the Gravesend supervisor, and McKane chafed under this curb. It took him two years to work his way with the legislature in Albany, but by 1881, with the authorization in his pocket, he was able to hire his own force, buy himself his own badge, name himself Chief, and build himself a shack in the heart of West Brighton to serve as his headquarters. Virtuously he proclaimed that he was serving at no salary. A salary would have been superfluous. The money to support the force came from licenses issued by him: soon anything on Coney required a license: the fees ranged from $50 for guess-your-weight concessions to $250 for layouts for ring boards or hoop tosses. Museums, carrousels, dancehalls and pavilions, music halls and saloons, shooting galleries and basket peddlers, high strikers and side shows, carryalls and hacks—all paid their tribute to the Chief. And all learned to err, when they forked their fees over to the Chief, on the side of generosity.

Would the investigators want to know who had gotten licenses? McKane must have winced at the thought. For the fact was, he had displayed a remarkable clemency in issuing licenses. The man who could not get or renew a license elsewhere was welcome here. From Hell's Kitchen, from the Tenderloin, from the Bowery, from every rathole of New York whence they had been flushed when the Tweed Ring

Picnic basket-lunches at Ravenhall's were a popular diversion in the 1880's and 1890's. Then to Brighton, for the racing.   THE BYRON COLLECTION, MUSEUM OF THE CITY OF NEW YORK

was at length ousted, they had formed a line and headed for
Coney. Grifters, bruisers, bouncers, pickpockets, and cracks-
men had filed through McKane's headquarters. Some got
licenses to run saloons, some operated flat-joints, some opened
fleabag hotels, some financed gambling houses, some joined
the police force.

What if the committee were to subpoena some from this
rogue's gallery? There was Joe Gorman, for instance. Gorman's
mugg was in the files of the New York Police Department,
labeled Number 329, for he had been lagged early and often
as a pickpocket. In selecting his profession he had displayed
at least some originality: his father was a fence, one brother
was a sneak thief and till-tapper, another brother was a
second-story man, and his wife Molly was a shop-lifter. After
attending to the redistribution of wealth for some years, Joe
and Molly had come to Coney to run the Hermitage, an inn
on the Creek near Gravesend Bay. It was a center for former
business associates. Another thief, who later published an
anonymous autobiography, described his idyllic trysts at the
Hermitage:

> Saturday nights in the summertime a mob of three or four
> of us, grafters and girls, would go to the Island and stop at
> a hotel run by an ex-gun [this was Gorman]. At two or three
> o'clock in the morning we'd all leave the hotel, with nothing
> on but a quilt, and go in swimming together. Sheenie Annie,
> Blonde Mamie, and Big Lena [here he gives the monickers of
> three well-known shoplifters] often went with us. At other
> times we took respectable shopgirls, or even women who
> belonged to a still lower class. What boy with an ounce of
> thick blood in his body could refuse to go with a girl to
> the Island?

What boy indeed? But even with mobs of such boys filling
his inn every summer weekend, Gorman found time to eke

out his income by joining Chief McKane's police force. He was a uniformed cop for several summers at $100 a month. It was healthy outdoor work. And never lonesome: he could always count on seeing the patrons of his hotel, busy at their work among the Sunday crowds.

Or what if the committee investigators knew about red-haired Kate Leary? Kate was more celebrated than Gorman, and McKane had given her a license to run a small saloon a few yards from the ocean, on land that was later to be taken over by Steeplechase Park. Kate was wife to John (Red) Leary, moving spirit of a gang of bank robbers that flourished for a quarter century after the Civil War. Red was an engaging figure in the criminal and sporting world of the time. A massive man, he weighed nearly three hundred pounds and was acknowledged by such experts as John Morrissey, the pugilist, gambler, and Tammany politician, to be the best rough-and-tumble fighter in America. But he was no ordinary thug: he was fluent in French, German, Spanish, and Italian; he had, moreover, his own punctilio: he forbade profanity or obscenity in the presence of women. With his considerable help, his gang did well. George Walling, who was superintendent of New York police when the gang was in its prime, is authority for the estimate that they engineered eighty per cent of the bank robberies in the United States between 1860 and 1884, snatching $500,000 from New York City banks alone and at least $7,000,000 altogether. Men who could spend even a tithe of this kind of cash on Coney could get themselves gaudy reputations. Leary was accused of complicity in some notable capers. When $1,500,000 in cash and securities was removed from a bank in Northhampton, Mass. in January, 1876, Red was said to be there; he was on hand, too, in October, 1878, on the historic occasion when the Manhattan Savings Bank was knocked off for $2,747,700, most of it in non-negotiable securities. This haul—it was to hold the record for several decades—provoked an unprecedented public squawk. Red was in cosy retirement on Coney, but one day he made the mistake of showing his face in Brooklyn and was at once picked up. He was released for lack of evidence on the Manhattan Savings Bank charge but immediately rearrested as one of the Northhampton bank robbers and carried away to Ludlow Street Jail. The notion was to extradite him for trial in Massachusetts, but the police were reckoning without red-haired Kate. She enterprisingly rented three rooms at 76 Ludlow Street, right next to the jail. She got hold of two men who knew how to operate a hydraulic jimmy and pointed to a spot on the wall. At noon of May 7, 1879 Kate was admitted to the jail to visit her husband; she was back with John (Butch) McCarthy to see him that evening from five until eight. She saw him again at nine p.m. but this time it was without the sanction of the prison authorities. This time Red had hurled his mighty shoulder against the final layer of brick and was climbing through a hole that led through five feet of masonry from the third-tier toilet of the prison to her tenement flat. It was a clean sneak. No warden realized that the Ludlow Street Jail was shy one bank-robber until two hours later. By that time Red, trussed up in wrapping-paper, was in the back of a wagon headed for Coney, driven by a thief named Ed Goodie, and hauled by two sorrel horses. Kate, wrapped up like her husband, lay next to him and all the way down Ocean Parkway to Coney and safety they laughed and laughed.

It was then McKane had given her a license to open a saloon. But her prestigious exploit made her bar too popular a hangout. She and Red fled to Europe. Home again, he was recaptured in Brooklyn by some Pinkertons. This time it stuck, but Kate kept her hand in. Her saloon, suggestively called the Red Light, rivaled the Hermitage as a hangout for thieves; once, only too recently, some Manhattan detectives had raided the Red Light and flushed a covey of loft-workers; after diligently delving in the sand in front of the saloon, moreover, they had turned up $30,000 worth of silk, safely wrapped in oilcloth. Only the greatest diplomacy of her local protectors had saved Kate's skin on that occasion.

McKane had permitted another prominent member of the same gang houseroom on Coney. This was Abe Coakley, a man whose benevolent appearance was enhanced by a Santa Claus beard. Coakley had had a hand in the Manhattan Savings Bank robbery. When a policeman on his rounds had glanced in through the bank's window, on the Sunday morning of the theft, it had been Abe who, in shirtsleeves, impersonating a janitor, had had the *chutzpeh* to give the cop a cheery and reassuring wave of the hand. The cop had returned the wave and strolled on, while the gang had completed the job. Abe retired to Coney on the proceeds of his share and, licensed by McKane, opened a saloon. By 1887, if historians of the period are to be trusted, Abe had taken a step up in the hierarchy of the underworld and was assisting in the play of various short con games devised to pluck Coney's visitors.

Was it possible the committee had never heard of those short cons? Several of them were invented at Coney in this period. Every other house along the lower end of Ocean Parkway was a late-hours gambling joint; one of the principal duties of McKane's cops was to direct the eager chumps to where they could play faro, keno, or roulette. As soon as the gamblers discovered that among these tourists were many who liked to get the best of it, they exerted their ingenuity and evolved tat (a crooked dice game), the tip (a crooked poker game), the last turn (a crooked faro game), and the huge duke (a crooked poker game played with a euchre deck); their profits were enormous.

McKane might have wondered if any committee investigator had been snooping around on Coney's newest street, the Bowery. If so, the investigator could have gotten an eyeful. He might have dropped in for the evening, say, at Solomon Perry's Glass Pavilion. Perry had formerly run a disreputable haunt on Broadway near Houston Street; when the New York authorities nailed it shut, McKane had welcomed him to Coney. The Chief himself never went into the place except on business, but his coachman was an enthusiastic patron and kept him fully informed.

In this early spring of 1887 McKane, if he thought about the Glass Pavilion, might have recalled a contest that had taken place there one night late in the previous summer. Miss Lilly Larkelle and Miss Clara Chappell, two of Perry's star table workers—that is, singers who were required to sit with the customers between numbers and urge on them more drinks—sang The Maid of the Mill for a prize of $10 offered by a book-maker from the Brighton Beach racetrack. The audience, for it was late in the season, included chiefly members of the year-round colony and a delegation of touts and jockeys. Inter-est ran high. Side bets were freely offered and covered all over the room. Then a hush fell as the professor banged out a vamp and Lilly sang a verse and then the chorus:

> *Do not forget me,*
> *Do not forget me,*
> *Think sometime of me still!*
> *When the morn breaks,*
> *And the throstle awakes,*
> *Remember The Maid of the Mill . . .*
> *Do not forget me,*
> *Do not forget me,*
> *Remember The Maid of the Mill!*

Deafening applause for Lilly. Again the expectant hush. Clara got the vamp and sang the song once more. An equally thunderous cheer and, rising shrilly above it, the high-pitched verdict of a jockey: "Dead heat!" But the official arbiter arose, a Paris come to judgment. This was a gentleman renowned for his discrimination. He was Cockeyed Leo, the eminent fence, successor indeed to Marm Mandelbaum herself. Cockeyed Leo's fame was enhanced by the fact of his being brother to Dutch Heinrich, who supplied him with much of the silk and lace and jewelry with which he dealt.

"I find," said Leo, "for Miss Larkelle," and the approving shout of her supporters could be heard all over West Brighton One hand held aloft, Miss Larkelle nevertheless clutched the sawbuck in her other. And presently, with an imperious gesture, she summoned a waiter and called for as much beer as her prize would buy. Not Coney beer, four-fifths froth, but bottled Milwaukee beer, a stunning treat. And she summoned to sit with her, to share in the fruits of her victory, a cross-section of Coney Island society. There was her defeated competitor, of course, and the bookmaker who gave the prize. Joe Gorman was at her table too, next to an old gambler who, afflicted with the palsy, could no longer deal faro. The Human Pincushion, from a nearby side show, joined her, as did a newspaperman. The last to be invited was a pathetic old drab in shabby clothes, who came to the table from a dark corner of the Pavilion where she was sometimes permitted to sit, quiet and humble, without being importuned to buy a drink. This forlorn derelict was Diamond Minnie, once, years ago, a reigning beauty of the Cremorne, the Buckingham, and the Argylle Rooms of the Tenderloin, once a lovely courtesan in Solomon Perry's own Boulevard, back on lower Broadway. Envy once was hers, pity now; and gratefully she drank her free beer.

The memory of the incident would bring McKane, in its

Joe Gorman was in the
rogue's gallery in the 1880's,
but he was a respected Coney
Island boniface a few years
later.

FROM T. F. BYRNES *Professional
Criminals of America.*
N. Y. PUBLIC LIBRARY

train, two associations. One concerned the old gambler. He
had died, a month or two ago, leaving a little money and a last
will and testament only one line long. McKane must have smiled
as he thought of that last request, so faithfully executed by
the gambler's friends. It was that no one should go sober to his
funeral. Three or four dozen of Coney's best had reeled hilari-
ously after the hearse to the old burying ground in Gravesend,
and Joe Gorman had toppled into the grave while trying to say
a prayer beside it.

The other memory, and here McKane must have scowled,
concerned Cockeyed Leo. He had done the Chief dirt, precisely
how was never learned. It was enough that McKane had turned
his hand against him. About that time a committee waited on
the Chief to solicit his contribution to a charity. McKane had
bristled. "I won't give you people a dollar," he had vowed,
"so long as Cockeyed Leo, who's one of you, remains on earth.
But," he had added, "I'll give fifty dollars to the first man who
brings me news of his death." And before the week was out

McKane was awakened, late at night, by a crowd come to collect the money.

In the main what went on along the Bowery, while occasionally rough, was all in the spirit of fun and the patrons of cabarets like the Glass Pavilion were, even when a little criminal, at least the aristocracy of the underworld. But McKane suffered as well an underworld slum, a noisome cluster of shacks and firetraps cramped together in a long shallow hollow reaching north from the dunes alongside and to the west of Ocean Parkway. This was called the Gut, and McKane knew there was no hope that it would be overlooked by an investigating committee. The Gut owed its population to Coney's thriving racetracks. The first of these had been the one-mile oval at the Brighton Beach Fair Grounds, where races were run beginning in 1879; the next year the Coney Island Jockey Club had opened a richer and more fashionable course at Sheepshead Bay, in 1886 there had appeared the Brooklyn Jockey Club's track at Gravesend, to the north. Thus in short order there had been need to find semi-permanent roosts for a great flock of touts, exercise-boys, jockeys, racetrack riffraff, and their camp followers. Most of this crew thronged congenially into the Gut, and they kept the night hideous with their carousing from early in May until late in October. Off the evidence, the Gut ranked well up among the contenders for the palm as a latter-day Sodom. "It was the wickedest place in all America," wrote one scandalized commentator, after a nervous tour of the area. He added that "wild orgies . . . beggaring those of a low Paris concert-hall, could be seen [every night] in public . . . There was license," he concluded with a shudder, "utter and complete." After a testimonial like that, quite naturally the Gut had had a vogue. Its nightly orgies had begun to get overcrowded. The semi-permanent population had been obliged to resort to knock-out drops to thin the ranks of the prurient. At length McKane himself had been forced to take action. He had conducted some perfunctory raids and had sent packing off to jail all those who had no influential friends. Later, describing his actions to a reporter, McKane had been tolerant, even amused. It was as though he took pride in such a superlative concentration of vice in the very middle of his bailiwick, as though the Gut made Coney even more of a tourist attraction.

McKane, puffed up with self-importance, always had a hard time keeping his mouth shut around newspaper men. The Chief made juicy copy: every weekend three or four reporters would find their way to his headquarters and get him talking. He was a man among men; too often he forgot that he was also a police chief among reporters. On the subject of gambling on the horseraces within his jurisdiction, an activity that was sternly interdicted:

"I don't propose to interfere with the pool-selling at Brighton Beach and Sheepshead Bay."

On the subject of prostitution:

"Houses of prostitution are a necessity on Coney Island."

Impolitic remarks like these, coming from an official sworn to uphold the law, were an open affront to the righteous. Their self-appointed spokesman, Anthony Comstock, of the Society for the Suppression of Vice, then at his most officious, had engaged with his customary zeal to teach the Chief a lesson. In those days, the public debate as to the ethics of gambling on horse races was at its height. To Comstock there was no doubt, no debate. Gambling was a vice. He had been horrified to realize that at the three tracks in Gravesend alone the handle was an annual $15,000,000, a frightful source of sin and corruption, and every last penny of it illegal. He had rushed down to Coney with a sheriff's posse, bent on smashing the gambling at the Brighton Beach track. He had leaped from the train at the

Brighton depot before it came to a stop, thinking to catch the pool-sellers redhanded. But of course McKane had been tipped off in advance and had thoughtfully arranged to have a welcoming party on hand. Comstock had been booed on arrival, fleered at the track, hooted the more derisively when it developed that all the gambling paraphernalia had been momentarily hidden away, razzed as he bustled off to raid the pool-selling room in Paul Bauer's West Brighton Hotel, and jeered to the echo when he could find nothing incriminating there either. All very well, but McKane could not accord the same treatment to a committee of the State Assembly.

The committee met in the chamber of the Brooklyn Common Council, and it was there, responsive to his subpoena, that McKane sat, hostile and arrogant, on a Saturday morning in March, 1887. He was entitled to some misgivings, but he had determined to brazen it out. The committee chairman was an earnest Brooklyn Republican, a West Point graduate, Alexander Bacon, but the hearings were dominated by the chief counsel, John Parsons. Parsons was a chilly and forbidding man, intellectual, aristocratic, and an exceedingly able lawyer. At fifty-seven, he was recognized as a leading member of the New York bar. He was a co-founder of the New York City Bar Association and had been counsel to the association in its proceedings against the Tweed Ring judges. Actually, however, civic reform was for Parsons only a side-line, like his interest in Bible and tract societies. He was to make his reputation as one of the nation's foremost proponents of trusts and industrial combinations. Later in this same year he was to draw up the agreement that was the basis for the Sugar Trust, a combination that would occupy him professionally for the rest of his long life. With this committee hearing, Parsons was taking his leave of active participation in civic reform. His attitude toward the witnesses under subpoena was that of a biochemist

In 1879 Culver Plaza was gas-lit. Paul Bauer's West Brighton Hotel is at left, Cable's in the background, and at right the Inexhaustible Cow, from whose impartial udder pretty maids could draw either milk or lager.
COURTESY THE FRANCIS K. MOORE COLLECTION

who strives to isolate a deadly virus: something loathsome that must nevertheless be regarded with scientific detachment. He studied the Pooh-Bah of Coney Island without relish as McKane took his seat in the witness chair.

Parsons's task was to induce McKane to make for the record a statement of his own corruption, misfeasance, and malfeasance. He went about it with implacable efficiency. He and his associate counsel made McKane's witness chair into a meatgrinder.

The Chief was on the stand, that first day, for about three hours. He was taxed severely, as he had known he would be, for his slapdash attitude toward the Gut. On the matter of houses of prostitution running full-blast within a quarter-mile of his police headquarters: "I do not make inquiries," he said lamely. On the matter of gambling joints at Coney: "[There are] none that I know of," said the Chief, and stared out angrily at the audience when the wave of laughter swept the room. He claimed he had attempted to stop gambling at the tracks, but "I am not positive whether I went myself or whether I sent officers," he said, perhaps reflecting on the possibilities of his being indicted for perjury. He admitted that he had been paid upwards of $142,000 by the three tracks for various construction work he had done for them, and that among these buildings were at least 125 bookmaking booths, the purpose of which he understood quite clearly. Parsons permitted his distaste to show only in his icy formality. "Did you have any doubt that pool selling was going on?" he asked.

McKANE: No, sir.

PARSONS: I want to find out whether, when you saw that this pool selling was in full play, you then and there did anything to stop it.

McKANE: (*Sparring for time*) When I saw it myself?

PARSONS: Yes.

McKANE: (*Valiantly*) Yes, sir.

PARSONS: What did you do?

McKANE: (*After squirming thoughtfully for a time*) The way, as I understand the law now, is that you can't go and grab a man and do just as you please with him, without a warrant, and I generally try to be as cautious as I can, and at the same time do my duty; I may have perhaps went and got the warrant and then afterwards, if the racing was done for that day, I may have went the next day, or the day after that. . . .

Parsons declined to be moved by this touching display of respect for civil liberties.

PARSONS: Is there any doubt that a police officer has the right to stop the commission of crime which is going on under his own observation and in his own presence, without a warrant?

McKANE: (*As though impressed by a novel proposition*) If he sees the crime committed himself, I suppose he has the right to arrest them.

PARSONS: [Have] you ever exercised this right [when] you have seen pool selling in full play?

The question was uncomfortably close. In desperation, McKane, forgetting that he had but a moment before stated that he had personally witnessed the gambling, veered off at right angles.

McKANE: Mr. Parsons, I might just as well try to go to a furnace and not get hurt, when it was red hot, as to try to walk towards that race track and attempt to arrest anybody. As soon as I would go anywhere near the race track, if they were selling pools they would stop while I was there.

PARSONS: Your mere presence there stopped the pool selling?

McKANE: (*Vastly relieved*) There is no question about that.

PARSONS: Then why were you so careful to stay away?

McKANE: (*Inspired*) I had no business there unless there was complaint!

Before Parsons had done with him, the Chief had convicted himself of dereliction of duty, venality, and complicity in the violation of a half-dozen statutes. Then he was permitted to stand down. He took a chair in the rear of the room and there, in the succeeding days, he alternately glowered and winked at the parade of Coney witnesses that followed him to the stand. Most were his henchmen; most of those who were not he could control by virtue of the mortgages he held on their property. Over one-half of the buildings in West Brighton were so clamped under his thumb. And so each filed to the chair, protested he knew nothing or perjured himself, and passed on. The committee's lawyers seemed to be much interested in the fate of Gravesend's common lands. And this astonished McKane, for he had thought that that was all old history, since he had managed to sell all those lands five years before, to his friends and political allies. Just how he had managed those sales would, McKane hoped, never come out.

John Y. McKane

And, he reflected, it was just as well his old friend Garry Katen had managed to duck a subpoena. Katen was McKane's man in charge of the common lands. When the committee's sergeant-at-arms had come into Katen's gambling joint, a few weeks before, he had approached Katen, standing behind the bar. He had asked, "Is the boss in?" And Katen, wary, noticing the stiff, folded paper the sergeant-at-arms held in his hand, had said, "Sure. I'll go fetch him." And he had walked out the back door, kept on walking till he reached the end of Norton's Point, climbed into a boat, and passed over to Staten Island and thence to New Jersey, where he proposed to stay till the committee left town.

But still the stories of bribery and fraud came out. McKane glared helplessly as one witness, an executive of a railroad company and therefore not beholden, testified that he had had to pay the Chief a $4,000 bribe in order to buy one small parcel of land. And this was never denied. Indeed, so damaging was some of the testimony about the rigged sales of Coney real estate that a respectable young lawyer, William S. Gaynor, was obliged twice to take the chair to deny that he had had any part in the crooked dealings. He had been the lawyer for the trustees of the Gravesend common lands, and he was under a cloud, no doubt about it; his explanations had to come smoothly and fluently, for he was already launched on the political career that would one day make him mayor of New York City. But he was able to clear his name. Frauds there had unquestionably been, but without his knowledge or connivance.

Not until the next-to-last day of the Coney Island hearings did McKane discover who had been his secret opposition, the man who had so accurately singled out, for the committee's investigators, the most corrupt of McKane's henchmen. On that day Peter Tilyou's older son George took the chair.

George Tilyou was then twenty-five years old, and he was scared stiff. He knew that to testify against McKane was to invite the death warrant for any dreams he might have of doing business on the Island; he knew, as well, that he was placing himself in personal jeopardy, should McKane be able to ride out the storm of the committee's inquiry. He also stood alone. He was the only resident of Coney Island who dared, flatly and without qualification, to blow the whistle on the Chief. He sat in the chair for an hour and he blew the whistle without cease. As a resident of West Brighton for twenty-one years, as a man actively engaged in the real estate business, he knew what he was talking about. He named the houses of prostitution, and placed them; he told how a doctor who was McKane's assistant police sergeant and health officer got a weekly fee of $2 for each prostitute he examined. He had seen McKane's justices of the peace in gambling places and named names and dates. He had seen McKane's captain of police in regular attendance at one bagnio; the same man had tried to rent land from him to run a gambling joint. He had been

present when the trustees of the common lands had engaged
in a flagrant fraud. He had seen one of McKane's justices of the
peace leaving his courtroom after a trial, and—

Q: What was his condition?
TILYOU: Well, I should judge he was intoxicated.
Q: How grossly intoxicated?
TILYOU: Well, he came from police headquarters and went to
[a gambling place], and when he went to go up the stoop he
fell down and they had to pick him up.

In short, he reported what was common knowledge, giving
chapter and verse. And when he was done, McKane, trembling
with rage, stood up in the audience, demanding to make a statement. Parsons waved him delightedly to the witness chair
and minced him a second time. McKane desired to deny all
that Tilyou had said; he ended by convicting himself anew
for dereliction of duty, and by perjuring himself into the
bargain.

The committee's work was done. They filed a report with
the Assembly assailing Coney Island as "a source of corruption
and crime, disgraceful . . . and dangerous," and stigmatizing
McKane as "an enemy, and not a friend, of the administration
of justice." They recommended that Coney Island be made a
part of Brooklyn and called for "the immediate indictment
and the prompt prosecution of John Y. McKane, in order that,
if convicted, he may not only be punished but be removed
from the offices whose trust he·has so completely betrayed."
These conclusions of the committee were reached on May 11,
1887 and spread across the front pages of the newspapers.

It was one thing for the committee to recommend, but quite
another for the Assembly to act in such a way as to make it
stick. Besides, McKane was protected by the sturdy shield of

Brooklyn Boss Hugh McLaughlin. In truth, McLaughlin was disturbed. Some very dirty linen had been spread out and was dancing on the line. Corrupt though he was himself, McLaughlin had no stomach for graft that came from prostitution, nor for any protection of prostitution. He cooled toward McKane, but he kept his shield extended. In Albany, the committee's report was pigeon-holed.

Back at Coney, the Chief grinned broadly. His victory proved there was nothing could pry his grip loose from Coney Island. That summer he was tendered a vast testimonial party. It was held at Bauer's Casino in West Brighton. One thousand followers showed up to do homage to the Chief. A great picture of McKane, decked out in red, white, and blue bunting, dominated the room. He was called to the bandstand, toward the end of the evening, so that he might be presented with a gift: a gold badge with a diamond star within a circle, and upon it enameled, Chief of Police, Gravesend, Long Island; a laurel wreath worked in diamonds and emeralds surmounted an eagle with outstretched wings set in diamonds; on the back was engraved, "Presented to the Honorable John Y. McKane by his friends at Paul Bauer's Casino, Coney Island. Veritas Vincit." The badge held 229 brilliants and 110 emeralds. It was worth $1,500. It was presented to a beaming McKane by the same justice of the peace who had tumbled up a flight of stairs, falling down drunk.

George Tilyou found it necessary to retire from the real estate business.

It seemed to McKane that he was in the flood-tide of his prosperity. Who was there to challenge him? Now that he thought it over, had he ever really needed McLaughlin's help? Certainly not! He chose, capriciously, to be guilty of the crowning perfidy. He backed, on a whim, a Republican assemblyman. One of McLaughlin's lieutenants summoned the

Chief to Willoughby Street and bade him resign from the Democratic state committee and from the board of supervisors as well. "I suppose I can keep my clothes, can't I?" asked McKane, sardonically, and strode out.

Back at Coney, he sought out John J. O'Brien. O'Brien was family. Not only was O'Brien the father-in-law of McKane's closest crony, Paul Bauer; O'Brien's granddaughter Katie had married McKane's brother. O'Brien was also Republican politics. When he was not summering at Coney, he was New York City's Republican boss and New York City's election commissioner. There was much that he could whisper into McKane's ear. The Chief's unwonted silence during the presidential campaign of 1888 began to puzzle his followers. A committee of the John Y. McKane Association was appointed to wait on him and ask what was his pleasure. The members of the committee were back within ten minutes; they had been told that the citizens of Gravesend would be instructed as to how they should vote on the morning of election day; this remarkable report was received with a dutiful outburst of applause.

McLaughlin sniffed even greater perfidy. He mobilized three thousand loyal Democrats and had them poised on the border of Gravesend with each man holding a locust club; at the last minute he decided against a showdown battle.

On the morning of election day, 1888, the Chief spoke. His instructions were: Vote the straight Republican ticket. Throughout the long day he sat in Gravesend's town hall, eyeing his faithful as they trooped past to do his bidding. And not only his faithful: O'Brien's as well: for the two had evolved a delectable system. The good Republican waiters and bartenders and bouncers and thugs from O'Brien's New York Bowery district repeated as often as they dared in New York and were then transported to Coney to repeat all over again.

In turn, Coney's fragrant population of freaks, floaters, fortune-tellers, gypsies, touts, and resident thieves voted early and often and were thereafter shuttled to New York to repeat the process. My, what a vote they rolled up for Harrison!

And once again it was a close election. Cleveland had a popular plurality, but Harrison won in the electoral college. It was New York's thirty-six electoral votes that won for him, and once again New York was carried by the most slender of margins. This time there was no doubt about it: McKane's switch was responsible. It was the triumph of corruption.

McKane handpicked one hundred members from the John Y. McKane Association; he bought for each of them a cane, high-yaller gloves, a gray Prince Albert, and a stovepipe hat. Exultant, he led them north to Brooklyn and posed them for a photograph on the very steps of Hugh McLaughlin's City

The Chief celebrates his triumph. Here, complete with banner, is the John Y. McKane Association, on the steps of City Hall.   COURTESY KINGS COUNTY CLERK'S OFFICE

Hall. Then he paid their way to Washington, that they might march in the jubilant inaugural parade. On every Coney Island hip a flask of whiskey, in every Coney Island hand a flourishing cane, on every Coney Island nob a tall silk hat. They were a brave sight, marching down Pennsylvania Avenue.

And when the word came back to Coney of their triumph, of how President Harrison himself had swept off his hat and acknowledged Coney's crucial contribution with a graceful bow, my, how proud were the trollops, how proud were the pineapples, how proud the sports and the grifters and the double-bankers, the claws and the prattmen, the blisters and sharks! It was corrupt Coney's finest hour. McKane, twirling his stick, doffing his stovepipe left and right, had answered every critic and confounded every foe. He was in solid.

Puck, 1881. N. Y. PUBLIC LIBRARY

~Rapscallion~

AT four o'clock on the morning of November 7, 1893, the fire
bell in the Gravesend Town Hall began all at once to clang
urgently. Peal after peal rolled out. But there was no fire in
the town. The bell was a warning signal. "Wake up," it clamored; "out of bed! Now is the time for all good knaves to come
to the aid of John Y. McKane!" For this was election day, and
all the good knaves had been alerted that unfriendly strangers
were coming to town to pry into the masterful election prac-
tices of Coney Island. And so, on this morning only, the bell
was by prearrangement the town's alarm clock.

It was dark and raw and bitter cold outside, and the polls
were not scheduled to open till sunrise, at 6.38 a.m. Yet in a
very few minutes the wagons and buggies began to clatter
up to the Town Hall; men stamped into the lighted bar-and-
grill of Hoerlein's Hotel across the street; presently there were
over a hundred gathered on the walks outside. McKane himself was on hand, moving through the crowd with the insufferable self-esteem of a man who has just brought off a seven-horse
parlay. He was flanked by the men who, in the past four years,
had come to be his most influential lieutenants: Dick Newton

Kenny Sutherland

Dick Newton

and Kenny Sutherland. Both were considerably younger than the Chief. Newton was a dapper, foxy man, much taken with his own wit and shrewdness. Sutherland was shorter, plumper. He had been a bricklayer in New York, then a barkeep in a Coney Island saloon; now, like Newton, he was one of Mc-Kane's Justices of the Peace. These were the triumvirs whose rule, in 1893, was absolute over the town of Gravesend and, in consequence, over Coney Island, the nation's most celebrated and most popular seaside resort.

As these three moved through the assembled crowd of toughs and rowdies—special officers, most of them, of McKane's personal police force—they handed out orders. Men were detailed to stand, one hundred and fifty feet away, at every approach to the Town Hall. Inside that line, no stranger should pass. Any attempting to pass should be arrested. The men nodded and moved off, most of them hefting the fearsome Coney Island policeman's nightstick, a lead-filled four-foot club. So outsiders thought they could come to Coney and tell honest folks how to run their affairs, did they? They would soon find out.

McKane glanced at his heavy gold watch. There were still ninety minutes before the polls were to open. On the other hand, the intruders might arrive at any moment. They were coming, he had been told, to be Republican watchers at his polls. It was intolerable interference. He, McKane, had already personally appointed all the watchers necessary—both Democratic and Republican—good, safe men, all beholden to him. And now these pushing, officious, meddlesome reformers were going to show up. They were coming, McKane knew, at the behest of William Gaynor, who was running for Justice of the State Supreme Court on a reform ticket. McKane knew him well, for this was the same Gaynor who only a few years before had been on McKane's own payroll, as counsel to the trustees of the town's common lands. The Chief had never trusted the young lawyer. Gaynor had been meticulous, fussy; proper; too proper. Yet he had been so intimately involved in the town's affairs that he must have learned about all McKane's tricks for winning an election. He was, in short, a menace. McKane vowed he would snow Gaynor under a great deep drift of Gravesend ballots. And he could do it. He was supremely confident, he was invincible. Satisfied with the precautions he had taken, he strode into Hoerlein's to get a cup of coffee. Newton and Sutherland followed on his heels.

If the unswerving fealty of his henchmen meant anything, the Chief had reason to exude confidence. It was not a simple phenomenon, this loyalty; it was compounded, in about equal parts, of respect, fear, gratitude, and admiration. They respected him because he was a devoted family man and a pious Methodist Sunday School superintendent, but most of all because he worked hard on their behalf. They knew they could find him in his office early and late, ready to get them jobs, give them advice, settle their disputes, loan them money (properly secured, of course, with mortgages). During the summer season, he would linger in the Coney Island police headquarters long after midnight to deal with miscreants, and if he often capriciously reversed the judgments of his justices of the peace this was not because he lacked respect for the processes of the law but only because he *was* the law.

Tales of his summary justice led as well to fear of the Chief. Especially in the last few years, and encouraged by the long uninterrupted string of victories over his enemies, McKane had engaged to punish as well as sentence. He had wound thread tight around a thin, supple steel rod; he enjoyed swishing it reflectively as he eyed some unfortunate sneak-thief caught operating on Coney without proper authorization; he had even come to enjoy laying it across a plump rump. He was indifferent to his victim's rank or potential influence. McKane himself told the story of how once, when he was dispossessing a widow with whom he had had some trouble, a strapping young reporter from a New York newspaper had strolled up and presumed to voice criticism. "I'd like to see him try to evict me like that," the reporter had said; "I'd tell McKane what I thought of him." And McKane, standing close by, had lifted his hand in signal, whereupon one of his cops had instantly sent the reporter sprawling and had kept on beating him till McKane lifted his hand again. McKane, telling the story, would add gravely that the reporter himself, before limping off, had agreed he had been properly punished for interfering. Nor did respectable Coney Island businessmen dare to object to such indecorous incidents, even when they happened to be eye-witnesses. For the example of those who had objected was fresh in their memory: there was George Tilyou, forced out of his real estate business, and his father Peter Tilyou, one of Coney's pioneers, stripped of his property and nearly pauperized. Moreover, the respectable businessmen were uncomfortably aware that at any moment the Chief might decide to compete with them at their own business. He could be, they knew, a doughty competitor. It had occurred to him recently to launch an artificial-ice company; to insure his monopoly, he had his excise commissioners saddle every iceman on Coney with a $200 tax; no iceman had required a second hint; McKane's enterprise was proving deliciously profitable.

And yet the Coney Island businessmen had reason to be grateful to the Chief. For had he not paved Surf Avenue, and thereby enhanced real estate values throughout West Brighton? Even more important, had he not approved the development of Coney Island's own Bowery? And the Bowery, only a few years ago a narrow alley boasting a half-dozen disreputable cabarets, had blossomed into a narrow alley jampacked with half-a-hundred disreputable saloons, cabarets, and "hotels," each of them yielding pickings lush beyond the dreams of avarice. The respectable businessman most jubilant over this turn of events was a portly old scoundrel named Anson Stratton. Stratton was another of the New York saloon-keepers who had found that, sure enough, there was a pot of gold at the foot of the rainbow. He had arrived on Coney in 1884 to open a dancehall on the Bowery. Within two years he was speculating in real estate. Now, in 1893, having dutifully called on McKane whenever he needed any construction work, Stratton owned Bowery property worth more than $500,000—all safely in his wife's name. Stratton and his associates were not concerned with beauty. The buildings they had gotten McKane to throw together for them suggested, to a contemporary journalist, "a Western mining camp in its palmy days, with a most wonderful leaning toward the Moorish, [featuring] Alhambraic turrets and minarets, garish decorations and gilded domes, utterly at variance with all other styles." Inside these curious structures, girly-shows were the lure, beer the paramount commodity, short-changing the accepted method of barter, and force the chief factor in social give-and-take. Waiters were here the supreme powers, the sole criterion for their employment being a complete set of monstrous muscles. Bowery businessmen were twice grateful to McKane: that he had helped build up the half-mile alley, and that he had since so resolutely turned his back on what went on there.

His henchmen respected McKane, they feared him, they were grateful to him, but most of all they admired him. Their admiration was the ungrudging tribute of neophytes to a grand master. On Coney flimflam had always been routine business practice. The man who had never in the course of a long life made a single dollar save by fraud or deception was not extraordinary. Yet each man, when it came to skulduggery, bowed his head in homage to McKane, acknowledging him to be without peer. Their chicaneries were petty, calculated only to separate the chump from his ready cash; they never approached the grandeur and sweep of McKane's frauds. He, after all, had hoodwinked an entire nation. He had accomplished this stupendous deception, moreover, with only the most modest of resources. Other bosses had great cities full of voters whose ballots they could steal. McKane was obliged to effect his black magic with a measly couple of thousand. His henchmen considered that the Chief was not properly appreciated. His talents, they agreed, deserved greater scope. Some of them grumbled that he should have been appointed postmaster-general in Harrison's cabinet; later they had insisted that he should be nominated as governor of New York. But McKane himself was content to rule supreme over Gravesend and Coney Island. And this, in the face of every effort to unseat him, he continued to do.

The state legislature had for a time vetoed every Gravesend bill in an effort to snarl his purse-strings; he had found a loophole that gave him access to the town's funds and had thumbed his nose at Albany.

The legislature had aimed an electoral reform bill directly at his election-day practice of sitting in the Town Hall where he could eye each voter in a meaningful way and personally supervise each vote. The law had stipulated a separate polling place for each of the town's six districts. The Chief had lost no sleep. His town board had unanimously voted to redistrict the town so that each of the six districts ended in a ribbon of land that led into the Town Hall. McKane had cut six new doors into the building; himself, he still sat in the middle, the watchful spider in the web. Blandly he had announced: "The people of Gravesend must not be interfered with, but must be let alone to do their own voting in their own way."

Why should he not be confident?

To be sure, there had been, in the recent past, a few troublesome gnats buzzing about his august head. For one thing, there were the newspapers, among which McKane singled out the *New' York Times* and the *Brooklyn Eagle* for his special indignation. Earlier this year there had been a convention of volunteer firemen held at Coney; the Chief had passed the word that there should be no arrests of these visitors for drunkenness. If, when they got drunk, the firemen were the more easily fleeced by grifters and con men, was that a reason for the newspapers to attack him, and charge that he had deliberately encouraged them to drink?

And then there was the matter of the prize fights at Coney. They were regarded with horror by all decent folk, considered to be more degrading than cockfighting or bearbaiting. Brutality was the mildest term coupled with them. They were strictly forbidden and ruthlessly suppressed. Indeed, a year or so earlier McKane had himself halted some bootleg fights. He had driven, alone and unarmed, down to Norton's Point to stop the championship middleweight scrap between Jack (the Nonpareil) Dempsey * and Fulligaines. Some out-of-town sports had pulled their guns on him, but McKane had stood his ground and the fight had been canceled. But then Newton and Sutherland had pointed out to him how they could all make some money out of these prize fights. Call them exhibitions, they had urged, and stage them in Paul Bauer's Casino. Bauer was dead by this time, dead in an insane asylum, and McKane was executor of his estate. Newton and Sutherland had explained how McKane stood to profit: they would form a Coney Island Athletic Club, Newton would be matchmaker, McKane would be paid $5,000 a year rental on the Casino. The Chief had agreed. They had promoted a few fights; nothing spectacular, but enough to prove that they could handle a heavyweight championship match between Jim Corbett and the Englishman, Charley Mitchell. The papers had been signed. The fight had been announced. And it had touched off an uproar. The *Times* had taken dead aim on McKane. Protests were winged at him from all directions. The clergy, the YMCA, petitions, mass meetings—McKane had never experienced such a rumpus, and all right in the middle of the 1893 election campaign. He had been summoned to a meeting of desperate Brooklyn politicians who already were savoring the sour taste of defeat in November. The Governor himself had stepped in to demand that the fight be canceled. McKane, surly, had agreed only ten days ago to call the whole thing off.

And now there was Gaynor, the peskiest gnat of all, the man responsible for getting these intrusive Republican reformers to come down and snoop into Coney Island's election.

---

* Not, of course, to be confused with the Jack Dempsey who would be heavyweight champion a generation later.

Just the thought of Gaynor brought a black scowl to McKane's brows. Throughout this last week Gaynor, gnat-like, had been circling about, darting in for a quick nip, then skimming off before he could be slapped down. It was imperative that Gaynor be severely trounced, so imperative indeed that Mc-Kane had been forced to take a desperate gamble: he had registered 6,218 voters in Gravesend, more than 3,200 of them from Coney Island alone. But the town's population was only 8,400: taking into account the women and children, there could not have been more than perhaps 1,500 legitimate voters. Had he taken too big a chance? The *Times* had promptly attacked his figures; as promptly Gaynor had sent men to Coney, armed with a court order, demanding that they be permitted to copy the registration lists. But of course this was insufferable: McKane had them arrested on charges of vagrancy and drunkenness and lodged them overnight in the town jail. Another victory. And as far as this morning's intruders were concerned, these men sent down by Gaynor to be his watchers at McKane's polls—

But here a man stuck his head in at the door of Hoerlein's bar-and-grill. "They're coming!" he shouted. At once the barroom was all but emptied. Only two men were left. One was young Hoerlein, languidly wiping the bar with a rag. The other, as it happened, was one of Gaynor's watchers, a man most interested in the feverish preparations for his reception. And now he, too, ambled slowly out into the cold early morning air, to see what was afoot.

Outside, gray clouds scudded low before a raw breeze off the ocean. The crowd had grown. Three hundred men, fifty of them in police uniform, packed the yard in front of the Town Hall and spilled across the tracks of the Prospect Park and Coney Island Railroad. They were all looking north, for here, on their way from Brooklyn, came three carriages filled

The reception committee gathers to greet the men appointed as watchers. Three of the six doors McKane carved into the Town Hall can be seen along the side of the building in background.   *N. Y. Herald* N. Y. PUBLIC LIBRARY

with strangers. Newton, ever the eager beaver, leaped forward to catch the bridle of the near horse drawing the first carriage. But the coachman touched his horses with his whip and Newton lost his hold. The crowd gave way, and the carriages moved up to where McKane stood. The door of the first burst open. Out climbed Colonel Alexander Bacon, the same man who, five years before, had been chairman of the legislative committee charged with exposing McKane's corruption. "Good morning, Mr. McKane," said Bacon somewhat nervously, eyeing the sullen crowd that was bellying up to him. "These gentlemen with me are watchers and they place themselves under your protection." "Ah, yes, Mr. Bacon," McKane answered. "I've been looking for you. Get out of this."

The crowd edged closer. All three carriages were drawn up now, and out of them had emerged a dozen or so men: lawyers, physicians, clergymen, merchants: men who had been riding for two hours or more through the bleak, chill

"Injunctions don't go here!" A fateful moment in Coney's history, presaging the Chief's downfall and the resort's most brilliant era.　*N. Y. World*

night to insure an honest vote. They had been warned that their reception might be as bleak.

"I won't get out," retorted Bacon. "We are here lawfully, and we have an injunction from Judge Barnard."

"Injunctions don't go here," said McKane.

Bacon stared at him. It was as though he had said the sun does not rise in the east. "Oh, yes, they do," he said, and held the court paper out to the Chief. McKane shrank back, but Bacon lunged forward and slapped him with it on chest and shoulders, effective service of the injunction.

McKane was livid. "Hustle them off!" he ordered.

His police surged in. Bacon's party was knocked about, mauled, pushed, tripped, slugged. An ugly rumble filled the air. Bacon went down. "Are you arresting me?" he cried, and he heard McKane answer, "Take him away." Stillman Doubleday, a writer, pushed forward. He held up his injunction order. "I want you to understand, my dear fellow," he said, "that you are running up against the Supreme Court of the State of New York. This is Judge Barnard's signature." He was knocked sprawling. "You get to hell out of here, you and your orders," he was told. A lawyer, Herbert Worthley, was grabbed, thrown down, yanked to his feet, beaten, knocked down again. "Tell me where you want me to go," he begged them, "but don't beat me this way!" They told him. "Hit him anyway," McKane ordered. Worthley was slugged again, from behind, cruelly, by one of the lead-filled nightsticks. McKane moved away, followed by Newton and Sutherland. A clergyman, Robert Kent, heard him say, "I would have knocked that Bacon down myself if it hadn't been for the looks of it. Are there any more of 'em here?" Kent stepped forward, holding up his copy of the injunction order. At once he was slugged, knocked down, and sent sprawling again while he was struggling to get up. He put up his hands to protect his face, but a nightstick caught him wickedly in the eye. He ran. Pursued for a half-mile by the mob, Kent ran till he was gasping for breath, then walked the rest of the way home to Brooklyn. The last words he had heard were McKane's: "They're all drunk, take 'em away, take 'em all away and lock 'em up!"

The incident had taken perhaps ten minutes. Now the sun had risen. McKane ordered the polls opened and the repeaters put to work. He strode back into Hoerlein's bar-and-grill, his pack at his heels. His lawyer, a man named George Roderick, followed him in carrying a certificate snatched from one of Gaynor's watchers. Roderick clamored for quiet, then derisively read from the back of the certificate Section 102 of the election law. His audience roared with laughter. McKane called for coffee. "Did you hear that fellow holler about his order of the court?" he asked. Someone else asked: "Who was that tall man?" "Why," said McKane, "that's that Colonel Bacon. We've got him where he won't bother us again today. He's locked up." The Chief turned, noticing a strange face in the throng. "Who's that man standing there?" he demanded. Silence. All eyed the stranger. "Get out of this town," growled McKane and, when the man hesitated, "Hustle him," the Chief commanded. Ready hands tossed the stranger out into the street.

On Coney Island they celebrated McKane's latest triumph. He was winner, and still champion.

But back in Brooklyn, the story was carried to St. Clair McKelway, the righteous editor of the *Brooklyn Eagle*. Before noon, the *Eagle* was out on the streets with an election day extra. McKane's dictum "Injunctions don't go here!" was a feature headline in Brooklyn; it was picked up by the wire services; the whole country was reading about it before the day was over.

Notoriety did not faze the Chief. For what, after all, could the busybodies do to him? If he had broken some law, so what? The district attorney of Kings County was a good McLaughlin Democrat and an old personal friend. No one would ever prosecute him. But it is likely that McKane shrugged off the possibility that he had broken a law. For he had reached the euphoric point where he believed he could do no wrong, that what he did was right because he did it. In any event, he was confident the whole thing would blow over a day or two after the elections. And so McKane was unconcerned.

To be sure, the election returns were disconcerting. The Chief was forced to conclude that perhaps the headline in the *Eagle* had had some effect. He had grudgingly given Gaynor 105 votes in Gravesend, but nevertheless the hated reformer won his place on the State Supreme Court bench by 23,000 votes. Moreover, a reform mayor was elected in Brooklyn and a reform attorney-general was sent to the state capitol in Albany. And as if all this were not enough, it now appeared that the reformers were not content with their election victory.

They were still howling for blood. A mass indignation meeting was called by McKelway, at Brooklyn's Academy of Music; the hall was jammed with folk bent on scuttling McKane forthwith; Gaynor spoke and was cheered to the echo; a committee was named to raise a fund to prosecute the Chief. It said much that such a step was considered necessary: it showed how mistrustful were the citizens of McLaughlin's district attorney, how impressed they were with McKane's record of invincibility, and most of all how shocked and dismayed they had been by the events of election day morning, in front of McKane's Town Hall. William Ziegler, reputedly the second richest man in Brooklyn, whose money came from the Royal Baking Powder Company, knew about McKane's fraudulence at first hand: a few years before he had entered the highest bid for Norton's Point, only to be by-passed when he failed to sweeten his bid with an additional bundle of money passed under the table. Now he announced: "Draw on me to the extent of $100,000 for the punishment of the Gravesend scoundrels." Gaynor wrote the Governor: "I have been elected to an office which disqualifies me from prosecuting the perpetrators of these crimes; but I cannot and shall not sit silent and see these gross outrages against honest people go unredressed. I shall resign the office first." He urged the Governor to appoint one or more special assistant attorneys-general. The newly-elected reform mayor of Brooklyn was likewise pressed to name special district attorneys. Both officials agreed. Benjamin Tracy and Edward Shepard accepted the jobs. Tracy was a leading Brooklyn Republican, a former Secretary of the Navy. Shepard, an independent Democrat, had been one of the counsel to the Bacon Committee in 1887: he knew McKane's record at first hand. An extraordinary grand jury was summoned into session.

And still the Chief seemed unconcerned. Reporters called on him at his office. He sat rocking slowly in a great swivel chair, pushing himself gently back and forth with the toe of one polished boot. His attitude was one of mild reproach. He took note of the hot newspaper attacks. "Some of them have gone too far," he said. "They will have to pay when this thing has quieted down." He announced he was bringing suit against two newspapers for damages of $100,000 apiece. The reporters brought him back to the fracas in Gravesend on election day. McKane wagged his head tolerantly. On his shirt bosom, a three-carat diamond winked. "All this talk about my having defied the law," he said deprecatingly, "is the veriest rot. Does anybody think that I'm such an idiot as to throw myself within the meshes of the law in such a reckless, crazy way as has been attributed to me?" Gravely he informed the reporters that the first he knew of the Supreme Court's injunction was when he read about it in the newspapers the next day. His plans? He was going on a hunting trip, down in Virginia; he expected that by the time he returned this whole fuss would have long since been forgotten.

But it was not forgotten. By the time he returned from Virginia, he had been found guilty of contempt of court for

Gaynor, newly elected Justice, demands swift action against McKane. *N. Y. World* N. Y. PUBLIC LIBRARY

flouting the injunction, and fined $250 and sentenced to thirty days in the county jail. Nobody, however, paid any attention to this conviction and judgment. A stay of execution was promptly granted. Down on Coney Island, McKane's henchmen nodded sagely and winked. The Chief, they knew, would never have to pay a fine, much less ever go to jail. The reform decencies required a certain limited amount of heat; there would be one or two stories on the front pages of the newspapers; then all would be as before. What county official was not beholden to McKane? To McKane, who was president of the board of county supervisors? But the extraordinary grand jury was still in session. His friend the district attorney was not privy to the deliberations of this jury. What were they up to? For the first time McKane began to fret.

On the next-to-last day of the year the extraordinary grand jury handed up its indictments. There were eleven counts, including oppression, conspiracy, assault, contempt of court, misconduct of registry, and aiding and abetting election officials in violations of the election law. The indictments caught in their net McKane, Newton, Sutherland, and eighteen prominent citizens of Coney Island who had been named by McKane as election officials. McKane, the whale among these minnows, was the only one to stand before the bench to answer the indictments. He was vexed, his face was flushed, he resented the throng of reporters standing in a semicircle around him, but he was determined to act unconcerned. While Justice Willard Bartlett read the indictments aloud, McKane slouched before him; deliberately he let his bored gaze wander about the Court of Oyer and Terminer; when once he stifled a yawn, Justice Bartlett was obliged to give him a verbal rap across the knuckles. It was as though McKane could not warrant the possibility of an actual trial. Had not something always turned up? And so it would again.

But on January 23, 1894, a gavel rapped in the old Brooklyn Supreme Court House. The trial was under way. In a formal sense, it was the People of the State of New York *versus* John Y. McKane *et alii* for various infractions of the election laws. But to the press, to the clergy, to the public generally and especially to those sections of the public who were on the one hand God-fearing, moral, right-minded citizens, and were on the other hand easy-going, cynical, live-and-let-live folk, the trial from the first took on emotional colorations that all but completely obscured the formal issues. McKane, to press, to clergy, and to an appreciable segment of the public, was not simply an individual: he was Vice Incarnate, naked and arrogant. To a less articulate and less well organized segment, the Chief represented a reasonable approach to man's primary pleasures. The virtuous who crowded into the courtroom desired McKane's absolute perdition. One woman asserted, with mathematical imprecision but with high moral fervor, that she knew ten thousand mothers and sisters who were praying that the jury would convict. As she spoke she was surrounded by a gaggle of gamblers, minor politicians, sports, and pugilists who, if they had heard her, would have stared at her blank and uncomprehending. In their view McKane was a model of tolerance and indulgence, a man who had permitted innocent gambling at horserace tracks, who had winked at tiresome Sunday blue-laws, who had sanctioned manly prizefighting. He was a man who recognized that his fellows liked to blow off occasional steam but did not himself go off like a rocket when he encountered evidence of their mortal weaknesses. As for the alleged infraction of election laws, his sympathizers shrugged: didn't everyone steal a vote, wherever and whenever the opportunity presented itself? The partisans of these wildly clashing viewpoints could, however, agree on one thing: McKane personified Coney Island: it was Coney Island's way of life that was on trial. And the contrary factions shared, as well, intensity of emotional commitment. They fought enthusiastically for seats in the courtroom. Upstairs, in the gallery, the Chief's Coney Island henchmen were so thickly packed that they seemed to one reporter to be standing on each other's shoulders. Here each chawed on a cud of tobacco, each clutched a sandwich wrapped in wax paper: the seats in the gallery would not be vacated at the lunch hour for the duration of the trial.

The prosecution was alert to the danger that some prospective juror might have been approached. It was three days before the jury box was filled. Meanwhile McKane sat attentive in his chair, for the most part impassive. When the panel was completed, he was satisfied, even cheerful; at the press table the reporters noticed his good humor; a discreet speculation crept into a few of their stories: this jury would never agree.

The first witnesses were the men who had been sent down by Gaynor, armed with a court order, to get copies of the registration lists. They had arrived in the evening. One of them told how he had been arrested. "John McKane was there," he said. "McKane asked me what I meant by coming down to a peaceful little village like Gravesend at that time of night." When the witness reached the word "peaceful" the crowd in the courtroom started to laugh. His last words were drowned out. McKane glared up at the gallery at his adherents. But it was difficult for them to quench their merriment. It was to be so throughout the trial. They had been his appreciative chorus down through the years on Coney, loyally roaring and clapping their thighs at each McKane witticism and on every occasion that showed, as they thought, how clever was their Chief; they would never understand that here in the courtroom the ground rules had changed.

Another of Gaynor's copyists had been collared by McKane.

"How much are you getting paid by Gaynor?" the Chief had demanded. And, when the man had refused to answer, McKane had peeled off his overcoat. "I'll bounce you off the floor," he had shouted, "and stamp and jump on you till you tell me what I want to know!" The man, glancing nervously at the encircling ring of McKane's toughs, had told McKane what he wanted to know. The copyists had been thwarted in their task by a dozen of McKane's Coney Island heelers who had been pretending to copy the registration lists themselves, at the behest of the Chief. One of these was now invited to the witness stand. Each of McKane's Coney Island witnesses, when he advanced to testify, engaged in certain rituals, as who would avert some smart-aleck big-city devil. Each removed his chew of tobacco, gave the Bible a condescending smack, and fell back into the witness chair, tilting it to a forty-five degree angle, left hand carelessly thrust in pocket, right hand free to gesture grandly. Each then bent on the judge a look of ineffable familiarity, as though at any moment he might chuck the judge under the chin. Counsel for the people requested that the first McKane copyist write his name. Painfully the witness hunched over a piece of paper. His tongue stuck out at one corner of his mouth. His concentration was immense. At length he looked up triumphantly. He had written his name. It had taken him two minutes.

There was laughter from McKane's chorus during this laborious process; Kenny Sutherland and Dick Newton both sniggered, as though tickled by the spectacle of their own chicanery; but McKane remained impassive. Upstairs the gallery rocked with laughter when prosecution witnesses testified to the events of election day morning. Most comical was the clergyman who testified that his whiskers had been unmercifully yanked. But McKane never grinned. He kept his gaze on the twelve men in the jury-box and his expression was

Justice Willard Bartlett

thoughtful. The stranger who had been so abruptly booted out of Hoerlein's Hotel was a damaging witness. He turned out to have been one of Gaynor's watchers; McKane flushed and talked nervously with his lawyers while the young man was on the stand.

The Chief was the first witness to take the stand in his own defense. He was clad in sober black broadcloth; a white necktie was demurely draped over his celebrated diamond stud; his demeanor was grave; his tone was modulated and suggested mild reproof. It was a muted performance. Of course he had not threatened Gaynor's copyists; they had been jailed because they were drunk and prowling about long after midnight; they were young men and, no doubt, knew no better; as for Colonel Bacon's party, he had heard that a large group of armed men had planned to deploy in Gravesend for the purpose of interfering with an orderly election; no, he had never said he was "going to down that man Gaynor;" on the contrary, Gaynor was an old, valued, and trusted friend. He really knew nothing of the details of election procedure, all that was left to the proper election officials. No, he had never actually seen the registration lists himself. Yes, he was quite sure: he had definitely never inspected them.

And now McKane had tripped. Inelegantly he had fallen flat on his phiz. For the special attorney-general, Benjamin Tracy, now pulled out of his sleeve McKane's own affidavit, in which, only two months before, he had sworn that he had personally inspected all Gravesend's registration lists. McKane flushed a deep brick-red. Ponderously he began to flounder, stammering out flabby explanations. But the gavel banged. The court stood in adjournment. It was Saturday noon. The jury—and the newspapers—had the whole weekend to recall the picture of McKane trapped in perjury.

And on the next Monday, when he took the stand again, he was again caught up in the snarl of his own lies. He was a badly flustered man. He knew that the case was not the same as that which had obtained for the legislative investigation, seven years before. This time it was not merely for the record but for a jury, this time a jail term attached. Anxiously his eyes wavered down along the faces in the jury-box. The reporters, watching, read into his nervous glance a measure of uncertainty. The cross-examination continued. It was established that the Coney Island policemen who had so heartily thwacked Gaynor's watchers were paid by checks drawn on McKane's personal bank account; that whereas in 1878 the police payroll had amounted to $1,000 in 1892 it had amounted to $30,000; that he had padded the registration rolls, increasing them by more than two hundred per cent in three years; that no election inspector lifted a finger save at his bidding; that in Gravesend he was boss not only of the Democratic party but also of the Republicans, who could not be said to have a party at all. Their leader was the same Anson Stratton who had so profited from the development of the Bowery. This old rascal, Gravesend's only member of the Republican general committee for New York state, now took the stand and said, of the most recent election: "I never saw a fairer election on the face of the earth;" when he was reminded by counsel that the Republicans had got only ten of 1,512 votes cast in the 2nd (Coney Island) election district, "Humph," said Stratton, "I'm surprised they got as many as that."

Stratton was the first of a string of character witnesses called to testify to McKane's probity. A Methodist clergyman took the stand, but scurried off again after mouthing a few dutiful platitudes. McKane's bankers took the stand; one of them, the president of the Hamilton Trust Company, was dismayed to find that, on the day after his appearance, his company's stock dropped seven points on the exchange. And, in payment of his considerable debt, Austin Corbin, the promotor of Manhattan Beach, likewise took the stand. He came clad in a fur-trimmed overcoat; his hat he handed to a court officer, who deferentially held it for him until he should have stood down. Benjamin Tracy, on cross examination, had no difficulty establishing for the jury the nature of the intimate relationship between Corbin and McKane:

TRACY: Didn't you have the consent of the Gravesend authorities to cross Coney Island Creek with your railroad?
CORBIN: I never needed to ask them.
TRACY: (*With a smile*) Oh, you never needed to ask them.

Tracy had been of counsel for the defense in the celebrated Beecher-Tilton trial, held in this same courthouse a few years before. On the last day of McKane's trial, just before he was to close the case for the people, Tracy remarked to a reporter that the crowds were even greater on this occasion, that the interest was greater. There was no question about the relative size of the stakes. Tracy, rising to the occasion, orated in high gear for six hours; his peroration was so impassioned that, at its conclusion, he collapsed; he required a stimulant before

Benjamin Tracy, McKane's chief prosecutor. Ironically, Tracy would never have been Secretary of the Navy if McKane's election frauds had not put Harrison in the White House.
Leslie's Weekly

he was able to leave the courtroom. The righteous and virtuous among the spectators applauded this effort so persistently that they were cleared from the courtroom with difficulty; McKane's adherents departed willingly and gathered in knots in the corridors, where presently one or two of them started making book on his chances. McKane himself was taken in charge by the sheriff, a youngster named William J. Buttling who, although a Republican, was nevertheless the Chief's buddy. The jury likewise withdrew and the wait began.

When the period of uncertainty reached through the afternoon, the evening, and late into the night, McKane's friends plucked up their spirits. The odds on his conviction went down. By the time the deadline had been reached for the morning newspapers, bettors were offering even money that the jury would acquit. On Thursday, February 15, the newspapers freely predicted that at least three jurors had been bribed to hold out for McKane's acquittal. Snow fell Thursday morning, on streets covered with slush, but foul weather was not enough to keep the crowds away from the court house. The corridors were jammed before seven o'clock; most of the early arrivals were Coney Islanders. As it happened, on that day the court commenced a new term. A new justice was scheduled to take his seat on the bench. The gods in charge of orchestrating the ironies had seen to it that this new justice would be William Gaynor. He proceeded at once with the case on the docket. It was, as so often is the case in the New York Supreme Court, a liability case: a Brooklyn woman and her daughter had been injured by a runaway horse in Grand Street, Manhattan, and they were suing the owner of the horse for heavy damages. Plaintiffs, defendant, and counsel looked wonderingly over their shoulders at the great throng in the courtroom.

At 11.25 a court officer slipped in and whispered a message to Justice Gaynor and then hurriedly retired. Gaynor tugged at his mustache and glanced up at the packed gallery. At once the crowd in the courtroom divined that the McKane jury was about to come in. A moment later the word had reached the corridors outside: a hundred more men pushed their way in through the great swinging doors: they pressed along the walls on either side of the room, some of them climbed up on the radiators. The lawyer trying the indemnity case was unnerved. Justice Gaynor halted him with a wave of his hand. As he did, Justice Bartlett, the trial judge, slipped in and took a seat next to Gaynor. The two men whispered together. Justice Gaynor was clearly excited and nervous. Justice Bartlett's face was flushed.

The jury filed in. But neither McKane nor his lawyers were present. Justice Bartlett dispatched a court officer to fetch the defendant. Ten minutes passed before he arrived, flanked by Sheriff Buttling. McKane walked to a seat in front of the jury, staring straight ahead of him, and folded his hands. The sheriff gave him a consoling pat on the shoulder. And still the Chief's lawyers were not to be found. Justice Gaynor wheeled this way and that in his high-backed chair on the bench. Justice Bartlett fumed about the tardiness of McKane's counsel. At length, out of patience, he instructed the clerk to proceed. The clerk, having called the jury to stand, asked for the verdict.

"Guilty," said the foreman.

McKane stared, unbelieving. The jury was polled; as each repeated the word, McKane's head shook in negative puzzlement. He turned. Sheriff Buttling's consoling hand was on his shoulder. McKane whispered something and shrugged. Then he smiled. There were, that smile seemed to say, still a few rabbits in the old master's top hat. He was too old a hand to have put all his trust in one or two fixed jurors. (It presently would come out that at least one of his jurors had been reached, with a promise of a free house and lot. But the others had shamed him into agreeing to convict.) And indeed even now that his guilt had been formally pronounced, the press, the clergy, and the right-minded citizenry were apprehensive that somehow McKane would escape punishment. He had, to be sure, been finally lodged behind bars in the Raymond Street Jail to await his sentencing on the following Monday, but his residence there scarcely qualified as punishment. He dwelt in the warden's private apartment; his meals were specially catered; his political cronies came and went freely while reporters were unprecedentedly barred from the jail; the rumor even spread that he had been taken in a closed carriage to spend the weekend with his family at Sheepshead Bay. Other tales circulated: that a gang of his Coney Island catchers were plotting to raid the jail, snatch their Chief, and whisk him off to Cuba, as had been done with Tweed; that he was seriously ill of Bright's disease and would avert payment of his debt to society by dying before the month was out; that his lawyers had found a loophole through which he might wriggle to freedom.

Indignation and sympathy packed the courthouse again on Monday, February 19 with crowds come to hear sentence pronounced. So jammed were the corridors that Sheriff Buttling had trouble bringing his prisoner in. "Come, boys," said McKane, "let me get by," and, "All right, Chief," "Sure, Chief," "Good luck, Chief," cried his Coney Island chorus. He was asked if there was any reason why sentence should not be pronounced. The crowded courtroom fell quiet. McKane licked his lips. "I don't know that I can say anything," he began, with a show of his old assurance. He glanced at his lawyers, then looked again at Justice Bartlett. "I merely repeat what I've said on the stand, that I've never in my life done anything wrong to anybody that I know of." It was his credo; he was wholly sincere. "I had nothing to do," he went on, more uncertainly, "either directly or indirectly, in relation to the matters as charged. I never counseled or advised any of the election in-

The Chief is sentenced. Justice Bartlett sits at left; Chief Clerk Byrne faces McKane; Tracy and Shepard are just behind him.   *Leslie's Weekly*

spectors to do anything against the law"—here he paused and swallowed, his fire damped, his eyes downcast—"and I say that I am not guilty of this crime." Justice Bartlett declared that McKane's punishment must be severe enough to express stern condemnation but not so severe as to excite sympathy. "Six years," he said, "in the state penitentiary, at hard labor." The Chief's cheeks were sallow. His fingers twitched.

But still the sentence was not executed. The next day he was arraigned with two dozen Coney Islanders on still further indictments of fraud. Meantime his lawyers, mum, scoured the state in search of a Supreme Court Justice who would grant a stay of execution and a certificate of reasonable doubt as to the fairness of his trial. To Troy they went, to Albany, to Watertown and Oswego and Syracuse and Little Falls and Kingston. The newspapers grew increasingly critical of his extended residence in the warden's apartment of the Raymond Street Jail. It was explained that he might be wanted as a witness by the prosecution in the trial of his two lieutenants, Sutherland and Newton. And on the last day of February he was brought back to the courtroom where Sutherland was on trial. But there was a hitch; he did not take the stand. He sat alone inside the inclosure while the lawyers wrangled. He was very pale. Twice tears ran down his cheeks, and he tried to hide them. "I am reconciled to my fate," he murmured to a reporter, "and I now know there's no help for me. I must go to Sing Sing. I have sent a carriage for my wife and family . . . My wife is ill and mayn't be able to come to the jail, but I want to see her before I go away." His voice trailed off to a whisper.

Next day, a few minutes after noon, Sheriff Buttling drove him from the jail yard in a closed carriage. There was a throng in the street, but they could not see him. Over the Brooklyn Bridge he went. At the New York end of the bridge stood a man whose fair hair had turned white. He was smiling and rubbing his hands. He cheered as McKane's carriage rolled by. Reporters, following McKane in a second carriage, paused to question the man. It was Peter Tilyou. "This is my revenge," he said. "John Y. McKane is on his way to Sing Sing and Peter Tilyou is a poor but free man. Don't you bet he'd change places with me now?"

Sheriff Buttling was supposed to get his prisoner to Grand Central Station in time to put him aboard the 1.10 train for Sing Sing, but his carriage went slowly over a circuitous route. For McKane's lawyers were hopeful of one last chance: Justice Barnard, whose injunction McKane had flouted four months before, had said that he would rule on a stay of execution at two o'clock. But the reprieve never came. McKane was taken to a smoking-car on the 2.15. He sat down next to a window. At once a crowd gathered around, pointing and grinning. McKane pulled down the blind. Four policemen tried to keep all other passengers out of the car; reporters had to get the station agent to let them in. There were crowds gathered at Yonkers, at Tarrytown, at Ossining. McKane was led through the snow, over the railroad ties, to the penitentiary. A warden bid him take his hat off. The three-carat diamond stud was unscrewed from his shirt front. His head was shaved, his peanut-colored goatee shorn off. He was in prison.

At the weekly meeting of the Methodist Ministers Association, reporters asked for comment: what had Methodism to say now, about the erstwhile Sabbath School superintendent? Heretofore McKane's congregation had sedulously avoided prejudging him. Now they indicated cautious approval of the course of justice. One minister quoted Shakespeare's speech for Brutus: "As Caesar loved me, I weep for him; as he was fortunate, I rejoice at it; as he was valiant, I honor him; but as he was ambitious, I slew him."

And now that the Chief had been toppled, the jackals

scuttled for safety. Kenny Sutherland,* tried and found guilty, jumped bail and fled to Canada before he could be sentenced. Dick Newton, cannier, turned state's evidence and pleaded guilty. All the lesser Coney Island fry, consternated by Newton's opportunism, likewise pleaded guilty, turned state's evidence, and were let off with relatively light sentences. Once the cover had been lifted from the garbage can, it was discovered that McKane had himself gotten off very lightly indeed. For the extent of his frauds had scarcely been imagined. Now it turned out that the Chief had never placed his sole reliance on repeaters and stuffed ballot boxes. At the Presidential election of 1888, for example, when Gravesend's votes had elected Harrison to the White House, McKane had waited till the polls were closed and then had simply instructed his election officials: "Give Harrison so many, give Cleveland so many, and fill out all your papers to prove that it was so." After the most recent election, that of 1893, when one Coney Islander repeated at least fifty times and Kenny Sutherland personally stuffed at least 1,000 ballots into the boxes of two election districts, McKane had ordered the election inspectors locked up in his Brooklyn office on the day after the election so that the lists might be fixed to correspond with the vote.

With the Chief safely in jail his followers no longer needed fear him, or respect him, or admire him. Paul Bauer's widow brought suit against him, complaining that while he had for five years profited as executor of the Bauer estate to the extent of $200,000, he had given her only a microscopic $3,700. An opposition to McKane sprang up overnight and, in the annual election for supervisor, swept into office a slate of candidates dedicated to extirpating every last trace of the Chief. Ac-

* Another Kenneth Sutherland, nephew of the man described in this chapter, subsequently became Democratic leader in Brooklyn. The two should not be confused.

countants went to work to estimate McKane's thefts from the
town of Gravesend. They could never come close to the full
truth, for they were obliged to accept as honest his frauds in
the sale of the town's common lands. The *Brooklyn Eagle* put
his peculations in excess of $500,000.

On April 26, 1894, a bill passed the New York state legislature
annexing Gravesend—and Coney Island—to Brooklyn. Early in
June the reporters went down to the beach to see what they
could see. They found a gay and orderly resort. The Brooklyn
police in charge were bored. There was little for them to do.
The thieves had fled. Gone were the pickpockets and grifters,
the con men and bruisers. Sunday laws were being observed.
The bagnios were shuttered. The gaffed roulette wheels were
stilled. On the shore the surf broke unceasingly, and children
built sand castles. Coney was at peace.

McKane was released from Sing Sing on April 30, 1898. He
had not been a particularly popular prisoner among his fellows:
they held against him his special favors, his private icebox filled
with fresh milk and butter, his cushy jobs. For four years he
had exerted all the influence at his command for an appeal, a
reversal, a pardon, but to no avail. Changed, he came back to
a changed Coney Island. As for him, he was old and tired and
embittered. As for his island, the fix was no longer in and his
old gang had departed. He was destroyed; he was shattered;
there were new faces on Coney, and they ignored the old man.
He tried to pick up his building business again, but with his
political connections at loose ends it was hard sledding. He took
up the business of selling life insurance. It was not that he
needed the money: there were mortgages in his wife's name
on more than half the buildings on Coney Island: but the in-
activity oppressed him. One of the last policies he wrote was
for William Gaynor; it was for $50,000. He suffered a stroke

in August, 1899; in September he was hit by another; he died
the next day in his sleep. In death, all his old friends returned
to him. His body lay in a Sheepshead Bay church for a day
while the barkeeps and the gamblers and the politicians trooped
by to do him homage. The fear and the respect and the admiration had been transformed into pity. Good Baron John was
dead and they could reflect on his meager virtues and strive to
ignore his infamies. Of these, the most significant could never
be properly assessed. For the fact was that he had stolen something more important than a half-million dollars. He had stolen
Coney Island's good name. He had tainted the lovely beach
irrevocably. When, in October, 1893, the *Times* had brought to
bear against him its strongest guns, their writers (and notably
one who signed himself Monsieur de l'Épée) had borrowed from
some of Brooklyn's more indignant preachers the tag they had
hung on the Island. They had called it Sodom-by-the-Sea, and
the *Times* broadcast the demeaning nickname. McKane would
ever bear responsibility for that sneer. He had earned for it
the insult.

Puck, 1894. N. Y. PUBLIC LIBRARY

~Splendiferous~

In the shade of some comfortable, middle-aged elms, beside an ample, sun-dappled meadow, a group of hostlers and stable-boys lounge at their ease, idly gossiping and pitching pennies. At this moment of a lazy, hazy August midday, they are minor figures in a most favored landscape. Off to their left is the warm red brick of a grandstand; beyond, horses nicker and paw impatiently in their stalls, and small, tight-faced men are dressing in gaudy silks amid loud, nervous talk and the smell of sweat and liniment and smooth-worn leather, and here the atmosphere is charged. But in the cool, deep green shade the stable-boys yawn. Now from the distance there comes a compelling sound: *Taa-ta-ta-ron, ta-ta-ron!* It is a horn blown from an approaching tally-ho. The boys scramble to their feet. For the rest of the afternoon they will be on the go. Before long they are busy with tally-hos and four-in-hands by the dozen, and busy with victorias and drags and two-wheeled buggies. The broad meadow comes alive with pink and azure and yellow and mauve frocks, and gay fringed parasols bob, and here a hem is lifted to show an ankle, and white linen is spread on the grass, and out come wicker baskets laden with tender fowl and chilled wine, and Berry Wall, the most dedicated fop of his time, strolls about, splendid in vivid checks, nodding to a Belmont and a Withers and a Lorillard, and here comes Ward Mc-Allister, who invented the phrase, The 400, to describe New York society, bowing to a Vanderbilt and a Lawrence and a Cutting and a Jerome and an Oelrichs, and everyone is eager and happy and excited. The world of leisure and fashion has come down to Coney Island's doorstep, for this is Futurity Day at Sheepshead Bay.

For a quarter-century Sheepshead Bay reigned as queen of American racetracks. Here the fleetest and best-bred horses ran, here the infield and paddock grew greenest, here the stables were the most comfortable and the crowds the biggest and the stakes the richest. And the two brightest jewels in Sheepshead Bay's crown were the Suburban, the country's ranking handicap, and the Futurity, the two-year-old championship. Today's Futurity was to be the thirteenth renewal of the classic, and while horsemen did not regard the colts as anything special, there was, as everyone was whispering, more involved in the race than simply a decision as to which horse could run fastest. This one was for blood. Over their luncheon and later, in the Gold Room of the Coney Island Jockey Club, down in the betting ring, out in the paddock, wherever the knowledgeable gathered, the talk was about the chances of the three-horse entry from the stables of James R. Keene against the two colts nominated by William C. Whitney. Keene, in this period, dominated the country's tracks. He had lavished a fortune on his stables; he had engaged the best trainers; he had first call on the services of the most promising jockeys; he was to the American turf what Calumet Farm was a few years ago. Whitney, on the other hand, was a newcomer, but coming very fast and clearly intent on challenging Keene's supremacy as the leading money-winning owner. He had started racing his

LEFT. James R. Keene (with beard). The man with Keene is Robert Pinkerton. CULVER SERVICE
RIGHT. William C. Whitney (in top hat) at Sheepshead Bay.
BROWN BROTHERS

own horses only three years before; now, in 1900, for the first time his string was running under the Whitney name and carrying the Eton blue and brown cap (today, of course, these are C. V. Whitney's racing colors). This 1900 Futurity, then, would be the challenger against the champion.

But the sporting rivalry, while it held a certain interest, was not a patch on the financial enmity between the two men. What their fellow members of the Coney Island Jockey Club knew, what indeed was a matter of common gossip on every hand, was that, just a few weeks before, Whitney and Keene had been locked in one of the most savage struggles in Wall Street's history. Keene, whose fortune and reputation had been won as the most fearsome bear on the Stock Exchange, had for years taken delight in pounding various stocks in which Whitney was a heavy investor. It was provoking, but Whitney bided his time. He could settle his scores with Keene later; in 1899 he was preoccupied with his efforts at getting a lock on New York City's transportation system. By the end of 1899 Whitney and his associates had a stranglehold on every streetcar railway in the city, save only one. This was the Third Avenue, and early in 1900 Whitney found himself in the gratifying position of being able to grab off this last streetcar line while simultaneously gaining revenge on his old enemy. For Keene had launched an ursine attack on the Third Avenue. He had corraled 20,000 shares; he dumped them on the market and went short by many more thousands of shares. Nothing could have better suited Whitney's book. He and his associates, concealing themselves behind the beards of various respectable brokers, cornered the market without Keene's ever being aware of it. Gleefully they set their bear-trap: whenever Keene borrowed more shares to go short, it was the Whitney interests that loaned them to him from behind their beards and the Whitney interests that promptly bought them from him again. By the time the trap was snapped, Keene had borrowed thousands upon thousands of shares that he could never return; he could only throw himself on the mercy of the Whitney syndicate and hope for a cash settlement. Rumor had it that Keene was forced to pay $5,000,000; the most conservative estimate put his obligation at $2,000,000; in any case, a severe wallop was handed his bank account. Could there be any doubt that in all Keene's long and successful career as a horseman—and such doughty competitors as Domino, Colin, and Sysonby carried his colors—he ever wanted to win a race as fervently as he wanted to win the 1900 Futurity? For his part, Whitney was just as anxious. The rancor born of their battle on Wall Street reached into Sheepshead Bay, on this August afternoon of 1900, and perhaps would lighten the impost carried by one of their colts. The question was: which colt? And this lent a zest to the day's affairs.

The fashionable had only one complaint: neither Keene nor Whitney was on hand. Keene had gone to England on business —the unkind view was that he had withdrawn to lick his wounds. Whitney had also gone to England, but his paramount concern had been with this race, this thirteenth Futurity. He had gone to secure the services of a jockey, Tod Sloan.

At the turn of the century there was no more colorful jockey than Tod Sloan. His permanent fame rests on the fact that he was the first to ride "monkey-on-a-stick," huddled far up on his mount's withers; moreover, having taught American jockeys a lesson, he had crossed the ocean to take the wind out of the English jockeys' sails. George M. Cohan later celebrated this achievement in his "Yankee Doodle Dandy"—"Yankee Doodle came to London, just to ride the ponies . . ." But Sloan's contemporary fame was as a cocky, devil-may-care, flamboyant sport, guaranteed to roll higher, wider, and handsomer than anybody in town. And he also won races. Whitney wanted him badly, but when he saw him he wasn't so sure. Sloan had taken a tumble in a race for the Liverpool Cup; his head was swathed in bandages and one eye was closed. Whitney stared, then burst out laughing. "What happened to the other fellow?" he asked. The Futurity was then only some two weeks off but Sloan, cocky as ever, insisted he would be able to ride—for a price. Whitney gave him $5,000, and Sloan hurried to board a ship. He chucked up quite a swell when he arrived in New York, still wrapped in bandages, and took up residence at the Waldorf-Astoria at $100 a day. The other riders who had been assigned horses in the Futurity took malevolent notice of all the fanfare attending Sloan's homecoming; they winked to each other; they nodded sagely. Sloan, they agreed, would get his comeuppance.

Of the other riders, the three most important were those riding Keene's three colts, and they were all first-rate. Henry (The Iceman) Spencer was to be up on Cap and Bells, which was known to have a lot of early foot; Milton Henry was riding Olympian; and Winnie O'Connor had been assigned the favorite, the horse carrying top weight of 129 pounds, Tommy Atkins. In this thirteenth renewal of the Futurity, someone was in for some bad luck, and these three had a good idea who that someone would be. As post-time for the feature race approached, down in the betting enclosure the horseplayers agreed: they made the Keene entry an odds-on favorite. And everyone, as he placed his bet, did so with a special relish.

Not that there was any need to whet interest in a horserace on Coney, around the turn of the century. Sheepshead Bay was merely the most fashionable track, but by no means the only one. There were, as well, Brighton Beach and Gravesend. The three tracks competed enthusiastically for the crowds. They were never able to dovetail their schedules to everyone's satisfaction. In theory, each had a spring and a fall meeting, but in practice this meant that Gravesend had an early spring and a late fall, while at Brighton Beach spring and fall were both elbowed into the summer and the first meeting had scarcely closed before the second was ready to begin. Brighton Beach was obliged to lick up the crumbs, for if Sheepshead Bay had its Suburban and its Futurity, at Gravesend there were the Brooklyn Handicap and the Brooklyn Derby (what is known today as the Dwyer Stakes) and even, for a period of fifteen years, the Preakness; but the governors of racing at Brighton Beach were never able to come up with a stake race as attractive as any of these. The horseplayers cared not a rap for such conflicts. As far as they were concerned, there was racing in or near Coney from May through October, a circumstance approximating the horseplayer's Heaven; moreover, in those days the Winter book had meaning, what with as many as two hundred bookmakers offering fluctuating odds from December till April on the Suburban or the Brooklyn Handicap. Come spring, and the New York newspapers would turn over their entire front pages to these races, and sometimes their second and third pages as well; the assassination of a European monarch or a Latin-American revolution would be scratched before post-time.

The racing fever infected everybody, young as well as old. Directly across the track from the grandstand at Sheepshead Bay stood a big red brick building. This was P.S. 98, and the little scholars soon discovered that the standard punishment for errant behavior—being sent to stand in the cloakroom—afforded a splendid view of the finish of the first and second races. For a time juvenile delinquency knew no bounds, but presently

There was nothing posh about the Brighton Beach track, but for the $2 bettor in summertime it was a fine home away from home.
BROWN BROTHERS

Miss Drumgool and Miss Mullaly, sensing that the mischief always seemed to begin around post-time for the first, required of the embryo chalk-eaters that they repair to the office of Principal George Tappen, who would sportingly offer them their choice of a whack across the hand or the pants.

Every right-thinking boy in P.S. 98 envied Jimmy Fitzsimmons. Jim had been born on a farm spang in the middle of what later became Sheepshead Bay racetrack; his father's barn stabled the horses used in clearing and grading the land. With such an in, Fitz was walking hots almost as soon as he could walk himself; by 1885 he had been hired as an exercise-boy; in 1889 he was a jockey; and now, in 1900, only two weeks before, he had nonchalantly stood in the winner's circle at Brighton Beach with the first winner he had ever trained, a filly named Agnes D. Every right-thinking graduate of P.S. 98 believed, in

No tote-board, no tax-bite, but a hundred bookmakers in the betting ring to pick and choose from. And Gravesend was handsome, too.
BROWN BROTHERS

1900, that Sunny Jim Fitzsimmons had done nothing *he* could not have done, if only *his* father's farm had become the infield of Sheepshead Bay.

About the time Jim Fitzsimmons was walking hots at Sheepshead Bay, Joe Weber and Lew Fields were twelve-year-old entertainers at Phil Duffy's St. Nicholas Hotel ("one of the liveliest spots on the island") for a joint thirty dollars a week. They were bitten by the bug. They used to get up early to watch the morning works at Brighton Beach, and one gray day they were touted on a sure thing by a stable-boy their own age. They went for the whole thirty dollars—food money, to their families—and wept when they learned the stable-boy had not even bet their roll. Duffy only grinned. He wondered out loud what Weber would do to the stable-boy if he ever saw him again. Weber vowed he would slaughter him. Duffy grinned the more broadly, saw to it that the young tout was enticed to the St. Nicholas, and himself referee'd the slugfest, held in the middle of a circle of shouting horseplayers down from the track. The sports raised a purse of thirty dollars for the winner, Weber, whose family was able to eat again.

It was obvious even before 1880 that Coney needed a race-track. As a smart resort, it had everything else. The patrons were already there, and in profusion. Every weekend in season the wealthy and fashionable crowded into the Manhattan Beach, the Oriental, and the Brighton Beach; they wanted diversion. These long, rambling, wooden hotels were uniquely the expression of their era; they have no modern counterpart. Stretching, each of them, a furlong along the beach, with deep verandahs reaching down the whole length, set back from a wide esplanade of green turf, begirt with beds of gay geraniums and heliotropes and lobelias and broad curving walks, flanked by bathing pavilions and scallop-shell bandstands, they were characteristic creations of a gracious and leisurely day. And they were immensely popular. (They were also, in their day, select and expensive. The Manhattan Beach, particularly, took pride in its cuisine, boasting that such dishes as whitebait and oyster crabs were served in its dining room for the first time in America. In the season of 1880, a couple dining at the Manhattan Beach off littleneck clams [twenty-five cents a portion], crab bisque [twenty cents a portion], baked bluefish [forty-five cents] or roast lamb [sixty cents], the appropriate vegetables, salad, and meringue glacée [thirty cents a portion], would be lucky to get away from the table before they had spent $3.85.) Some idea of the popularity of these hotels may be gathered from one small set of statistics: in 1877 the Manhattan Beach Bathing Pavilion offered to its public 117 bathhouses; the next year this number had leaped to 800; the next to 1,500; in 1880 there were 2,350 single bathhouses and 350 larger rooms, for groups of a half-dozen bathers at a time—for by 1880 the Manhattan Beach had been adopted as a summer headquarters by the Union Club, the University Club, and the Union League Club, as well as by the recently formed Coney Island Jockey Club. To the west, the Brighton Beach offered summer shelter to the Bullion Club and the New York Club, and here the facilities were likewise taxed. Hotel managers grew accustomed, in the 1880's, to weekend trains seventeen cars long, with every passenger headed for the east end, and cots by the dozen being set up in the hotel corridors.

And everywhere there was music. Senator Thomas C. Platt, Republican boss of New York State, who made the Oriental his summer headquarters for many years, would stroll in the evening down to the Manhattan Beach, accompanied by Chauncey Depew, Chester Arthur, or whoever happened to be running errands for him in the governor's mansion at the time, to hear Patrick Gilmore's 22nd Regiment Band, featuring Signor Raffayello on the euphonium trombone and the celebrated Jules

Levy on cornet. Levy, a dashing figure who had been lured away from the band at the Brighton Beach when Austin Corbin raised his salary from $350 to $750 a week, was extravagantly adored by ladies who have subsequently failed to understand why their granddaughters should swoon over Sinatra. The cornettist considered it standard operating procedure when one day he was handed a perfumed billet-doux. "I met you at Brighton Beach recently," wrote his admirer, "and your glances gave me courage to address you. I am a married woman and therefore cannot invite you to my home. Will see you Monday morning at 10.30 at the corner of Fifth Avenue and Eighteenth Street. I will come closely veiled and, if possible, please have a coupé in readiness, as I would not be recognized for anything." Giving himself over to riotous fantasies, Levy hastened to the rendezvous only to discover that his correspondent was in fact his booking agent, bent on serving a summons so he might collect his ten per cent of the salary increase. All New York giggled, but Levy, unperturbed, continued to stab the air with his brilliant variations. At the Brighton Beach the concerts were provided by Admiral Neuendorf and his Naval Band; at Cable's by Downing's 9th Regiment Band, featuring an equally celebrated but more circumspect cornettist, George Washington Arbuckle; at the Sea Beach Hotel it was Carlberg's Orchestra; at Paul Bauer's Hotel it was Conterno's 23rd Regiment Band; at Feltman's ever-expanding gardens and restaurants it was the 6th Regiment Band and, in addition, *sängerbunds* and *schützenverein* by the dozen, singing through the evening hours. And on the Iron Pier there was Graffula's 7th Regiment Band.

The Iron Pier was Buel T. Hitchcock's contribution to Coney Island gaiety. A writer for *Scribner's* who went out to have a look at it in 1880 was enchanted. It was, he wrote, "an interminable dainty palace, pinnacled, gabled, arcaded, many-

John Philip Sousa leads his band. He played at Bauer's in 1890 but proved so popular that he was booked by the Manhattan Beach. L. H. BOGART COLLECTION, MUSEUM OF THE CITY OF NEW YORK

storied, raised on slender columns above the water, like a habitation of some charming race of lake-dwellers . . . All is festooned, floating, honeycombed, with the free air blowing through." Steamboats pulled in to the Iron Pier every twenty minutes over the summer weekends; the crowds on Coney grew steadily.

And, too, there was Professor King's captive balloon. Those who did not suffer from acrophobia could be wafted aloft fifteen at a time, up twelve hundred feet in a wicker basket, a dazzling experience.

Coney Island was, to the *Scribner's* writer, "a Centennial of pleasure, pure and simple, without any tiresome ulterior commercial purposes, held amid refreshing breezes, by the sea. The same gay architecture, the same waving flags, the same delightful distracting whirl, the same enormous masses of staring, good-natured human beings." It was, he concluded, "the greatest resort for a single day's pleasure in the world."

But all this, beguiling as it was, still was not enough. Still the rich and the fashionable craved a racetrack. For they were all, in those days, necessarily enthusiastic and knowledgeable horsemen. At a time when getting from here to there involved a horse, men fancied themselves as expert judges of horseflesh, even more than today they believe they can, unassisted, diagnose and treat their automobile's whooping-cough. In the 1880's, moreover, they were even quicker to back up their judgment with money. Every Sunday there were staged a hundred impromptu races, along Ocean Parkway, before thousands of onlookers who clustered around to bet on the outcome.

Gaslights and greenery bedeck the New Iron Pier, the second of four ocean piers built to handle the big crowds bound for Coney. COURTESY THE FRANCIS K. MOORE COLLECTION

(Down at the foot of Ocean Parkway, Lucy Vanderveer annually gave a champagne supper to the first sleigh party to reach her restaurant from Brooklyn after the first fall of snow.) To be sure, these Parkway races were contests between trotters or pacers, but it called for no great vision to perceive that he who built a better racetrack would shortly be combing horse-players out of his hair.

The first who undertook to meet this public need was William Engeman. There was no Jockey Club when Engeman formed the Brighton Beach Racing Association, but even if there had been he was not the Jockey Club type. He was, how-ever, a man who knew horses, having bought and sold them by the thousands to the Union Army during the Civil War. He was also a man who moved quickly. Within six weeks, from a stand-ing start, he built his racing plant at Brighton Beach in time for an opening in June, 1879. The first day's racing was, from the horses' point of view, discouraging. The only records set were track records. The horses were fetlock-deep in sand all after-noon. But Engeman was cheerful. He had observed that Bar-num's axiom held up: the crowds had battered his gates down to bet on his frightful day's card of races.

The Coney Island Jockey Club, led by such men as August Belmont, Jr., Leonard W. Jerome, A. Wright Sanford, William R. Travers, and D. D. Withers, was already at work carv-ing the Sheepshead Bay track out of a forest of oak and maple and elm. When the track was opened, in June, 1880, the judges were such well-known horsemen as J. H. Bradford, W. K. Vanderbilt, and J. G. K. Lawrence, whose memory is kept alive today by the Lawrence Realization Stakes; from that day on, Coney was off to the races. The advent of the Sheepshead Bay track helped establish Coney's tone for the next thirty years. It meant, first, that almost at once wealthy men moved into the neighborhood. It was their playground, they meant to make it as well their part-time home. The whole stretch of shore on the north side of Sheepshead Bay was gobbled up in huge bites by one millionaire after another: they built docks where they could moor their yachts, lodges where they could live and entertain during the race meetings, and stables for their horses. Their trainers and jockeys found homes in the neighborhood. Jimmy Rowe, Sam Hildreth, Uncle Henry McDaniel, Father Bill Daly, William Lakeland, Max Hirsch, George Odum, all names celebrated in American turf history, all found homes in Sheepshead Bay. A somnolent village had been tendered a lucrative industry: overnight stables, hotels, and restaurants sprang up and started to cope. It was the restaurants that acquired the most lustrous reputations, for all those who follow in the train of the securely wealthy—the playboys, the beauties, the gamblers, the get-rich-quicksters, the actors and theatrical managers, and the politicians—needed a fashionable place to congregate after the races, since they could scarcely afford opulent lodges of their own. They created three great restaurants: Tappan's (in later years, for undiscernible reasons, this was spelled Tappen's), Villepigue's, and Lundy's.

Actually Tappan's, in 1800, was already a venerable inn and chophouse. Twenty years before, Charles Dickens had sampled seafood delicacies there; it was one of the few experiences he had in this country of which he did not write with condescension. Soon after the racetrack opened, the restaurant concession at Tappan's was turned over to a man who had grown comfortably fat in the business of feeding horsemen. This was Big Jim Villepigue, a 335-pound gourmand up from Camden, South Carolina, who had shown that he knew how to victual the rich by running the clubhouse restaurant at Morris Park. Beardless Kips and Sanfords, juvenile Jeromes and Hitchcocks, callow Belmonts and Keenes, who had been weaned on Big Jim's terrapin soup at Morris Park, flocked eagerly into Tappan's front porch and parlor to graze off Big Jim's okra and collard greens. And in their train came the Freddie Gebhards, the Lily Langtrys and the Lillian Russells, the Diamond Jim Bradys, the Jesse Lewisohns, the Abe Hummels, the Maurice Barrymores, the Bet-a-Million Gateses, and the Dick Crokers. So dense was the crush that at length Big Jim had to buy a set of his own dinner silver and open his own place. The most colorful eaters followed, their tongues hanging out. Of these, surely the gaudiest was James Buchanan (Diamond Jim) Brady. A steel salesman, Brady did most of his business with railroads; one of his more *gemütlich* customers was A. J. Cassatt, who was president of the Pennsylvania. Cassatt was also president of the Monmouth Park Racing Association; one thing led to another, and presently Brady was racing his horses under Cassatt's colors. But the newly-formed Jockey Club eyed such ventures askance, and especially since one of the Brady colts, Gold Heels, was winning everything in sight, including the Brighton Handi-

Constant companion to Lillian Russell, gourmand extraordinary, gambler, racehorse owner, apotheosis of the Golden Age, this is Diamond Jim Brady, down for the races at Sheepshead Bay.
BROWN BROTHERS

cap, the Suburban, and the Brighton Cup. For business reasons, Brady decided he would sell out: he celebrated his decision with a monstrous banquet at Villepigue's. Earlier he had mentioned to Big Jim that he liked scallops, he liked mussels and shrimp and clams on the half-shell and clam chowder and steamed clams, he liked crabs, he liked lobster, he liked bluefish and flounder and sea trout, within reason he even liked scungili, and he liked all the trimmings that customarily went with these several dishes. But he had just one complaint. Nowhere had he ever been able to find the man who would serve him all these goodies at one sitting. Big Jim proved to be his man. They called the result the Shore Dinner. On his night of celebration, just to make sure he wouldn't skimp, Diamond Jim rolled up his sleeves before he began to tuck away eight lobsters. According to the legend, at some stage of this gargantuan glut Brady was dismayed to find that he was minus one diamond cuff link. It was a moment to delight the student of conspicuous consumption: which superfluous and incontinent ostentation would prove more important—a seventh lobster or an umpteenth chip of carbon? Tradition alleges that Brady called for the doors to be locked while the waiters searched the scullery and ransacked the garbage can; himself, he chomped indomitably on.

Lundy's, the third of Sheepshead Bay's celebrated restaurants, specialized in seafood and politicians who were serious eaters; Fred Lundy was content to forgo the high jinks.

Meantime, in August, 1886, the Brooklyn Jockey Club had launched the third track at Gravesend, just off of Ocean Parkway. The first jockey to be weighed in was Edward (Snapper) Garrison, whose hard-whipping finishes had already added an expression to the language. Garrison had married a Brighton Beach girl and now made his home there; in consequence every Coney Islander exulted when he romped home first in Gravesend's first three races. The Brooklyn Jockey Club included some of the same men who had formed the Coney Island Jockey Club; most influential were Phil and Mike Dwyer; they had been at pains to build a commodious and handsome plant on the site of the old Prospect Park Fair Grounds; the one-mile track was considered, in its day, the finest in the country; from the first their stake races were attractive.

And now, with three tracks going full tilt, and Coney the horseracing capital of the country, and every horseplayer pleased, and only an occasionally absconding bookmaker vile, one after the other each of the three tracks faced difficulties. Eminent sportsmen, governors of jockey clubs, distinguished financiers, leaders of society—all began capering about as though they were standing on hot bricks. The problem was with the preachers, who considered racehorses to be playthings of the Devil. First Engeman was arrested and indicted, in 1885 and again in 1886. Then the governors of the Coney Island Jockey Club were served with subpoenas and actually put on trial for permitting gambling on their premises. It was difficult to judge who was the more mortified: the assorted Belmonts, Vanderbilts, Lorillards, and Lawrences who were obliged to stand trial, or the district attorney who, by virtue of the statutes on the books, was required to prosecute them with the full majesty of the law. The district attorney, the compliant creature of Brooklyn's Boss Hugh McLaughlin, was also a man with social pretensions; he belonged to the same clubs as his (Ugh!) accused. The statutes insisted that gambling was illegal. Yet as any who could read the newspapers knew full well, there were as many as one hundred bookmakers operating at each of the three tracks on every day of the meeting, and each paying the management $100 a day for the privilege. Fortunately, at this desperate moment in the history of the

American turf, the commonsense of the average horseplayer
was asserted. It was impossible to impanel a jury of twelve
good men and true without at the same time impaneling at least
three good horseplayers and true. In the circumstances, it was
impossible to convict. In 1887 the Ives betting bill became law
and all hands breathed easier. But still the reformers scowled
and shook monitory fingers. In 1894, on the very day that Dr.
Rice upset Henry of Navarre in the eighth running of the
Brooklyn Handicap, Phil Dwyer was arrested; handcuffs were
waved in front of the judges' stand. It was too much: it tried
the railbirds' patience: their irritated clucking could be heard
for two furlongs, all along the straightaway in front of the
grandstand. Next day, however, a loud laugh went up, for it
developed that the lawyer retained to prosecute Dwyer was
Abe Hummel and the judge before whom he would be tried
was William Gaynor. Both men were well-known figures around
New York at the time: Hummel was perhaps the most celebrated criminal lawyer of his day and Gaynor a rising political
power on his way to the mayoralty. More important, each was
a regular at the big races. Hummel's performance as advocate
for the prosecution was a parody; Gaynor peremptorily tossed
the case out of court.

For those who are touched by the spectacle of courage en-
listed in a hopeless cause, the wistful attempts to halt betting
on the races at Coney must stand unrivalled as the most affect-
ing example in our history. Not merely quantitatively but also
qualitatively the betting was extraordinary. The three tracks
were a home-away-from-home for men who gambled in the
grand manner; it was with them a point of honor; more, a way
of life. One such was the slim, mild-mannered George E. Smith,
the refugee from a cork factory who won fame as Pittsburgh
Phil. When he showed up at Sheepshead Bay in 1888, for the
inaugural Futurity Stakes, he was as close to fury as he ever

The finish of the first Futurity (1888) at Sheepshead Bay, with Proctor Knott by a neck over the storied Salvator. The winner's owner was so poor he slept in the horse's stable the night before the race. Next day he pocketed $40,900, and slept on pinfeathers.   PRINT ROOM, N. Y. PUBLIC LIBRARY

permitted himself to be. A newspaper had printed a story that his losses had been so severe as to drive him out of his mind. He was quite seriously contemplating an action against the newspaper; wasn't such a story, he demanded, a libel *per se?* Besides, he added crossly, the fact was that he was only a trifling $15,000 behind on his year's betting. This sum was promptly increased by the several thousand that he got down at five-to-one on Salvator, which lost to Proctor Knott by a neck.

Two years later Salvator came back to Sheepshead Bay to cop the Suburban in record time before a crowd of 25,000, who bet more than $1,000,000 (Pittsburgh Phil won $7,000 this time), but everybody was not satisfied that Salvator was the best horse in the race. There were those who thought that Tenny, a moody animal which had run third, was in fact Salvator's superior. And so a match race was arranged for the fortnight following, a race that witnesses have insisted was the race of the decade, if not of the century. It was also Prince Charming against the Ugly Duckling, the royal purple against the humdrum drab, and the rich against the common folks, for Salvator was a high-bred beauty owned by a millionaire horseman and Tenny a swayback of undistinguished lineage carrying the colors of a Chicago bookmaker. Salvator's owner was J. B. Haggin, a Kentuckian who for inscrutable reasons had seen fit to move to California; once there he had done this and that, and so turned up as principal owner of the Anaconda Mine, which is better than standing in line at a soup-kitchen. Tenny's owner was David Tenny Pulsifer, who was in a chancier business; he had bought his horse at an auction for a song. When it came to the jockeys, however, it was no longer a case of the hobnailed boot oppressing the downtrodden: up on Salvator was Isaac Murphy, the Negro jockey who was to ride three Kentucky Derby winners, and up on Tenny was Snapper Garrison, also one of the all-time greats.

Horseplayers dutifully turned out, and by the thousands. Little Abe Hummel was there, spick-and-span, to wager his $100 on Tenny, and gaunt DeWolf Hopper kept the bookmakers busy with bets on Salvator; Berry Wall was there, too, in what a sardonic journalist described as a "thrilling" suit of clothes; Leonard Jerome, Winston Churchill's grandfather, was in the box next to August Belmont; two boxes away sat Pierre Lorillard, the man who was so shrewd as to commission Tiffany's to hammer him out a set of horseshoes from the new miracle metal, aluminum; Charles Delmonico bowed stiffly to John Peacock, of the Hoffman House; and here were Freddie Gebhard and W. J. Arkell, the publisher of *Judge*, and T. Burnett Baldwin, the manager of Tuxedo Park, and Dick Newton, McKane's crony, and Henry French, the most successful theatrical manager of the year; and the word went round the betting ring that Dave Pulsifer had just bet $5,000 at five-to-seven on his own horse, Tenny; and then the horses were at the post, and then they were off.

Tenny was on the rail, but Salvator crept ahead, by a nose, by a neck, by a length at the three-eighths pole, by two lengths at the three-quarter pole; and now those men who were holding watches stared in disbelief at the time; at the mile Salvator was a full three lengths in the lead and running with a sure power and rhythm; there was another quarter to go, and Tenny's backers were shaking their heads.

Then the swayback made his move and Garrison was riding the finish of his life. In the last two furlongs Tenny made up a length, two, two-and-a-half; in the last moments the black head crept up alongside the chestnut, closer and closer, and then they were across the line and Murphy and Garrison were pulling up their horses and Garrison was saying to Murphy, "I got you on the last jump," and the expressionless Murphy was stolidly shaking his head, No, and caressing Salvator's neck and withers and, "No, you didn't," he said, "I won." And back in the grandstand boxes and along the rail the crowd was screaming and cheering and crying and laughing, and they were slapping each other on the back and stamping their feet, and hats and canes and fans and parasols were tossed in the air, and they kept on cheering for a good five minutes, just for the race, nobody was sure yet who had won, and then the official timer, Captain Conner, hung out the winning number on the judge's stand, and it was Salvator's and the thousands still had no chance to quiet down for now he hung up the time, 2:05, and himself, like a happy schoolboy, began to lead the cheers all over again, for this was a track record and very fast time indeed.

And the next day the eminent author of recitations, Ella Wheeler Wilcox, hauled off and wrote a piece that went over large for the next twenty years. It is an example of the artist, cool, controlled, perfectly in command of her material, yielding not a whit to emotion, simply setting down the bald, unadorned facts. Here are the last few lines:

> *There's a roar from the crowd like the ocean in storm*
> *As close to my saddle leaps Tenny's great form.*
> *One mighty plunge and with knee, limb and hand*
> *I lift my horse first by a nose past the stand;*
> *We are under the string now—the great race is won,*
> *And Salvator, Salvator, Salvator won!*
> *Cheer! hoar-headed patriarchs; cheer loud, I say,*
> *'Tis the race of the century witnessed today!*
> *Though ye live twice the space that's allotted to men*
> *You never will see such a grand race again.*
> *Let the shouts of the populace roar like the surf*
> *For Salvator, Salvator, King of the Turf!*

As the race of the decade or the century, the Salvator-Tenny duel lasted only a couple of years. Then James R. Keene brought his fine colt Domino to Sheepshead Bay for the Futurity. Domino went off at six-to-five and came home the winner by a head, but again there were horsemen who insisted a better horse had been beaten. Again it was the show horse, Dobbins, owned by Dick Croker, the head of Tammany Hall, which had its obstinate adherents, most of them Tammany henchmen. There was, of course, no photo-timer in those days, so if an owner squawked strenuously enough, he was likely to convince a few in his audience that he had indeed been robbed. Croker keened so shrilly that at length he got the match race he wanted. In August of 1893 Domino and Dobbins broke head and head, and raced head and head over the Futurity distance, and finished head and head. Croker chose to conclude that this proved his colt had not been beaten in the Futurity, but it did not cause Keene to split his Futurity purse of $49,000.

A year and six races later, Domino was still regarded as the champion of his time, with thirteen victories and a dead heat in fifteen starts; but again there were railbirds who were growling that his record was a phony, and that Henry of Navarre was his peer. Again a match was made, this time at Gravesend. Henry of Navarre was Kentucky born and bred, and this time most of the drama was played before the race, down in the betting enclosure. It began a half-hour or so before post-time when a thin, pale, beardless, boyish young man in shirtsleeves climbed up on a bookmaker's box and made a short but effective speech. "I am here," said he, "to bet some money on Navarre, and I will be glad to accommodate the gentlemen who fancy Domino." This was a Kentucky gambler named Riley Grannan, and as he concluded his speech he displayed a board on which he had chalked a laconic message: "3-5, Domino;" Henry of Navarre's name was also on his slate, but with no odds offered.

Hats were cheaper, in 1886.
The horse is Troubador,
winner of the Suburban at
Sheepshead Bay.
Leslie's Illustrated
N. Y. PUBLIC LIBRARY

Grannan's invitation attracted immediate interest. Someone bet $1,000, and it was accepted imperturbably. A bookmaker anxious to lay off some bets, put up $5,000; this too went into Grannan's book. And now the action stepped up in tempo. Mike Dwyer offered $10,000 and, when Grannan refused to change the odds on his board, another $10,000. The little fish stepped respectfully to one side and let the whales disport themselves Every big bettor in the East closed in and fired one commission after another into Grannan's book; all were cheerfully accepted. Keene's commissioner put in another $10,000. The action paused. "Come, come gentlemen," urged Grannan; "surely there is some more Domino money in the house?" He stared around. There was a pause. The biggest bettors in the East eyed him and then looked away. At length Grannan turned in disgust to his sheetwriter. "What do you think of 'em?" he asked. "They won't bet me!" He had taken in $62,000 against his own $37,200; he had begged for more, but to no avail; fretfully he closed his book and stalked off to the second tier of the grandstand. It was, at the time, the biggest book that had ever been made by an individual on any race in the United States. Grannan watched impassively, his complexion pasty as usual, while Domino and Henry of Navarre galloped the mile-and-one-eighth to another dead heat in 1:55.5; as, under the rules, the face values of the tickets were added together and the sum total divided, Grannan had to give back the Domino bettors $49,600. He won $12,400, "enough," as he remarked to Mike Dwyer, "to pay for my expenses from Kentucky."

Mike Dwyer was himself an impressive gambler. His partnership with his brother Phil was a curious thing: together they owned some fine thoroughbreds, of which perhaps the best was Hindoo, which won thirty-one of thirty-six starts in the early 1880's and never finished out of the money; but Phil was content to let Mike do all the family's betting. Mike thrived for some years on a diet of chalk. His idea of a good bet was $30,000 to win $10,000. Once, when he had made such a wager, he got so engrossed in a discussion with a friend that he clean forgot the race. Turning to a Pinkerton, "Say, boy," he inquired, "who won that race?" "Your horse got beat, Mr. Dwyer," he was told, "he run second." Mike paused. "Well," he is alleged to have said at length, but it is three-to-one that he never used at least one word attributed to him, "well, I'll be dinged, these ponies are a pesky bunch sometimes."

Mike and Phil Dwyer dissolved their partnership in the early 1890's, and Mike took his share, supposed at the time to be worth around $2,000,000, to England, for he and Dick Croker had decided that they could make a killing on the English tracks. They were not the only ones who have made the same mistake. Back at home, Mike suffered a stroke at the track one day; thereafter he had to be ladled into a carriage by his Negro valet whenever he wanted to go to the races; to a compassionate reporter who had asked him for his advice on betting, "I am not in the mood for giving advice," said Mike Dwyer, "and I don't suppose anyone would take it if I did." He looked out across his old track, Gravesend, and perhaps he saw and heard the lightning and thunder of a stretch finish. "If there are any fools, young or old," he said, after a time, "let them go ahead and take their chances as I took mine." His fingers plucked at the rug his valet had tucked around him. "And," he added, "with a similar result."

Not every loser took his financial reverses so bleakly. In the 1893 Brooklyn Handicap, James R. Keene's Diablo, seven years old and reputed to be a broken-down cripple, romped home over Lamplighter at forty-to-one, and thereby impoverished nearly everybody who lived south of the Green-Wood Cemetery in Brooklyn. The biggest song hit that year was "After the Ball," and some unsung but songful horseplayer went back to

Coney Island from Gravesend humming the lovely waltz music. The words came naturally and ruefully:

> *After the race was over,*
> *After Diablo won,*
> *After your pockets were empty,*
> *You by the bookmakers stung—*
> *Many a head is aching,*
> *Many a saddened face!*
> *Many a dollar has vanished,*
> *After the race!*

And this feeling plaint was greeted with dolefully sincere applause that night on the Bowery, at Inman's Casino.

But the most splendid attitude struck by any horseplayer, in this era of magnificent gestures, was, fittingly enough, assumed by an actress, one of the favorites of the day, Edna Wallace Hopper. Miss Hopper (she had married and divorced DeWolf Hopper, but had clung to his name) was the star of the musical comedy smash of 1900, *Floradora.* She was, in the words of the *Herald's* critic, "petite and dainty," and so offered a pleasing contrast to the hefty maidens of the celebrated Floradora Sextette. She was also an enthusiastic horseplayer, and a few days before that year's running of the Brooklyn Handicap she was touted on a sure thing. Nothing would do but that she be at Gravesend personally to root her horse home. But there was the matter of her Saturday matinee. She appealed to the company manager.

"Why don't you close down and give us a holiday on Saturday?" she urged him. "It's Handicap Day, and there won't be anybody in the house—and, oh! I've got such a tip!"

Company managers have changed very little over the years. "Nobody in the house, eh?" this one answered. "We'll do $1,600 worth of business on Saturday."

"Then," said Miss Hopper calmly, "I'll give you my check for $1,700 and we'll call the performance off."

One thousand, seven hundred dollars, just to see a horse-race? But manifestly Miss Hopper meant it. The producer was inclined to jib; grumbled it would only give Miss Hopper exalted notions of her importance to the show, were they to cancel simply because she chose to take the day off; but they took him to one side and, using only basic, primer words, patiently explained how the sensational publicity would more than compensate; and presently even he understood. And so a notice went up on the call-board of the Casino:

> Edna Wallace Hopper begs to inform the ladies and gentle-men of the Floradora company that she has purchased the entire house for the Saturday matinee performance, May 25, and no performance will be given that afternoon, permitting the members of the company to enjoy a holiday.

When word of her extraordinary motive got around, Miss Hopper was promptly besieged by an army of dear friends, former schoolmates, and distant cousins, each anxious to take a nibble at the prevailing odds. Miss Hopper was also mindful of the odds and she very sensibly kept her petite and dainty mouth shut. On the Saturday, the six impressive beauties who at the time comprised the Floradora Sextette were handed up to the top of a tally-ho that had been thoughtfully parked in front of the Casino. (At least, it had the general outlines of a tally-ho, but no one could be absolutely certain, so awash was it in muslin banners, each flaunting to the public gaze the magic word, Floradora.) At the turn of the century, these six young ladies were the most glamorous cupcakes in town; because of them the rear of the Casino was nightly encumbered with stage-door johnnies; nightly they made their regal entrances into Rector's or Shanley's for after-theatre suppers, carrying

Edna Wallace Hopper had to fight for the part of Lady Holyrood, in "Floradora." The producer thought she was too young, too tiny. She proved him wrong.

But the producer had no qualms about the hefty maidens of the celebrated Floradora Sextette. Nor did any other man in town.

bouquets into which would have been thrust—if the escort of the evening wished to be favored another time—a diamond necklace, or a $100 bill. A legend had been born around them: to be one of the girls in the Sextette was to marry a millionaire. Indeed, already on this Saturday four of the original six were gone: one to marry a millionaire silk manufacturer, another to marry a South African diamond magnate, a third to marry a stock broker, and a fourth—a canny miss, who had been given a tip on the stock market by James R. Keene and promptly ran it up to $750,000—to marry the most inveterate playboy of the decade, Freddy Gebhard. Even the two who still, after nearly two hundred performances, listened eight times a week to the question, "Tell me, pretty maiden, are there any more at home like you?" and answered sweetly, "There are a few, kind sir, but simple girls, and proper, too," were destined for greener pastures; one was to marry Andrew Carnegie's nephew, the other to marry an Irish peer and be presented at the Court of St. James's. On Handicap Day these favored six were the

Misses Sears, Relyea, Toland, Green, Winter, and Drake, off to the races atop their tally-ho, but bound first for Coney, for they were to have a champagne luncheon at Ravenhall's.

Miss Hopper drove down to Gravesend with somewhat less manufactured fanfare, in her brougham; she was radiant despite the steady fall of rain; six young men of distinguished appearance buzzed attentively about her. To one she gave charge of her wraps, to another her pearl-handled umbrella, to a third her notebook and gold pencil; a fourth was appointed her betting commissioner; she took the arms of the fifth and sixth and chose a box near the edge of the clubhouse. But if the rain failed to damp her spirits, the feature race did the trick; it developed that she had gotten down $3,000 on the favorite, Clarence Mackay's Banastar, but he had trouble in the heavy going and finished unplaced. "This is dreadful," said Miss Hopper. Her black plumed hat drooped disconsolately. A reporter from the *Herald* approached. "What about the young man who gave you the tip?" he asked. "Is he safe?" "I should like to see him," said the actress very slowly and calmly; "oh, I should like so much to see him." "And the Casino cost you $1,700," observed the reporter. Miss Hopper looked at him thoughtfully. "You have the faculty," said she, "of changing subjects with rare felicity." The pretty maidens of the Floradora Sextette were in no better case: each had permitted herself to be touted by Miss Hopper: that night the performance at the Casino seemed to lack spirit, except during the first of Miss Hopper's patter songs. She had learned that Clarence Mackay was out front in a box; she seized the opportunity to interpolate some scathing lines, and sang them resentfully in his direction, to his evident delight.

More than fifty years later, Miss Hopper was asked how much truth there was to the tale of her day at the races.

"All true," she said, "all true," and she wagged her head ruefully, as if in wonder at the follies of her youth.

It was suggested that it was by all odds the most scintillating gesture of a gay and spirited decade even if, as it must have seemed at the time, it was a trifle expensive.

"Oh," exclaimed Miss Hopper, bridling, "but of course it wasn't my money that paid for the theatre!"

There was a slight hissing sound, as of a punctured illusion.

"You surely don't think," Miss Hopper went on, "that I would spend that kind of money just to go to a horserace!"

Scottish blood courses through Miss Hopper's veins, and where $1 evokes admiration, seventeen hundred times as much admiration is due $1,700. But who, then, was the lightsome spirit who had so recklessly bought the house out on her account?

Miss Hopper paused. Then, "After all," she said, "it's more than fifty years ago." She mentioned the name of a gilded youth —or, to be more precise, of a youth who had gleamed like burnished copper, for his wealth had been extracted from the earth under Butte, Montana—"but, of course," said Miss Hopper, "we had to keep his name out of it. You see," she added, and there was a twinkle in her eye although her expression was demure, "his wife disapproved of horseracing."

But no matter who picked up the tab for that matinee at the Casino, it was picked up, and the *beau geste* was typical of the fashionable attitude toward racing at Coney's three tracks. Most of those who lingered in the Gold Room of the Sheepshead Bay clubhouse, just before the feature race, the Futurity, on this August afternoon in 1900, would have sympathized wholeheartedly. Some had lunched at George Bader's handsome roadhouse on the circle at the head of Ocean Parkway, some at the Riccadona Hotel, the hangout of politicians at the foot of the Parkway, some in the more elegant hotels on the shore, some at Ravenhall's, some on the lawn, but all were now eagerly looking forward to the race that was just the immediate aspect of the bloodshot rivalry between Keene and Whitney. In the betting enclosure the bookmakers cheerfully exploited the heightened interest, the odds tightened on the Keene entry, but there was unflagging affection for Whitney's Ballyhoo Bey, and there was concern, too, over Pittsburgh Phil's choice. The great gambler had not shown his hand; he was out in the paddock.

At Sheepshead Bay the paddock was an entirely delightful spot. Fountainous maple and stately elm shaded the deep green lawn and muted the brilliant silks of the jockeys; here trainers gentled their horses, and all about, leaning on whitewashed split-rail fences, clustered the last-minute horseplayers. Here, aloof, stood Pittsburgh Phil. Someone dared to ask him what was the inside information. "I have never had any," he answered, "and don't want any. My inside information is my eye. That's all. I can tell when a horse is fit and willing to run. I get to know him intimately, I keep close tab on him until, in my opinion, he is fit to run, and then I back him." He watched the colts before him intently as their trainers saddled them. "I don't pay much attention to a horse in the paddock," he went on, without taking his eyes off them. "I want to see him move. I want to see him warm up and know if he feels like running." A few yards away, Henry Spencer got a leg up on Cap and Bells, which reared and broke into an impatient canter. "There is one thing," said the greatest gambler of his time, his voice rising peevishly, "that upsets my most careful calculations, and that is the jockey. We have absolutely the worst bunch of jockeys riding races now that it's ever been my experience to observe. They are," he went on, anticipating the querulous complaint of every year's crop of horseplayers down through eternity, "totally incompetent. They ride a good race today and a bad one tomorrow. What's the sense of working out a horse's form if you can't depend on his jockey?" His questioner moved away, mumbling a polite nothing. Pittsburgh Phil's lips were still working. "You can't gauge a jockey by past performances," he was grieving; "he will upset your calculations every time . . ."

Up on Ballyhoo Bey, Tod Sloan was aware that Spencer, on Cap and Bells, Henry, on Olympian, and O'Connor, on Tommy Atkins, were gathered together around Keene's trainer, Jimmy Rowe. Presently they moved away from Rowe, walking their horses on close rein. Sloan might have wondered if these other three were talking about him. They were, and "Bighead" was merely the most printable epithet they were hanging on him. They were three against one, for the other colt nominated by Whitney was inconsiderable, and three against one, when three singleminded jockeys are involved in a race over only six-and-one-half furlongs, makes steep odds. There were eight other contenders in the race, but they were ignored, as one by one the field cantered down the straightaway past the grandstand to the foot of the chute.

Tod Sloan

Snapper Garrison

At the post, each of Keene's three jockeys in turn kept riding in front of Sloan, knocking Ballyhoo Bey around and generally making it tough for him. There were two or three false starts before Chris Fitzgerald's successful "Come on!"

At once Spencer took his speedy Cap and Bells in front. Henry was second. Sloan was on the rail, and O'Connor was at his side, so close that he could reach out and scratch Sloan's back. Sloan was, then, trapped, deep down in a pocket. The four horses, all others forgotten, stayed in the same relative position all the way down the chute, past the quarter-pole, past the half. With less than two furlongs to go, O'Connor shouted to Spencer, a length and one-half ahead of him. "Stay where you are," he called. "I'm coming up outside!" And he went to his whip.

But ahead of him, Spencer, The Iceman, had gotten greedy. He too moved up. Sloan, who had been cursing silently for a half-mile, saw a chink of daylight. His heels dug in, and he shot through. At the five-eighths pole he had collared Cap and Bells. It was Ballyhoo Bey by a length, ridden out, with Olympian second and Tommy Atkins third, and all the time Sloan was pulling his horse up he was gasping with laughter. O'Connor galloped past, furious, looking back over his shoulder at Spencer. "If you'd done what I told you," he shouted, "he'd never have had a chance!" The colts were walking now, and Sloan grinned. "You know," he said chattily, to O'Connor, "if your stable had only entered six horses in the race, you might have put me in a pocket." O'Connor was so angry he couldn't answer.

In the betting enclosure, Pittsburgh Phil strode purposefully toward his bookmaker with a handful of winning tickets.

The loser's son, Foxhall Keene, dispatched a laconic cable to his father. But what consolation could there have been in owning the place and show horses, when Whitney's horse had won?

At Villepigue's, the night of the race, the rumor flew around that young Harry Payne Whitney had proposed a match race, Ballyhoo Bey against Tommy Atkins, for a side-bet of $100,000; but if the offer was made it was never accepted. For both colts had in any event been entered in the Flatbush Stakes, to be run the following Saturday; the issue was already drawn; and this time William Whitney would be on hand to watch. There was another difference: Foxhall Keene took Winnie O'Connor off Tommy Atkins and replaced him with Spencer. O'Connor was miffed. He went privily to Tod Sloan and whispered a warning. At the post, Sloan spoke up to the starter, Chris Fitzgerald. He nodded, and raised his voice: "If I see the slightest thing out of the way here," he said, "I'll report the matter to the stewards and I tell you it will go hard with the boys who are guilty." The start was good, and Sloan fell in behind two other horses, with Spencer on Tommy Atkins just to the rear. The two jockeys setting the pace kept looking over their shoulders at Sloan; he smiled. At the half-mile post Sloan moved up as though he had ideas about going through. It was beautiful the way the two front runners amicably parted, but instead Sloan whipped

Ballyhoo Bey around outside and dashed ahead. Behind him, Spencer fell into the trap laid for Sloan: he tried to slip through, Tommy Atkins went down on his knees as the leaders closed in, and Ballyhoo Bey was off and running easily, three lengths to the good. Before the numbers went up, Foxhall Keene was up the stairs four at a time to the judges' stand, claiming a foul, demanding Sloan's disqualification. He was still white-lipped when, the judges having refused him, he stalked back to the clubhouse. He announced that he was withdrawing all the Keene horses from further contention at Sheepshead Bay. Whitney, watching him, was moved. Twice he started over toward him, to offer a word of consolation; each time he decided he had better not. Instead he made a firm offer: a match race between the two colts, with his purse from the Flatbush as part of the stake. The offer was frostily ignored. Whitney shrugged and walked away to find Sloan.

The owner and the jockey strolled around to the lawn in back of the clubhouse and sat down on a bench. Whitney could have been forgiven a moment of exultation and a pleasurable sigh. He stretched his legs out comfortably and looked at Sloan. "Let's see," he said. "I haven't given you anything for winning the Futurity except that five thousand you had in London for travelling expenses, have I?" He reached a hand into his pocket and pulled out an obese bundle of large, coarse banknotes. "It's all I have with me," he apologized, handing it to Sloan. It was a trifle more than $9,000. "No," added Whitney, correcting himself, "I *do* have something more," and he handed over his gold watch. It was a fitting tribute to the most piratical jockey of his day.

The Whitney-Keene feud faded and was forgotten, and each man went on to more laudable, if less bloodthirsty, ventures on the turf. Whitney headed the group of owners that saved Saratoga, in 1901; Keene, after recouping his fortunes, came back to breed and race two of the greatest thoroughbreds in history, Sysonby and Colin. Of each of these it could be said that he was a Coney Island horse, for eleven of Sysonby' fifteen starts (he won fourteen of them) were at one or another of Coney's three tracks; six of Colin's fifteen (he was unde feated) were there as well. The three tracks were to glory in one more triumphant decade, and their importance to the sea side resort was to be inestimable. How could it be otherwise when they brought down to the Island all that was wealthy and gay and fashionable? The great hotels were filled to bursting every season. At the Manhattan Beach, Gilmore's band gave way to John Philip Sousa's, and his in turn to Victor Herbert's and with each succession the crowds around the bandshell grew. And in the evening when the band wasn't playing, there were breathtaking displays of fireworks, spectacular pageant engineered by an Englishman, Henry J. Pain, who used the sea shore for a stage and the ocean and heavens for a backdrop to conjure up, in bursts of rockets and Catherine wheels and bombs scattering showers of gold and silver, such epic event as the defeat of the Spanish fleet at Manila or the siege of Vladivostock. And the race crowds meant, too, that light opera and vaudeville blossomed on the beach. In West Brighton, Fred Henderson introduced vaudeville at his Music Hall; the nex season, up went the Brighton Beach Music Hall, offering the headliners of the day, and attracting so many theatrical foll that Reisenweber was obliged to open a branch restaurant on Coney Island, just off Ocean Parkway; further east, there wa the Manhattan Beach Summer Opera House, where road com panies performed the hit musicals of Manhattan's winter season

Not, of course, that everything was peaches and cream. Espe cially the Brighton track had its woes. There was, for one, the elements: whenever a full moon coincided with a stiff offshore breeze, the tides would rise supernally high and the indignant

The Brighton Beach weighed 6,000 tons, according to somebody's estimate. On April 3, 1888 they started hauling it back. The job was finished
on June 29 with the hotel ready for business.   COURTESY THE FRANCIS K.
MOORE COLLECTION

horses would be loaded into rowboats and ferried from their
stables to the track. Indeed, the tides at Brighton worked havoc
on more than just the racetrack. Twice they cut away so much
of the shorefront that the owners of the Brighton Beach Hotel
were obliged to snatch their bathing pavilion back from the
clutches of the encroaching ocean. And once the entire hotel,
a several-storied structure more than five hundred feet long,
had to be jacked up on railroad cars and eased six hundred feet
inland. Six locomotives in two teams of three each hauled the
building so gently that not a pane in a window nor a mirror in
a room was cracked. The Brighton track also suffered from the
rapacity of man. Some shrewd scalawag early realized that he
was afforded a splendid view of the finish line from the top of
the nearby Iron Tower, imported to Coney in 1877 from the
Philadelphia Exposition. He required only field-glasses to make
out the colors of the winning jockey. Since wagers were ac-

cepted in the pool-room of the Albemarle Hotel for two or three crucial minutes after each race was won, it was a case, all over again, of money for jam. With the help of two confederates and a set of bandannas in different colors, his strategem functioned smoothly throughout almost an entire season before it was detected, and a lofty fence erected to block his view.

Later, at Gravesend, gamblers evolved a more complex plot. One man paid admission to the track and took up his position in a corner of the grandstand visible to a friend on the outside. While the horses were still pounding down the stretch, the inside man made a careful guess as to the winner and then a pre-arranged signal to his friend. This second man then signaled to a third standing at a telephone with an open wire to a fourth in Manhattan. The fourth took the call, ran next door to a horse-room, and signaled to a fifth, who then bet heavily on the gang's choice, across the board. No law was broken: the bet was made before the race was over: the tip had left the track before the horses had crossed the finish-line: the profits were enormous until higher and ever higher fences were set up about the Gravesend grandstand.

But these were very minor frets. The sorriest worm in the luscious apple made its appearance at the end of the century's first decade, when horseracing became an issue for the politicians. It was an unlikely turn of events, for politicians had been among the most determined producers for the game. Indeed, it had come to seem that the taxpayer was safest on Futurity Day or Handicap Day, since only then would the politicians in a body remove their hands from the public till, in order to repair to the racetrack. But in 1908 William Randolph Hearst undertook to run for governor, and he took as one of his liveliest campaign issues the mortal sin of gambling. Hearst swore that, if elected, he would forever end betting. An aroused electorate sent Charles Evans Hughes to the governor's mansion in Albany, but almost the first action taken by the new governor was to doublecross the voters by calling a special session of the legislature to enact legislation against betting on horseraces. Once again, arrests reached a peak; once again, it was almost impossible to convict; but once again, the nuisance was extreme. And this time the horsemen decided that they had had it. After two years of struggle, they quit. Brighton Beach closed in 1907; the others were shuttered in 1910. Coney Island was without racing for the first time in thirty years. And it never came back.

But Coney still has its memories of the great racing days, and with each succeeding racing season they are refreshed. For Sheepshead Bay's most important stakes were taken over by Belmont—the Futurity, the Lawrence Realization, the Suburban, and the Swift Stakes; and Gravesend's most attractive races were bequested to Aqueduct—the Astoria, the Brooklyn Handicap, the Dwyer Stakes, the Gazelle Stakes, and the Tremont Stakes. It is not much, but it is something. One day, perhaps some latter-day Widener or Whitney or Haggin will see fit to move that the Jockey Club revive the Coney Island Cup, and something more of the graciousness and leisure and gaiety of a by-gone time will return to the American turf.

N. Y. World, 1892. N. Y. PUBLIC LIBRARY

~Pugnacious~

THE closing years of the century were a golden age for professional fisticuffs. From featherweight to heavyweight, the names are a rolling of drums and a skirling of pipes to dreamy-eyed men still alive. George Dixon and Terry McGovern, the names run, Jack McAuliffe and Kid Lavigne and Frank Erne, Mysterious Billy Smith and Tommy Ryan and Kid McCoy, Gentleman Jim Corbett and Ruby Robert Fitzsimmons and Jim Jeffries. All these were champions, but the oldtimers insist that among the heavyweights there were some other magnificents—notably Peter Jackson, Joe Choynski, Tommy Burns, Tom Sharkey, Gus Ruhlin, and Peter Maher—any one of whom would have been, in his prime, the peer of today's champions. And nearly all of these venerated pugs fought at Coney Island. For the Coney Island Athletic Club, a cavernous wooden structure outfitted with seats for about ten thousand customers, was, during this period, the undisputed world's capital of the Sweet Science. Here in this barn the world's heavyweight championship was up for grabs three times within one year; here for the only time in fistic history a title changed hands beneath a roof. And here, on the night of November 3, 1899, the fancy gathered

154

from all over the country, for the issue was to be debated by the ex-sailor, Tom Sharkey, and the ex-boilermaker, Jim Jeffries.

That a fight could be held thus openly and without fear of interference by the police was due to the kindly ministrations of a Tammany statesman, the eminent solon Big Tim (Dry Dollar) Sullivan. This public benefactor had shepherded through the New York State legislature the Horton Act, a dispensation that authorized prizefights so long as they were limited to twenty-five rounds, and so long as all present subscribed to the amiable fiction that no fighting was going on, but only a theatrical entertainment. Since the police found it possible to participate in this suspension of disbelief, the promotion of fights proceeded merrily; the more important matches shouldered their way onto the front pages of the newspapers; each gate was successively bigger; the fights became a fad and were taken up by all classes and conditions of men. Indeed, although the weather on the night of this November third was unspeakably vile, with sheets of cold rain blown in on a stiff ocean breeze, it seemed likely that every seat in the Coney Island Athletic Club would be filled.

Everybody was coming. Some were coming by train, some by carriage; some were from the theatre, some from politics, some from Wall Street, some from jail; some were coming to gawk, some to bet, some for business, some for fun, some because it was the fashion. One-Eyed Connolly was coming: it was by no means the first big gate he was to crash in an illustrious career. Some who were coming were, as will be shown in a moment, up to no good. But all were excited, all were happy. And of all these thousands of happy and excited men it may be safely conjectured that none was quite so exhilarated as the gabby, cheeky, peppery young man-about-town called Billy Brady. Brady had many reasons to be happy. He was, for this night, important, sought after, a man on whose slightest word other lesser mortals hung goggle-eyed. All this attention tickled his vanity, but he had a source of even deeper satisfaction. He was the happiest man on Coney Island because, no matter what happened in the upcoming discourse between Jeffries and Sharkey, he, Brady, was bound to win. Of all the many excellent motives for watching two men whale the tar out of each other, surely the most profoundly gratifying for the onlooker is this: that with every savage belt those two men exchange they are coining money for the onlooker. This was Brady's motive: indeed, it was his motive three times over. In the first place, he was president and principal stockholder of the Coney Island Athletic Club, and as such was making money. In the second place, he was manager of Jim Jeffries, the champion, who stood to cop the lion's share of the purse, and as such he was making more money. In the third place, he was the producer of a proposed motion-picture of the fight, and as such he expected to make the most money of all. He was, in short, in high good humor. He had been foresightedly planning for this night for months. He figured to clean up.

Brady's preparations had been launched two years before, shortly after the passage of the Horton Act. He had leased the Casino from the Paul Bauer estate—the same building where, years before, John Y. McKane had permitted prizefights in flagrant anticipation of the law. Brady incorporated as the Coney Island Athletic Club, enlarged the hall's seating capacity, and set up as a promotor of boxing entertainments. Shrewdly, he took in as partners in his venture Alec Brown, a Brooklyn politician, and Martin Julian, who was manager of Bob Fitzsimmons, then the world's champion. Coney Islanders were delighted. They had been fight buffs for years and had always fussed over the celebrated pugilists who came down to the resort. Coney had ever been a favorite haunt of the mighty John L. Sullivan when he was still champion. He loved to visit a Bowery concert hall to watch the pretty girl who sang "Murphy Owes Me Rent," and who was celebrated for making her exit in a series of cartwheels. In the champion's honor, she would sing "It's Irish, You Know," interpolating some compliments to his brawn into her chorus. So the news that the old Casino had once again been refurbished brought a sparkle to eyes all along the Island.

A hitch, however, had developed. Brady needed more than a hall; he needed as well a license to operate. Now when Big Tim Sullivan wangled the Horton Act through the legislature, he had in mind his own sweet monopoly over the metropolitan fight business. The Coney Island A.C. dwarfed his New York boxing clubs. From these two premises, there was only one possible conclusion that Sullivan could reach: No license for Brady. In the next few months, while Brady was paying a stiff rental on his hall, it became an open secret that Sullivan meant to block the license until Brady caved in, then grab off the Coney Island club himself. Brady was young in years, but he was wise in the ways of a big city. Behind the ears, he was notably dry. After all, had he not been so prudent as to take in Alec Brown as a partner? Now he dispatched Brown to chat with his political crony Hugh McLaughlin, the Democratic boss of Brooklyn. McLaughlin had no love for Tammany Hall, nor for Dry Dollar Sullivan. He listened to Brown's story, then smote his desk with a great fist. "Tell Brady," he said, "they'll grant that license at their next meeting, or there'll be a split in the Democratic party of New York State!" Brady got his license.

But this had been a very limited victory. Hall and license were all very well; nice things to have; but meaningless without a drawing-card. As Brady saw it, what he needed was a world's heavyweight champion. Within a year he was manager of such a hero. It was the second time that he had been so blessed.

Jim Jeffries

Tom Sharkey

Since most prizefight managers consider one world's heavyweight champion to be the rough equivalent of the Holy Grail, and since no other prizefight manager in history has ever come up with two, it is instructive to reflect on Brady's technique. It was simple to the point of bafflement. It was to yearn for something quite different. Actually, Billy Brady had his eye on a far more distant star. His ultimate ambition was to become William A. Brady, premier theatrical manager of New York City, and it seemed to him, in 1899, that the shortest road to this eminence was as manager of the world's heavyweight professional boxing champion.

This course was, in those days, not so improbable as it would be today. In the eighteen-nineties the only way for a prizefighter to make money was to appear on the stage. The operative word here is "appear," for the prizefighters rarely performed. John

L. Sullivan established the precedent, in a thing called *Honest Hearts and Willing Hands,* and Peter Jackson, the Negro fighter whom Sullivan refused to meet, toured the country in *Uncle Tom's Cabin.* When Corbett battled Jackson for sixty-one rounds to no decision, it was like winning his diploma from the American Academy of Dramatic Arts, and it earned him a telegram from Brady offering him $175 a week for a role in Dion Boucicault's melodrama, *After Dark.* Presently Brady was able to maneuver his juvenile into a fight with the aging trouper John L. Sullivan, but even before the papers were signed for the match, Brady had commissioned a journeyman dramatist to confect a special vehicle, *Gentleman Jack,* for his tiger; while Corbett was still in training for the epic battle, Brady was harrying him to get up in his lines.

To Brady, the victory over Sullivan was no more than a regrettable nuisance, an onerous prelude to a triumphal tour of the theatrical circuit. The glib, fast-thinking manager was the first ever to realize how solidly a champion could cash in on his title. One day he found his thespian sitting stolid and patient, his right hand encased in a mold of plaster of Paris. Corbett explained that some man proposed to cast paperweights of "the hand that knocked out John L. Sullivan" from the mold. "For how much?" asked Brady. "It's a favor," Corbett answered. Brady smashed the mold and when the man from the glass factory showed up again sold him the rights to the paperweight for $1,000. In the first year after the victory over Sullivan, Brady said later, "Corbett and I cleaned up at least $300,000." Before the public had a chance to weary of *Gentleman Jack,* Brady was ready with another tailor-made melodrama, *A Naval Cadet;* he took his star touring to England, where they dropped £5,000, and then to Paris, where they grossed $10,000 in ten days at the Folies-Bergère. But all good things come to an end: sooner or later a champion heavyweight pugilist must defend his title: and in March, 1897, Fitzsimmons punctured Corbett's promising theatrical career with a right to the solar plexus. Thereafter it was the Cornishman's turn to don sock and buskin: he starred in *The Honest Blacksmith,* hammering out real horseshoes over a real forge, stage center.

Brady, once his actor had lost the championship, had professed to detect a waning of public interest in pugilism. He turned to the production of *Way Down East,* and announced that he was through with fisticuffs. It was evident he considered fighting to be undignified, too harum-scarum for a man in the legitimate theatre; and it is likely he would have persevered in his distaste had not the legitimate theatre come up with a severe case of the wobbles. This lamentable circumstance coinciding with the advent of the Horton Act, Brady found himself once again in the middle of the squared circle. It was, no doubt about it, a comedown. When he married the lovely actress Grace George, she made him promise, he revealed later, to give up the fight business. He married her on January 8, 1899, and it was not until January 9, 1899, that he was able to persuade her to let him once again undertake the management of a prizefighter. On that day he wired Jeffries in California that he would make him world's champion within a year if he would consent to fight under Brady's gonfalon. Jeffries agreed at once. Two days later, Brady issued a challenge in Jeffries' name to the regnant champion, Fitzsimmons. Since every heavyweight east of the Great Smokies had challenged Fitzsimmons, his defi did not, on the face of it, carry much weight. It was, however, bedizened with some attractive considerations. Brady controlled the largest fight arena in the metropolitan area; he had taken Fitz's own manager in as a stockholding partner; he was prepared to offer the champion sixty-five per cent of the boxers' share of the receipts. Moreover, so far as Fitz knew, Jeffries was nothing but a big oaf from the West

Coast. The proposition sized up as a remunerative pushover. It was beguiling bait. Fitz leaped clear out of the water to snatch at it. He had agreed to meet Jeffries on June 9, 1899, at Coney Island.

With a championship at stake, Billy Brady had moved with careful cunning. He retained Tommy Ryan, the cleverest boxer of the day, as Jeffries' trainer. Ryan had reigned from 1894 to 1896 as king of the welterweights and then, putting on a few pounds, had grabbed off the middleweight crown. He taught Jeff to coil his vast bulk into a perplexing crouch, he schooled him in footwork, he oiled the big man's gears so well that Jeff at least gave the illusion of speed. By June, the challenger was at physical peak. But temperamentally he was still torpid. He purred, but he spat not, neither did he snarl. Since Fitz was always supremely confident, and since on the eve of the fight Jeff was still sluggish and somnolent, Brady had decided that the occasion demanded some of his impudent dressing-room psychology. He delighted in these displays: they afforded him the opportunity to parade his theatrical virtuosity. In the Coney Island A.C., the fighters' dressing-rooms were under the stands, separated by a narrow corridor. Brady put Jeffries through a brief rehearsal and then, only an hour or so before the fight, rang up the curtain on his own little drama. The first scene was set in the corridor and called for an argument between Brady and Julian, Fitz's manager, over a technicality as to procedure when breaking from a clinch. The raised voices, as Brady had hoped, brought Fitz from his dressing-room. "Let's settle this in front of my boy," said Brady, and shifted the scene to Jeff's dressing-room. Fitz went in first. Jeffries, a monstrous mound of gristle, lay stripped on the rubbing table. Fitz had never before seen him close up. He blinked. Brady resumed the argument, then gave Jeff his cue. The fighter had only one line in the scene, and only one simple piece of business. He read the one and did the other to perfection. "Lemme show you what Brady means," he said. He swung off the table, clinched briefly with Fitz, broke, and, in the same motion, effortlessly bounced the champion off the wall. Fitz, as he picked himself up, swallowed hard. For the first time he realized that he was about to face the strongest man who had ever climbed between ropes.

Theatrically, Brady's drama could not have been faulted. Fitzsimmons' confidence was shaken and Jeffries' immensely bucked. But even as he was bowing gracefully from ringside, after the knockout in the eleventh round, Brady was preoccupied. He had his second world's heavyweight champion but he also had problems. For one, what kind of an actor would Jeffries prove to be? True, he had performed adequately in a supporting role, in the Drama of the Dressing-Room, but did that argue that he would be able to step into the starring role of *The Man from the West,* the charade contrived by Brady for his slender talents? The show was scheduled to open in a week's time, but Brady had misgivings. The words that occurred to him, as he thought about Jeffries, were: cautious, suspicious, young, and inexperienced. Jeffries lacked, he suspected, the spark. He gravely feared his new champion could do nothing but fight.

And there was still more to brood about. There was the matter of the motion-pictures of the fight. More than two years before Brady had sensed the value of such movies. He had tried to get a stranglehold on the picture rights to the Corbett-Fitzsimmons bout as his price for agreeing to make the match; he had been fobbed off with a paltry twenty-five per cent; moreover, through some devious corporate device, the rights had been so exploited that all Brady ever saw of the $700,000 gross was $80,000. He had determined, before the Fitzsimmons-Jeffries fight, that this would not happen again. But this time the fight was indoors, at night. Motion pictures were in their infancy. Nobody had ever been able to shoot a picture under those conditions. He had approached a knowledgeable young film expert, Albert Smith, of the Vitagraph Company. Smith shook his head doubtfully, but agreed to experiment. Miraculously, a few days before the fight, Smith developed an arc lamp bright enough to do the job. One hundred of his giant bulbs had been mounted over the ring; they shed a fine, hot, white glare. When Smith complained that the electric current was dangerously low, Brady himself, although he had a dozen more pressing matters on his mind, at the last minute had scrounged an auxiliary electric plant. He had paid Smith $5,000 out of his own pocket to do this one, simple thing: shoot him a picture of the fight. Yet while the fight was still only in the first round, the idiot had permitted half his arc lights to black out—inexcusable bungling. Six, maybe seven hundred thousand dollars out the window! Of course Smith had claimed it was a mechanical failure, unavoidable; but Brady had viewed his excuses dimly. He had at once engaged to forget, if possible, the name Smith.

Now, on the evening of November 3, Brady was satisfied there would be no more slip-ups. He had Smith's arc lights (for had he not paid for them?); this time there were not one but four hundred strung in banks above the ring; instead of Smith and the Vitagraph Company, he had retained a crew from Biograph, Smith's bitterest competitor. Just to make sure, Brady had demanded a rehearsal under actual fighting conditions: four nights before, the lights had been turned on and the cameras had rolled while two middleweights boxed in a regularly scheduled match; the next morning Brady had inspected the prints and found them excellent. To be sure, the fighters had been a mite querulous on the subject of the fierce heat generated by the arcs, but Brady shrugged them off. He, after all, would not be fighting under those lights. To him, they

William A. Brady

represented a handsome financial harvest—maybe as much as $750,000. As he thought of them, his face wreathed in smiles. Billy Brady was dreaming of a mink-lined future.

And now, though it grieves the historian to report it, it must be revealed that there were others bound for Coney Island on this blustery, miserable, rainy evening to whom it had also occurred that motion pictures of the Jeffries-Sharkey fight might be profitable. They were not greedy, these other men; they did not covet three-quarters of a million; they were ready to settle for, say, a paltry quarter-million; but even this modest sum beckoned imperatively. It cannot be said in their defense that they were unaware their course was larcenous; they knew it; worse, they reveled in it. The only consideration that at any point in their dark and dire deliberations had slowed their footsteps was this: Will we be caught? Indeed, so lost were these men to the dictates of conscience and a sense of the proprieties that ever since they have been zealously vying with each other as to which among them was the most shameless malefactor, as to whose was the original idea to bootleg a film, even as to whose hand turned the crank on the illicit camera (or, as it may have been, cameras). Their contrary contentions are so clamorous as to make us wonder if they were, indeed, spectators at the same fight. A great mythopoeic cloud has been fluffed up and it obscures what in fact happened on this night and who in fact was responsible for the mischievous events. To follow their disputed paths through the next few hours will be as difficult as to decide under which shell is the pea. For the moment, then, let us be content with their names and their motives for their desperate deeds:

Joe Howard, a talented young vaudevillian and songwriter. Today Howard has an A.S.C.A.P. rating of AAA, with a long string of evergreen melodies like "I Wonder Who's Kissing Her Now" to his credit. In 1899 he was still scrambling about, diligently plugging his own songs wherever he could, when he was approached by

Thomas Jenkins, a shadowy figure described by Howard as "the man who built the first moving picture machine in this country." * After persuading Howard to use movies with his vaudeville turns and song-plugging, Jenkins took him into partnership in the production of early movies. The two bid for the rights to the Jeffries-Sharkey fight and, when Brady turned them down in favor of Biograph, Howard wondered out loud why someone should not just go ahead and take his own pictures. His speculations were overheard by

James White, the head of the motion-picture department of the Edison Company. White was also simmering because Brady was doing business with Biograph. He had no camera small enough to be smuggled conveniently into the Coney Island A.C., but he knew a man who did. This was

Albert Smith of the Vitagraph Company. If White was simmering, Smith was seething. Brady had, he felt, wilfully and spitefully pilfered his lighting ideas if not his very lights. Smith

---

* Howard, in his memoirs, calls this man Thomas Jenkins. But it is likely he meant C. Francis Jenkins, a man who was for a time in partnership with Thomas Armat. One or other of these men—or both; the facts as to patents are cloudy—invented the motion-picture projector.

was more than ready to join in any plot aimed against Brady. He at once summoned

Jimmy French, a trusted Vitagraph lieutenant. The three men agreed to tackle the proposition. Smith wondered what Brady would do, should he see their camera at work. White vowed he would have twenty Edison men on hand, ready to head off twenty Bradys. And so they planned to meet at Ben Cohen's Albemarle Hotel, across Surf Avenue from the Coney Island A.C., at nine that night, to perfect the details of their slippery scheme.

Of all the hotels on Coney, the Albemarle was by far the gayest and the most thickly thronged, on the evening of the big fight. To the east, of course, the great hotels of fashion were dark; their season had closed nearly two months before; their owners ignored the prizefight crowd. The hotels and saloons along Ocean Parkway were, however, doing a brisk business. It was not often that Coney Island could count on fifteen thousand off-season visitors, and the Islanders were making the most of it. The champion and his entourage were stopping at Martin Dowling's; Sharkey was at the Sagamore; but every sport who could jostle his way in was at the Albemarle. Throughout the period of Coney's ascendancy in the fight world, this hotel would be headquarters for men who liked to lounge around, trade fight gossip, cut up old touches, make matches, and bet. Here on this night, in opposite corners of the saloon, the two dethroned monarchs, John L. Sullivan and James J. Corbett, held court. Each had been retained as an expert journalist by competing newspapers. Fitzsimmons was also on hand (he lived just a step away, in Sheepshead Bay). The air was heavy with cigar smoke and clamorous with talk. Tammany politicians, actors and theatre managers, professional baseball players, pugilists, jockeys, and bookmakers formed a congenial fraternity. An hour or so before time for the main fight, a woman, the wife of a Virginian sport, appeared in the bar wearing men's clothes. She hoped to pass muster and so get in to see the fight, but almost at once she attracted attention. An amused whisper; an elbow jogged against someone's ribs; a pointed finger; and up went a laugh. She blushed, turned, and fled back upstairs to her room. Something new for the men to gossip about, but they had plenty else. Most important, there was the condition of the fighters.

Sharkey was in the pink. His manager, Tom O'Rourke, glowed with confidence. The challenger was a thick-set scrapper. He stood only 5' 8½", but he weighed 185 pounds. His barrel chest measured 48 inches but he could expand it to 56 inches and did so, to the delight of the crowd, whenever he stepped into the ring. He was the darling of the New York fight crowd for he was Irish-born; moreover, he was an ex-gob at a time when, because of America's glorious naval triumphs over the Spanish oppressor, all sailors were by definition romantic heroes. No question about it, Sharkey ruled the sentimental favorite.

Jeffries, on the other hand, was less popular. His size (6' 1½"; 215 pounds) and his reach (nearly seven inches longer than Sharkey's) were against him with everybody except the bettors, who had established the odds at four-to-five or seven-to-ten. Even these odds were subject to change, however, because of the rumblings of dissension at Jeffries' training camp. Indeed, the very fact the fight had been scheduled was indicative of tension between the manager and his fighter. Ordinarily, Brady would have held off for at least a year before agreeing to make any match, but his hand had been forced. The ugly truth was that his misgivings had been well founded. Jeffries had been death at the box-office. *The Man from the West* had laid an egg of epic proportions. Brady, remembering Corbett, listening in his mind's ear to Corbett's tuneful baritone, recalling how

Corbett had appeared as Armand Duval in *Camille* even before he had laced on boxing gloves, yearned for the good old days and cursed his luck in drawing a champion who couldn't even hold a spear without stubbing his toe. It was crystal clear that Brady had no way to make money out of Jeffries save by his fighting. But the champion had proven woefully recalcitrant. The match with Sharkey had originally been made for the late summer, but at that time Jeffries had, in Brady's view, developed "ring fear." In August, one of Jeff's sparring partners had tossed a medicine ball at him. The champion, turning, had lifted his left hand and the ball, as it struck, injured his elbow. The incident had thrown the whole camp into a swivet. A doctor had told the champion: "The bone is broken. You cannot fight for six months." Tommy Ryan had insisted on a postponement. Bill Delaney, a West Coast fighter who had been Jeffries' trainer before Brady engaged Ryan, had taken the position that Jeffries could lick Sharkey with his left hand tied behind him— or could have if his principles of training had been followed. To Brady the inevitable postponement had simply demonstrated that his tiger had turned chicken. "Fighting was the only way he could make any money," his manager commented later, with asperity, "and notwithstanding his efforts to sidestep the fight, we got him into the ring." Word of the disagreement had seeped out, of course, and had found its garbled way into the newspapers. But the sports viewed the rumors with suspicion, pegging them as attempts to whittle down the odds. When Delaney, interviewed by reporters on the afternoon of the fight, gave it as his opinion that Jeffries had been trained down too fine, his pronouncement was likewise disregarded. In the lobby and the saloon of the Albemarle, action was slow. Around nine o'clock, the crowd began to leave, bucking the wind and the rain that swept in across Surf Avenue, heading for their seats in the big, cold barn.

At about the same time, a man signed the register at the Albemarle, booking Room Thirty-three for the night. Presently he was joined by another, and then by a third and fourth. These were the conspirators. The door of Number Thirty-three closed behind them.

Smith and French were the last to arrive. Smith looked around unhappily. He had the camera, he had the film, but where were the twenty bodyguards White had promised? White smiled blandly. "First things first," he said. "How are we going to get into the club?" Smith stared at him, incredulous. "You mean," he asked, "you haven't even bought any tickets?" White grinned. Howard scraped his feet in embarrassment. There followed one of those pauses. The men eyed each other. Outside, the rain fell. At length, with a sigh, French ante'd up a five-dollar bill. "To get good pictures," murmured White, "we'll have to sit in the ten-dollar seats." Smith wagged his head in amazement. "You win," he said, and brought out the necessary $35.

Because White was the tallest, they strapped the camera between his legs. Thus encumbered, and surrounded fore and aft by the others, he waddled painfully across the street and into the foyer of the clubhouse. They counted on taking advantage of the last-minute bustle and confusion to make their way unnoticed to their seats. Fortunately, Brady was nowhere to be seen. Unfortunately, his lawyer was on hand. This was Manny Friend, a familiar figure along the Rialto and at the racetracks. He eyed the quartet of conspirators curiously as, huddled tightly together, they inched their way toward the turnstile. Joe Howard saw him and, on an impulse, peeled off from his position in the phalanx to distract his attention. In this he succeeded; indeed, he was doubly successful, for he seized the opportunity to put the bite on Friend for $100. Humming happily, he caught up with the others as they struggled awkwardly through the turnstile. In ludicrous lock step they clambered up a dozen rows to their appointed seats. Smith promptly dove under an overcoat to set up the camera. The others, with elaborately studied expressions of innocence looked about them.

The inescapable center of attention was the canopy of lights. hung from scaffolding so close over the ring that a good high jumper could have broken the bulbs. Fifty feet or so away, on the south, or ocean, side of the building, was a raised platform on which were the four Biograph cameras. Electricians crawled over the scaffolding, adjusting reflectors. Already one row of thirty-five lights had been turned on; their brightness glared down on the customers in the first five rows; hereabouts experiments with home-made visors to shield the light were already under way. Two Biograph men, one in the ring and one on the raised platform, each equipped with a megaphone, were earnestly and incessantly exhorting the crowd to stop smoking a demand which, under the circumstances, rivaled that of King Canute. Brady anxiously presided over the whole scene, now fussing at an electrician, now conferring with a cameraman now bidding the police to enforce the No Smoking edict, now consulting with his friend Bob Pinkerton. In addition to two hundred uniformed policemen, there were fifty Pinkertons on hand, for Brady, while he had no reason to know about the plot that was afoot to gouge into his motion-picture grosses, nevertheless harbored a generalized suspicion. It would be slighting his keen intelligence to report that he was complacent. Where money was involved, Billy Brady was remarkably intuitive.

Now, turning away from the scaffolding for a moment, he spied One-Eyed Connolly attempting to hurdle the wire fence that separated the peasants in the bleachers from the gentry in the reserved seats. Brady was scandalized. He summoned a policeman. "Throw this man out of the building," he ordered

1 the manner of the Red Queen. The cop collared Connolly
nd dragged him, bleating, out toward the turnstile. Tom
)'Rourke, Sharkey's manager, observed this summary dis-
ipline with approval. "That's right," he said. "Toss him out into
he rain. He's a nuisance. How in thunder did he get in here?"
'Where's Alec Brown?" cried Connolly, latching on to a seat
nd digging his heels in. "He's my friend! He's the guy that let
ne in here!" The cop tugged. Connolly hauled. "I says to Alec,
ays I," pleaded Connolly, addressing himself to the general
ssemblage, " 'Alec, I ain't got a cent, but I can't miss this fight
or me life. If you can let me sit up in the corner of the house
omewhere I'll keep me mouth shut and I'll never forget ya.'
ays Alec to me, 'All right, Connolly,' says he, 'come right in,'
nd that's the way I gets in here tonight, and if Alec was
round he'd see to it that I wouldn't be pitched out of here
ike a bag of oats." And, like a merciful dispensation, here came
Alec Brown. "Let him stay," he said. "I'll stand for him." Brady
vas disgusted, but the cop loosed his prisoner, who ran, like a
nonkey for the tree-tops, up to the bleachers. A minute later,
ne confided to a reporter that before long he would be back in
a box-seat. "Me swell friends," he said, "will be down there with
ll their diamonds putting them lights out, and if I don't sit
lown among them they'll feel slighted. If I don't sit within ten
eet of the ring Jeffries and Sharkey won't want to fight. It's me
oresence that inspires those pugs, and if they knew I was
:ooped up amongst this bunch of cheap skates they would send
or me."

Connolly was the first and most spectacular celebrity to
arrive, but others hurried in as the hour approached ten o'clock.
Every pugilist of any consequence was there; and Tony Pastor,
he Toots Shor of his day; and Charles Frohman, the theatrical
nanager; Big Tim Sullivan, of course, and his cousin the alder-
nan, Little Tim; Wilbert Robinson, then still of the Baltimore

Orioles, not yet manager of the Brooklyn Superbas; his close friend John J. McGraw, then still manager of the Orioles; George Schaefer, owner of the St. Louis Cardinals; and Tom Navin, owner of the Detroit Tigers; Phil Dwyer, owner of the Gravesend racetrack; Sam Hildreth and Jimmy Rowe, the greatest racehorse trainers of their time; Pittsburgh Phil, the gambler; Joe Vendig and Joe Ullman, both celebrated book makers; and Fred Taral and Snapper Garrison, the jockeys. Garrison, late to arrive, had to be satisfied with a $10 seat; he picked his way up the incline and sat down next to the con spirators; he was looking for some action. Joe Howard was agreeable. Garrison wanted to know only how much and on whom Howard would bet. "A hundred dollars on Sharkey," said Howard. Smith emerged from the overcoat under which he had been getting his camera in readiness. He caught Howard's eye and shook his head. With Garrison's cheerful assent, Howard switched his bet.

At ringside far bigger bets were being freely offered and accepted, but only at the prevailing odds of ten-to-seven on Jeffries. As time wore on, it developed there was a scarcity of Jeffries money. Betting commissioners working for big Tammany bettors circled the ring a half-dozen times, shouting "$350 to $500 Sharkey," but finding no takers. The club was packed by now, and the crowd was beginning to chant, "Bring out the fighters!" In the ring, the man from Biograph pointed his megaphone in all directions. "Please stop smoking," he implored; "oh, please stop smoking!" He could not be heard. Johnny (Frogvoice) Dunn, the club's announcer, decked out for the first time in his career in a dress suit on account of the cameras, stepped forward, disdainfully rejecting a megaphone. "Order, please," he thundered. "Can't yez give order? Now then, all of yez! Stop yer smoking!" But he was ignored.

And now, one row after another, the raw, hot, carbon arcs

were turned on. Even packed as it was, the clubhouse had been chilly, but the ring swiftly became an oven and the heat spread. Around ringside, men promptly peeled off their coats and their jackets. To those accustomed to watching fights in a smoky murk, these lights seemed as hot and bright as the sun. Back in the bleachers, where seats cost only $5, a great cheer went up as the crowd realized they had never before had such a brilliant view. And another roar: for here came Sharkey, emerald green lights showing under his brown bathrobe. In his corner, two electric fans were turned on. When Jeffries entered, a minute or so later, his reception was mild. The two men shook hands and sat down, each in his corner. In accordance with the custom, challenges to fight the winner were pitched into the ring, picked up, and read out by Frogvoice Dunn: from Fitzsimmons, from Corbett, from Kid McCoy. Then Dunn introduced the referee, George Siler.

Siler was a man whose roots were in Coney. He was captain of the Iron Steamboat Pier. He was also, in the circumstances

The canopy of lights over the ring was a startling innovation in 1899. Inset, drenched sports crowd into the Coney Island A. C.   *N. Y. Herald*   N. Y. PUBLIC LIBRARY

of prizefighting in those days, omnipotent. There was no Boxin
Commission, no official physician at ringside, no judge. Th
club supplied a timekeeper, but he was regarded as so open t
influence that each fighter, in addition to his seconds, trad
tionally supplied his own timekeeper. The only impartial ma
present, presumably, was the referee. If the fight went the di:
tance, the decision as to the winner rested on his shoulder
alone. Siler was a man of unimpeachable integrity. He wa
perhaps the best-known and best-trusted referee of his time
The crowd, reflecting their confidence in him, cheered h:
name. He bowed. And now a telegram was handed up to hin
He ripped the envelope open, at the same time patting h:
trousers pockets in search of his eyeglasses. But he had left ther
in the pocket of his coat, in a dressing-room back under th
stands, where they might be safe during the fight. Since, in th
great American tradition of umpires and referees, his visio
was somewhat defective, without his eyeglasses the telegrar
meant nothing to him. He was obliged to ask Billy Brady t
read him the message. "Bet one thousand for us," Brady reac
"on Sharkey at any price. We have some good inside infor
mation." Brady's voice, as he read, went up, so that he seeme
to be asking a question. He glared at the referee. Siler glare
back, nearsightedly. Brady glanced again at the wire. It wa
addressed to George Schaefer, the owner of the Cardinals, i
care of Siler. "Somebody's idea of a joke," growled Siler. Brad
crawled thoughtfully out between the ropes. The bell rang fc
the first round.

In the annals of boxing history, the Jeffries-Sharkey matc
at Coney Island is generally regarded as the roughest and mo:
gruelling, and considering the length (twenty-five rounds) an
the savagery of the fight and the scorching heat from the prim
tive, low-slung arc lights, this view is entirely reasonable. Bu

when it was all over the weariest man was surely Billy Brady. The fighters started fast, exchanged freely throughout, and twenty-five rounds later were still on their feet, still indomitably slugging away. The same could be said for Brady. In the ring, the only knockdown came in the second—Sharkey was upended for a count of seven—but this was more a tribute to the fighters' physical condition and endurance than an indictment of their punch. Outside the ring, Brady never scored a knockdown either, but this was more a tribute to the physical condition of the $10-ticket holders than an indictment of Brady's determination and willingness to mix it. At first Brady was content to work at close quarters, staying near Jeffries' corner. In the fifth, when Sharkey landed a punch after the bell, Brady was up screaming "Foul!" But a moment later, a Pinkerton having reported to him that there were unauthorized cameras all over the hall, Brady was himself all over the hall, in a frenzy. In the eighth, Jeffries split Sharkey's ear with a right cross and in the tenth he opened a cut over the sailor's eye; by this time Brady was back at ringside, again claiming a foul. By the twelfth, Brady had located the conspirators and was attempting to lead a charge of Pinkertons through a dense and unyielding mass of $10-ticket holders, but in the thirteenth he was obliged to return to ringside to claim another foul. He was dismayed in the fifteenth when Sharkey bloodied the champion's nose with a beer-mallet right, concerned when the blood kept flowing through the next three rounds, and gleeful in the seventeenth when Jeffries, with a savage right, fractured two of Sharkey's ribs. In the eighteenth, Brady again sought to personally throttle the picture pirates; again he was flung back by a crowd on its feet and yelling to the fighters for the kill. Distractedly, in the twentieth, he looked toward the ring; saw Sharkey butt his man and once again start his nose bleeding; and dashed back again, to claim yet another foul. He was betwixt and between: on the one hand, he felt he had to protect his lucrative picture rights; on the other hand, he knew he had to protect his lucrative fighter's rights. This time he held his ground, for it appeared to him, as to every other hoarsely shouting man in the club, that Jeffries was about to land the clincher. In the twenty-second, the champion reopened the cut above Sharkey's eye; the sailor was groggy but game. In the last round, during a wild melee, Jeffries' left glove flew off and Sharkey, while Siler was trying to push it back on, kept slugging away. The hall was in an uproar, the din of the crowd was deafening. Just now, when excitement in the ring was at its height, Brady stiffened as though he had been stabbed. He had just seen that the Biograph camera was jammed. Film was spilling out in great, twisting coils. Billy Brady uttered a searing oath.

And then he was obliged to stand in his champion's corner and wait for the referee's decision. When Jeffries was declared the winner on points, Brady was not comforted. Over his shoulder, he had seen the conspirators melt into the crowd. He was in a torment. How successful had they been? Had they gotten a picture of the entire fight? Or had they been too far away? Had they gotten the last round? Had Biograph bungled? Where was Pinkerton? Why was there no one whom he could trust to perform one single, simple service? In short, was there no justice? Glumly, he acknowledged the congratulations of the hangers-on; sourly, he stalked off with his champion to the dressing-room.

As for the conspirators, they had dismantled their equipment and disappeared. Howard and Smith, each a truthful man, each claims the honor of having actually turned the crank of the smuggled camera during the course of the fight. With the years each has refreshed his memory; in the process, bewilderingly, the discrepancies in their stories have multiplied: the historian is constrained to suspect that one or other of these two reliable

The weary leaning Tower of Pisa at the left is the champion, Jim Jeffries; the man in the benny is George Siler, the referee; the bloody gladiator at the right is Tom Sharkey. This is a still from the proper, honest, ethical motion-picture filmed by Biograph. INTERNATIONAL NEWS PHOTOS

witnesses has inadvertently stretched the truth a trifle. The weight of the evidence indicates that the conspirators agreed to separate and meet again, later, in Room Thirty-three of the Albemarle. Snapper Garrison was pressed into service to sneak the precious negative out of the clubhouse. (This detail seems doubtful at best, for who can imagine a jockey getting involved in anything larcenous?) Smith had to carry the camera; again he and French were the last to reach the hotel room, having come by a circuitous route. While waiting for them, Howard had wasted no time. He was rolling high. Having collected on his bet with Garrison, he had called for champagne; corks had popped; everyone was congratulating each other and especially Garrison. The jockey was rollicking. The situation called for

madder music and stronger wine. Unnoticed, he slipped from
the room.

After a few glasses of wine, Smith decided that it must be
back to business. He and French packed the boxes of film
lovingly, for they were worth, the brigands had convivially
estimated, at least $200,000. But even as they were slipping into
their overcoats they paused, hushed. Downstairs, in the hotel
saloon, they could hear the rumble of angry voices. Smith stole
to the door and crept down the corridor, listening. There was
one thin, piping voice he could recognize. It was Garrison's
gleefully boasting about the smuggled film. And that deeper
throated, more wrathful baying—that could come only from the
men gathered to celebrate Jeffries' victory—Brady, Bob Pinker
ton, Jeff's handlers, maybe the world's heavyweight champion
himself. The conspirators had just time to swing out the window
and down a rope-ladder fire escape before Brady and the other
came charging up the stairs in full cry.

Smith, laden with the film, lagged behind his friends. He
fancied that he could descry Jeffries' huge bulk leading the
pursuit. Somewhat anticipating the technique of a man fleeing
from the Keystone Kops, Smith ducked into a dark alley, waited
for his pursuers to pound past, then popped out and ran the
other way. Jim White caught up with him; the two men found
a cab to take them to the Vitagraph offices in New York. While
White slept, Smith busied himself developing his films. At
length, exhausted but happy, he stretched the precious negative
on the drying drums and went to sleep himself.

White was the first to wake. The negative was dry. Moving
quietly, for he was a thoughtful man and did not wish to dis
turb Smith's rest, White wound the negative on a spool and
hurriedly left for the Edison offices in Orange, N.J. He was also
careful to send a print down to Washington, so that the twice
stolen film was the first to be copyrighted.

Smith, when he woke up and found the negative gone, went
raight to Orange and confronted a grinning Jim White. On a
unch, he snatched a film box off White's desk and ran; he had
he first print, and he leased it to Riley and Woods, a vaudeville
utfit. And now prints began bobbing up all over the place:
our days after the fight, while Biograph was still busy proc-
ssing their miles of film, Edison had booked the Theatre
omique, on 29th Street just off Broadway, and announced a
rst showing of the fight picture; in Philadelphia Riley and
Voods four-sheeted their Vitagraph print. The Theatre Comi-
ue was jammed for the first showing of the Edison print, and
oe Howard was on hand to take a bow and introduce it. The
lm was still only in the fourth round when Brady arose in the
arkness. His voice, hoarse and passionate, drowned out the
lm's piano accompaniment. "These pictures are a fake," he
houted, "stolen at the Coney Island Athletic Club! The real
ictures will be shown at the New York Theatre, beginning next
eek!" Howard appeared from the wings. "How can they be a
ake," he demanded, "if they were stolen at the Coney Island
lub? You're a liar, Brady, and you know it!" Angry members
f the audience, wishing only to concentrate on the pictures
efore them, howled their disapproval. "I defy anyone here to
y a hand on me," Brady protested. He stomped out and, on
he sidewalk outside, breathed defiance in all directions. He
nd his lawyer, Manny Friend, got injunctions against the
dison print, against the Vitagraph print, against another Edi-
on print that turned up in Professor Huber's Museum of
reaks on 14th Street, against still another Vitagraph print that
as released in Boston, from city judges and from Federal
dges. It was like Jason and the dragon's teeth, all over again.
or every print that Brady slew, two more jumped up, one or
wo hundred miles away, each doing excellent business.

The nub of Brady's difficulty was the breakdown of the Bio-

graph camera, during the twenty-fifth round: it made his copy
right claim imperfect. There was only one course open: to re
take the last round, making sure it was just different enoug
from the bootlegged film to warrant a unique copyright, bu
similar enough to appease the fight buffs. Brady had littl
difficulty persuading the fighters to cooperate: each stood t
profit to the extent of fifteen per cent of the gross. Sharkey, wh
had belatedly decided he had been robbed by the decision
made one or two noises about how he would now knock th
champion kicking, but this was only blarney. On November 16
thirteen days after the night of the fight, Brady went back t
Coney Island to try again. He filled the house with pugilists
fight managers, exercise-boys from the Brighton Beach race
track, drifters, grifters, and hangers-on. He deployed his Bio
graph cameras. This time he was able to enforce the rule agains
smoking. His two fighters, properly costumed, took the ring
(Since there have been so many flights of fancy about the cir
cumstances of this fight, it is appropriate that the myths shoul
have proliferated even about this twenty-fifth, and phony
round. This time, the story goes, both Jeffries and Sharkey
when they entered the ring, were bald. The lights under whicl
they had fought two weeks before, it is alleged, were re
sponsible for having baked the hair right off their scalps. Thi
tale, like the notion that hair can turn white overnight, die
hard.) Brady faced only one major difficulty. Siler had gone t
Chicago. Brady, an embittered promotor-manager-produce
engaged to become for the occasion an actor as well. Siler wa
a stocky, dumpy man; Brady lean and wiry. Siler affected broad
black mustaches; Brady was clean-shaven. But Brady was no
to be daunted by such details. He stuffed a small pillow withi
his pants; with the help of spirit-gum he appliquéd som
thunderous mustaches. The cameras rolled. They rolled, in al
four times. Each effort was worse than the last. "Mr. Brady, a

eferee," commented the prizefight critic of the *New York Tele-graph*, when he reviewed the ultimate release, "is as full of umps and jerks as a bunch of snakes."

If Brady teetered and vibrated, his performance was pardonable. What had seemed two scant weeks ago like a $100,000 gate for the Jeffries-Sharkey fight had turned out to be a sodden and disconsolate $70,000 gate. To be sure, every seat had been filled, but only because a distressing amount of paper had been handed out. And this blow had been as nothing compared to he whack dealt his hopes for stunning motion-picture grosses. Brady did his best in the role of Siler, but his heart was never n it. Gloomily he had already guessed that, no matter how well his film of the phony last round turned out, the bootlegged prints would long since have skimmed the cream off the market. And so it turned out. The Biograph picture played the New York Theatre for three weeks to discouragingly sparse audiences; on the road it fared even worse.

The Jeffries-Sharkey championship match was Brady's last best chance to make a killing, and he was robbed. He was o promote one more big fight at the Coney Island Athletic Club, that between Jeffries and Corbett the next year, when Gentleman Jim essayed a comeback. Corbett almost brought it off, too, carrying the champion into the twenty-third round before succumbing to two sledgehammer rights. But by that ime Brady could take little joy in the occasion. In training or the fight, Jeffries had proven more dour and mistrustful han ever, insisting that his manager eat some of all the food prepared for his plate, making no bones of his suspicion that Brady was out to doublecross him. The fight was held in May, 1900; it was the last of the great mills at Coney Island; three months later Governor Theodore Roosevelt signed a bill repealing the Horton Act, and prizefighting in New York came o a halt. When it was revived, a quarter-century later, Coney

was in no position to grab off the big fights. The Tilyou fami[
bid for the Dempsey-Carpentier match in 1921, but Brady
successor, Tex Rickard, correctly guessed he would find
million-dollar gate on the Island. By that time, Billy Brad
was a premier theatrical manager on Broadway, and no long
confusing fighters with actors.

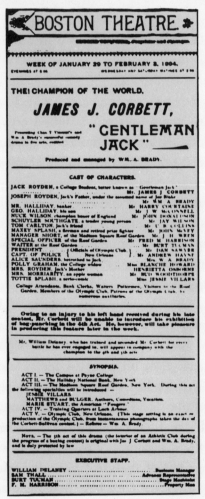

THEATRE COLLECTION, N. Y. PUBLIC LIBRARY.

~Spectacular~

FRIDAY, May 26, 1911 was a fine, mild spring day; the skies were clear and the temperature was in the low seventies; the man in the weather bureau, moreover, promised that Saturday and Sunday would be just as benign. As usual, the citizens of New York rejoiced, but none more so than the thousands of concessionaires, acrobats, hotel owners, animal trainers, weight guessers, restaurant managers, diving-girls, pitchmen, gypsies, singing waiters, sideshow freaks, musicians, sellers of hot dogs, fortune-tellers, renters of bathing-suits, ticket-takers, and barkers who staffed the hundreds of enterprises, large and small, at Coney Island. At Coney the weather has always been a matter of driving urgency. The Island's economy is based on a gamble. Those who own, rent, or work there wager that the weather will be pleasant, if not hot as the hinges, for as many as possible of the fourteen weekends that make up the season. If there are three rainy weekends, the concessionaires may merely break even; they may go bankrupt if there are five. They have grown bitter, betting on the weather. They are persuaded that a man can get rich by laying odds against the weather bureau. Only the previous weekend, for example, the

183

prediction had been for sunny weather, but sullen showers had streamed perversely from chilly skies throughout Saturday and Sunday. No more than a thousand visitors had ventured to Coney Island and these, sodden, had kept their cash in their pockets. But on this Friday evening the concessionaire and the carnival folk were more hopeful: the sun sank in cloudless sky across the bay, and the stars came out, and the variable breeze was a caress from the south. On the morrow the season was to open officially; a fine Saturday, a fine Sunday, and—who could tell?—perhaps the weather would hold through Monday and into Memorial Day. As many as two hundred thousand persons might be expected on each of these holidays. The Islanders rubbed their hands and prepared for the morrow. The welcome mat was out.

Every Memorial Day weekend is a time of decision at Coney Island. This truism is, again, a reflection of the peculiar weather economy. He who rents at Coney, whether it be a modest soft drink stand or a colossal Mile Sky Chaser, must pay his rent in three equal installments: the first when he makes his lease, the second on Memorial Day, and the last on the Fourth of July. The custom came into existence of necessity. Too many landlords found that their tenants were prone to take a skip if the early season weekends were washouts. Indeed, occasionally a timid rascal would abscond after one or two early season landfall weekends, presumably on the theory that to gamble further when he was ahead of the game was to tempt fate too rashly. In self-protection, the landlords clubbed together; gradually all the concessionaires were forced into the dispiriting position of having to pay for the life of their leases before they had half run. Since all of a winter's savings may have to be spent on the first two rent installments, the Memorial Day weekend must yield rich returns or some concessionaires are likely to go hungry until after the Fourth of July.

But this particular Memorial Day weekend of 1911 was even
more critical than usual. For the first time in a quarter century
and more the Island would have to draw crowds without the
powerful assistance of its three horse racing tracks. The shadow
of the reformer had fallen athwart Coney Island. In Albany,
strict laws aimed at gambling had been passed. In earlier
years the owners of the fine restaurants and roadhouses and
the managers of the three great amusement parks had taken as
a matter of course the influx of free-spending patrons in the
evening after, say, the Futurity had been run at Sheepshead
Bay, or the Brooklyn Handicap at Gravesend. Now, they knew,
only the quality of their food and the glitter of their entertainments could be depended on to attract the throngs.

It was a cause for very real concern. In a sense, the Island
stood at a crossroads in its history. The hope had been that
Coney could be transformed into a permanent playground, the
most radiantly coruscant on the Atlantic coast, if not in
America. But the Islanders were uneasily aware, in the spring of
1911, that the capricious world of fashion, the sporting and
theatrical world which had so extravagantly supported Coney
during the past two decades, might easily decide to turn elsewhere for amusement. To be sure, at the eastern end of the
Island, the staid and sniffy Oriental Hotel was certain once
again to fill up. The Brighton Beach Hotel would surely not
lack for clients. But the Manhattan Beach Hotel—once summer
headquarters for the Union League Club, for the University
Club, and for the late lamented Coney Island Jockey Club—
most fashionable of the Island's hostelries, was, so went the
whispers, already slated for sale or destruction.

Moreover, Coney was still haunted by the spectre of its
raffish past. The determined effort, launched around the turn
of the century, to stress the good, the clean, the wholesome
aspects of Coney's attractions had met with considerable suc-

Artistic, with a great big A, that was Dreamland. This entrance to the park led past a Biblical entertainment called "Creation." COURTESY THE FRANCIS K. MOORE COLLECTION

cess; the eminently respectable Albert Bigelow Paine had, in the pages of the eminently proper *Century* magazine, noted his astonishment at finding the crowd at the resort to be "well mannered," "even cultivated . . . a crowd as handsome and charming to gaze upon as any to be found at Newport or Long Branch." This, like approbation from Sir Hubert, was praise indeed. Nevertheless, the Island had never won a full pardon. It was, so to say, only out on parole, and the itch to violate parole was incessant. Only the summer before a posse of suspicious folk had ferreted out a dozen or so examples of those twin temples of evil, the disorderly house and the gambling hell, and there had gone up a great hue and cry from the pulpits of Brooklyn's many churches. A painful business; nor was it likely, on this Friday evening, that many of the Islanders had been able to forget it; for a week earlier they had read on the front

ages of their newspapers what punishment had been fitted to
he crime. The police commissioner had dismissed from the
orce John J. O'Brien, the inspector in charge of Coney Island.
n his stead there was Inspector Robert Emmet Dooley, the
ery name a harrowing memory to the more larcenous among
he Islanders; a few years before, as police captain, he had
veraged thirty arrests every Saturday morning before lunch;
he horses that pulled Dooley's paddy-wagon never cooled off
ill late Sunday evening.

All these considerations, in addition to each individual's
nore personal cares, worked in the minds of Coney's folk on
his Friday evening. But if, as they prepared for bed, these
eflections kept them restless, they had the consolation of the
air weather ahead to lull them and, even better, the prospect
f the crowds of well-heeled pleasure-seekers that would pour
ff the steamboats and out of the streetcars, fanning out to jostle
long the Bowery and throng through the turnstiles of Dream-
and and Luna Park and Steeplechase and cover the sands of
he golden beach. The Islanders were ready. All had been re-
urbished. Every concession, every refreshment stand and
musement park and pier and rollercoaster had gotten its lick
f fresh paint, its dab of hasty decoration. Everywhere things
vere new and shiny. In the offices of the *Brooklyn Eagle,* a few
niles away, a special Coney Island section had been prepared
or publication the next day; the advertising department had
unctioned smoothly with the editorial department; the section
vas swollen with advertisements of the goodies in store for the
isitor to Coney, and a banner headline was spread across the
ront page, proclaiming "Coney Island Expects New Season To
3e Most Prosperous in History of Great Amusement Park By
he Sea." It was no less than the truth. There was nothing left
o do, against the morrow. The Island went to bed.

Mrs. Lena Schwartz, who, with her husband, was to open

next day a small restaurant, made sure her baby was sleeping
soundly, kissed her husband good-night, turned out the gas
light by her bedside, and wearily laid her head on her pillow
Under that pillow was a wallet, as she knew, containing $110
the bulk of which was earmarked to pay the second installmen
of rent on her concession. Mrs. Schwartz hoped for sunny skies
and huge hungry crowds.

Julius Frosin was in a room of his brand-new hotel. For
fifteen years Frosin had worked as manager of various enter
prises at Coney Island, always saving his pennies. At length he
had saved enough of them to launch this modest hotel-and
restaurant, a monument to his years of toil. A week before, he
had taken to his bed, sick. His hotel was open, but there was
still not a dollar in his gleaming new cash register. But Frosin
did not repine. He was as certain as one can be of anything in
this life that his cash register would jingle on Saturday.

Many of the roustabouts, concessionaires, fortune-tellers, and
barkers had taken rooms in the boarding-houses along Sheri
dan's Walk, a promenade that ran from Surf Avenue to the
ocean almost in the shadow of the Giant Roller Coaster, a grea
scenic railway that flanked Dreamland on the west. In these
folk, hope and ambition stirred more sluggishly; the next day
was just another day, and it would bring what it might. Some
of them, however, looked forward to each next day as possibly
bringing them that precious moment when destiny would ac
cord them the guerdon for which surely they had been born
Thus here, on the Friday night, slept a lanky youth of thirteen
the son of circus people, whose name was Bud Abbott (Lou
Costello was an infant of three, asleep in a crib in Paterson
N.J.); a Dreamland barker named Marrener was asleep here
with his wife (his daughter, who would be Susan Hayward
was as yet unborn); a great, hulking youngster named Frank
Leavitt likewise rented a room here, to rest from his duties as

delivery boy for Erzinger's butcher shop (when he was old enough to grow a vast beard he would be known as Man Mountain Dean).

On one corner of Surf Avenue and Sheridan's Walk was a tin-type photograph gallery. Here the visitor to Coney could be photographed sitting in a Winton or astride a camel; here, against cardboard cutouts, the faces of a boy and girl could be photographed to simulate caveman and woman, or beau and belle of the Sixties. It was a successful enterprise, the property

When Dreamland first opened, there were chariot races run on a track around the tower and lagoon. But gradually concessions replaced spectacles. The Shoot-the-Chutes were always popular.   COURTESY THE FRANCIS X. MOORE COLLECTION

of the Sangunitto family. Old James Sangunitto was one of th
Island's earliest latter-day pioneers. He had been custodian o
Coney Island (Norton's) Point back in 1870, responsible fo
tending the beacon light before it was housed in a lighthouse
In the Sangunitto home, on this Friday night, affairs wer
merrier than usual: the family was reunited: Mabel Sangunit
to's husband, Matthew Kennedy, a police lieutenant, had afte
some years been assigned back to a tour of duty on the Island
He was, however, not at home; he was at the desk of the polic
station on West Eighth Street. All he wanted for the morrov
was peace; peace, and a quiet, orderly throng of well-behavec
trippers.

Nearer to the ocean on Sheridan's Walk was a wooden, two
story shack that housed a family of gypsies. They were not
strictly speaking, authentic Romany gypsies; the mother of th
brood, which numbered more than twenty, was a full-bloodec
Cherokee Indian named Mary Lee; but they dressed as gypsies
they passed for gypsies, they were maligned as are gypsies
they told fortunes in approved gypsy fashion, and they main
tained, as part of their establishment, two performing bears anc
a performing monkey, as gypsies are wont to do. Even this
lively entourage at length settled down to compose itself ii
slumber.

In Eileen Villa, the home of the Tilyou family, the olde
generation went to bed and to sleep. The younger generation—
two McCullough youngsters, nephews of the Tilyous—went to
bed but then, after a cautious pause, got up again and went to
the bedroom window. This day, Friday, had been one brother'
ninth birthday; the other was almost eleven. They had beer
permitted, as a special treat, to spend the night at Coney and—
most magical of all—to lark around on the morrow while the
Island came to life for the season. It was too much to expect
that they should go promptly to sleep. They hung out the win

low, listening to the music of imagined carrousels, watching
the light swing around from Norton's Point, and planning their
day, where they would go, where they would spend their
birthday money, what forbidden joys they would experience.
But they tired too, finally; they were asleep before eleven.

Off Norton's Point, the light still swung. There was a Marconi
wireless station here, too; the operator was an aspiring young
man named David Sarnoff; his ambition would in time enable
him to become president and then chairman of the board of the
Radio Corporation of America. On this night he sat huddled
over his telegrapher's key, listening to Morse code conversa-
tions between ships and shore. He yawned.

The owner-operator of Steeplechase, George Tilyou, was
asleep in an apartment in his park. The owner-operator of Luna
Park, Fred Thompson, was asleep in an apartment in his park.
But Dreamland had no one man as owner and operator. The
manager, Samuel Gumpertz, slept here. But the owners were
elsewhere.

Over in Long Beach, where he was spending the night at his
home in the newest of his real estate developments, Senator
William H. Reynolds was hoping for sunny skies and huge
crowds just as fervently as the lowliest of his concessionaires.
Senator Reynolds—the title was a courtesy dating from his one
term in the State legislature, seventeen years before—was the
principal investor in Dreamland, which was one of his most
ambitious projects. He was a big, dapper, cheerful man, given
to large ideas, prey to gusts of wild wrath, generous, friendly,
and harboring within him that special spark of a favored few,
the gift of making great gobs of money. While he was still in
his teens, Reynolds had in one year netted $40,000 in real
estate; he dropped it all in Wall Street at the earliest opportunity; back in real estate, he made it all over again and kept on
making it. Occasionally, his propensity for making it would land

him in water at least tolerably warm: he was to know what it is
like to be indicted on charges of grand larceny, even to be con
victed and sentenced to the penitentiary. But his sentence
would be reversed, he would escape jail. It is likely that the
scrapes he got into resulted from his lavish approach to life
Once, when he wanted to tour Europe, he took three friends
along, picking up their tabs, and, ever solicitous lest they grow
bored, hired a pair of blackface mummers to come along as his
court jesters. Years later, Reynolds was to find himself with a
comely bit of Manhattan real estate on his hands. He engaged
an architect to draw a picture of a glistening spire and, on the
strength of it, sold the plot at a handsome profit to Walter
Chrysler so that the Chrysler Building might spring from the
earth. When he died, Reynolds was a millionaire ten times over

It might be expected that a man of Reynolds' financial mettle
need not have worried, on this Friday evening, about a few
thousand admissions to Dreamland, more or less. Yet he did
The park had been like a contrary mistress to him. It had cost
him money, it had been a nagging nuisance, it had not yielded
so pleasurably as he had led himself to believe it would; but
still he lavished on it his attention and his money, still he hoped

He had come by his park through a combination of routine
canniness and routine political connections. His inspiration to
acquire it was just as commonplace. When in 1903 Luna Park
proved a bonanza, Reynolds cast a covetous eye first on the
soaring box-office take and thereafter on a tract of land between
Surf Avenue and the ocean that was vastly superior to Luna
Park's real estate. There were fifteen acres altogether, painfully
pieced together by the despotic chicaneries of the late John Y
McKane, the unlamented political overseer of all Gravesend. In
July of 1903 this land came up for auction in two packages, to
either side of West Eighth Street, a city property sixty feet wide
and 850 feet from Surf Avenue to the ocean. Possibly the hurdle

of this public land had daunted other would-be promoters, but not Reynolds. Somewhat concealing himself behind a pair of transparent dummies, he bought the land in, $200,000 for one slice, $247,500 for the other. Since he had reckoned on paying $500,000 for the two lots, he was already in pocket rather more than $50,000. Nor did he need to concern himself about the city property, for he had on his team such worthies as State Senator Pat McCarren, the Democratic boss of Brooklyn, and Big Tim Sullivan, a regnant sachem of Tammany Hall, and it was child's play for these statesmen to ram through the New York City Board of Estimate a proposal granting title not only to the city street but to the Old Iron Pier at its foot, at which were docked the steamboats from Manhattan.

After razing such memorable landmarks as the old Seaside Athletic Club, where a few years before Jim Jeffries had hammered Ruby Rob Fitzsimmons into stupefaction, thousands of workers busied themselves constructing the most splendiferous amusement part the world had ever seen. The notion at first was to call it the Hippodrome, for Reynolds hankered after chariot races around a lagoon; when he got his first glimpse of the architect's perspective drawings he switched to Wonderland; but Dreamland was the name that stuck. Everything—price, size, conception—was on an exuberant scale. The park cost, it was said, more than $3,500,000. The enclosure could accommodate two hundred and fifty thousand people. Its broad promenades and plazas fanned out from a lagoon; at the center of all was a beacon tower, three hundred and seventy-five feet tall, a copy, so ran the press-agent's allegation, of the Giralda Tower in Seville. Fruitier grist for the press-agent's mill was to be found in the lighting arrangements, for still in 1904 a prodigal consumption of electricity was calculated to make the eye bug. There were one million incandescent light bulbs in Dreamland; one hundred thousand of them were used to pick

out the tower against the night; it was estimated that the cos
of this lavish display added $4,000 to Dreamland's weekly nut

All this radiance was shed on flower-topped columns, a
esplanade where a band played seemingly without pause,
great ballroom built on a pier reaching out into the ocean wher
it sparkled at night like a gem-set casket, and a profusion c
concessions housed in buildings of light, airy design and so dis
posed about the fifteen acres as to cajole rather than inflame
Everything was painted a chaste white.

This garden of enchantment was for Senator Reynolds, unti
the day it opened, a true Dreamland. But from that day for
ward it grew thick with nettles. It troubled him. He was neve
able to make out why his park had not summarily eclipsed Luna
Park as competition. Wasn't Dreamland bigger? Wasn't it close
to the ocean, and the ocean breezes? Hadn't it cost more? Wasn'
it, indeed, crammed with attractions and entertainments lifted
bodily from Luna Park? Then *why* did more people insist on go

Dreamland's principal competition: Luna Park, run by a pair of con
summate showmen, Thompson and Dundy. This is Luna's lagoon.

ıg to Luna than to Dreamland? Dreamland had as many whirli-
ligs and turnabouts, as many tunnels of love, twice as many
hoot-the-Chutes, a scenic railway to transport the goggle-eyed
hrough the Alps of Switzerland, and a flotilla of gondolas to
vaft them along the Canals of Venice; Santos-Dumont was on
ıand with an airship, to take the more daring out over the
cean; a Lilliputian village had been confected on a scale for
.s three hundred midget inhabitants; whereas in Luna Park
ne thousand persons were employed to fight the imaginary
ames in a four-story building, in Dreamland there were two
housand on hand to save a six-story building. Where the lovely
valtz, "Meet Me Tonight In Dreamland," was an authentic hit,
Luna's counterpart, "Meet Me Down At Luna, Lena," was a
ulgar novelty. In every way Dreamland was bigger, better,
ewer, more spectacular, more (the word was not regarded as
umorous, in 1911) refined. If Coney Island was ever to be
ermanently ensconced as a temple of fun for the people,
enator Reynolds assured himself, it would be because of
Dreamland—wouldn't it? He could stand in the middle of Surf
Avenue: to the north were the glittering towers and minarets
f Luna, graceful and stately and many-hued; to the south were
he taller and more elegant towers of Dreamland, all a pristine
vhite. To a forty-four-year-old real estate magnate, the prefer-
nce was so simple as to be ridiculous. And yet a distressingly
arge number of pleasure-seekers continued to go north. Why?

One reason why resided in the difference between the man-
gers of the two parks. At Luna, Fred Thompson and Skip
Dundy were showmen from mazard to gizzard; for them, to
vhet a customer's appetite was instinctive. But at Dreamland
he bosses were venture capitalists and acquisitive politicians.
Vhen Dreamland opened in 1904, it opened three hours late;
ı the cashier's booths sat pretty young women demurely
arbed in long college gowns of white and topped by light blue

mortarboard caps. Luna Park opened on time with precision; i
the cashier's booths were luscious Mexican senoritas in son
breros and red bolero jackets; a marimba band played in th
street outside the entrance. And inside, no whit dismayed b
the fact that a half-dozen of their best concessions had bee
lured across the street, Thompson and Dundy had prepared, a
pièce de résistance, an entire Indian durbar, complete wit
procession of elephants, on the head of the largest of which wa
perched Senator Chauncey M. Depew, grinning and waving a
the crowd. Dreamland drew its share on opening day, but
was not the lion's share.

Nor, in succeeding seasons, did matters improve appreciably
Senator Reynolds did everything he could: he induced severa
authentic Broadway stars to take over concessions, accompanie
by a fanfaronade of publicity: Marie Dressler had charge of th
peanut-and-popcorn stands, and dressed up small boys as red
flanneled imps to act as her salesmen (Bud Abbott was one c
them, for a time); Peter F. Dailey, wooed away from Webe
and Fields, starred in something that was billed as A Parisia
Novelty but which every night turned into a crackling barrag
of improvisation and ad lib insult sufficient to pack his audienc
with appreciative fellow-actors; E. C. Boyce was the ballyho
talker for the Fall of Pompeii; and a popular singing Irish comi
of the time, Andrew Mack, guided the destinies of the little ti
fish propelled by clockwork in the Fish Pond, whence th
chumps tried to hook them. But the novelty palled; the cele
brated entertainers withdrew; admissions to the sumptuous par
languished.

Even the promotion stunts went awry. At Steeplechase, if th
fact that the mayor was coming on a visit failed to catch atten
tion, somehow the word would leak out that there was a plo
to assassinate him at the park, and business would zoom. A
Luna, if they announced (as they did) that, the big elephan

Topsy having become irretrievably vicious, she was to be publicly executed, the crowds came running; if she balked (as she did) at eating the poisoned carrots, they merely announced that the next week she would be electrocuted, and once more the crowds came running. But should Dreamland boast that a local eccentric had invented a new kind of airplane and that a local character had been prevailed upon to fly it from the park to Far Rockaway, it would invariably turn out that the plane would ingloriously plump straight into the drink, and the crowd would shrug shoulders and disperse, probably to Luna.

Moreover, since there were so many politicians involved in backing Dreamland, the park was considered fair game for other politicians, These clustered around, yapping and snarling like a pack of foxhounds in for the kill. The Dreamland pier was a fire hazard. Dreamland's buildings were built eleven feet beyond the right-of-way on Surf Avenue. The searchlight on Dreamland's tower was too much like and too close to the beacon lighthouse at Norton's Point. Borough, city, state, and even Federal politicians bedevilled the lovely playground.

Despite the unfriendly attacks, despite the regrettable tendency to sag into anticlimax, despite the dryrot at the box-office, Senator Reynolds, in May of 1911, was indomitably hopeful. Steps had been taken. Curt memoranda had been dispatched to each concessionaire, bidding each to be on his toes. The virginal white paint job had been scrapped: cream and firehouse red now assaulted the eye. Heads had rolled, new heads had been crowned: Samuel W. Gumpertz, once merely the manager of the Lilliputian Village, destined to be the managing director of the Ringling Brothers and Barnum & Bailey Circus, had been named to Dreamland's top executive post. Another $60,000 had been poured into the park to remodel, redecorate, revive. This was the year. Tomorrow was the day.

In the animal arena at Dreamland, Colonel Joseph G. Ferrari, assisted by his star lion-tamer, the dashing and glamorou Captain Jack Bonavita, and a staff of trainers, had bedded dow his troupe of eighty-odd wild animals for the night and was up stairs, in his apartment over the arena, with his wife an daughter. During the winter Colonel Ferrari had bought th entire string of Dreamland's animal acts from Frank Bostock Madame Morelli and her seven leopards; Professor Wormwoo and his performing monkeys, dogs, bears, and anteater; Herma Weedom and his assorted lions, leopards, hyenas, pumas, an wolves; a gaggle of noisy cockatoos; and Captain Bonavita an his lions—and he was understandably apprehensive about hi upcoming opening-day performance.

Not so Captain Bonavita, who also had an apartment upstair. The captain was a cool hand. He was magnificently cast in hi chosen role. He affected sweeping handlebar mustaches; h worked in a military uniform of unexampled severity, on whicl the only decoration was a single red rose pinned to the jacket most impressive of all, he had only one arm. That his other arm had been amputated was testimony to the footling ways o Dreamland's publicity, to the evil star that had winked over it destiny. A lion named Baltimore had, one day, clawed Bona vita's right hand; two fingers had had to come off. It was a natural accident, occupational; but then someone seized on the idea of wheeling the gallant lion-tamer into the arena and nex to the cage where his substitute was guiding the cats throug] their paces. From outside the bars, from within his swaddle o bandages, Bonavita could make faces at Baltimore, and Balti more snarl his retort. The surgeons at the hospital demurred For their patient to leave the hospital, they insisted, might cos him his arm. But the idea had caught Bonavita's fancy. Back a Dreamland, he knew, he would be closer to Marie Dressler, wh had lost her heart to him even before Baltimore's paw ha reached out and snatched; back at Dreamland he would have

onavita the intrepid can scarcely be picked out from amongst his twenty-
even great cats. But he is there, in the middle. COURTESY THE FRANCIS K.
MOORE COLLECTION

he heady roar of the crowd in his ears. He went back. The
rowd came, and applauded him wildly. Marie Dressler also
ame, at every opportunity. But the surgeons had been right;
he infection in his hand grew inflamed; he lost his arm at the
lbow. Predictably, his drawing power grew. Now, on this
'riday night, confident as a baby in his ability to charm the
ext day's throngs, Captain Bonavita went deep to sleep.

Bamboola, the animal act's Wild Man from Borneo who, after
pplying burnt cork to his face, frizzing his hair, and affixing a
reat gold ring to his nose, used to stand in front of the arena
nd ballyhoo by uttering grunts and meaningless ululations,
ad decided not to go home to his wife and family in the Bronx.
Bamboola was, in fact, a mild-mannered Alsatian of sedentary
abits, and the thought of the long trip home and back before
ext noon's opening was too much. He curled up on a couch in
n upstairs apartment, covering himself with a pouf despite the
lement weather, for he had a tendency to catch cold. He had
rought his rubbers with him, and his umbrella.

Downstairs, with the other animals, was a small but engaging elephant named Little Hip, in some ways the prize beast of the entire menagerie. He had been named for his birthplace, Manhattan's Hippodrome; he had, while still in his nonage, been a featured theatrical performer in an extravaganza called "Baby Mine;" he had taken tea with Edna Wallace Hopper, the popular musical comedy star, in her apartment; he could waltz, eat a meal from a table, and smoke a pipe, but most of all he enjoyed handing out programs, preferably to children, with his trunk. Children returned his regard; he was a great favorite. He was not, however, included in the sale by Bostock to Ferrari. Little Hip was a very overnight resident. Early Saturday morning he was to be taken to Hoboken and loaded aboard a ship bound for England, where he was to grace the festivities attendant on the coronation of George V. His keeper, Captain André, had blown him a goodnight kiss and withdrawn to Manhattan for a farewell party.

At about ten-thirty, that Friday night, there was a flurry of excitement at Dreamland's Baby Incubators, where prematurely born babies were cared for and, incidentally, exhibited. There were five infants on hand, three girls and two boys; but here at ten-thirty, came a sixth, a fourth girl, just a few hours old, rushed out from a delivery room in Manhattan. She was received by Dr. Fischel, handed over to a nurse, and assigned a crib near the others. Here the rhythm of her life would be as predictable as the measure of the tides lapping the beach a thousand feet to the south.

Lights burned at the end of the two piers thrusting out from Dreamland into the ocean. At the foot of the Old Iron Pier there was a fishing-shack and a small clam bar. Three island fishermen sat up late, on this Friday night, drinking Goldenrod beer and swapping lies; for all they knew of Dreamland they might have been at Land's End. Under the great ballroom, a the foot of the other pier to the west, William Atheer slept near the stalls housing his fifteen Shetland ponies. His was a popular concession; he had every right to dream of dimes in abundance, and children's faces tense with happy excitement, and children's fists gripping tight at his ponies' manes.

Others slept in small apartments scattered about the park— concessionaires, superintendents, their families—and three night watchmen patrolled their beats, but in only one Dreamland installation was there any urgent activity. This was in the concession called Hell Gate, owned by William Ellis. Here, for your pleasure, after climbing into a small boat, you were carried on a race through dimly lit caverns, swept through turbulent eddies, caught up by a great whirlpool, and then gently deposited at the exit. Ellis had, the year before, essayed a different sort of entertainment, one that foundered; heedful of Senator Reynolds' strict injunction that this year everything in Dreamland must be a surepop sockola or else, he had reassembled Hell Gate. But three days before, during a trial run, the bottom of the water spillway had sprung a leak. Ellis contracted with Samuel Englestein, a tinsmith, to make the necessary repairs. And so the lights burned late in Hell Gate, as Englestein and a gang of men strove hurriedly, with tubs of hot tar, to calk the leak.

At about one-thirty a.m., on Saturday morning, one of Englestein's workmen left Hell Gate, which was on the west side of Dreamland, and strolled out to Surf Avenue and then east to "Doc" Chambers' all-night drug store. He wanted his hand dressed. He had burned it with some of the hot pitch.

Minutes later, inside Hell Gate, there was a sudden, sharp report. Englestein's head jerked up. He looked at Emil Thur, one of his workmen. "What was that?" he asked. Thur shrugged. Englestein frowned. "Sounded like a pistol shot," he said. As he spoke there was another sharp report, then a third. They looked up. Overhead was a cluster of light bulbs, a dozen of Dreamland's vaunted one million. The bulbs were exploding, whether from the heat of the tar or from some sort of short circuit. All at once they were plunged into darkness. Englestein could hear his workmen's voices, raised in uneasy protest. In the black, someone kicked over a bucket of bubbling tar. A moment later, Hell Gate was in flames.

Coney Island was no stranger to fire. In the previous eighteen years there had been ten multi-alarm blazes, of which at least three were conflagrations. In May, 1899, $800,000 worth of West Brighton had burned. In November, 1903, a million-dollar fire had swept clean the five blocks from Steeplechase through the Bowery and east to Feltman's big brick-walled restaurant. In July, 1907, Steeplechase had itself been leveled, in an eighteen-hour conflagration. Each time, the showmen involved had waited only for the embers to be soaked down before moving in to rebuild. The day after the Steeplechase fire, George Tilyou had set up a large sign where the entrance had been:

> I have trouble today that I did not have yesterday.
> I had troubles yesterday that I have not today.
> On this site will be erected shortly a better, bigger, greater
> Steeplechase Park.
> Admission to the Burning Ruins—10 cents.

And Steeplechase's celebrated Funny Face had been lifted above the smoking ashes, crossed and recrossed with plaster patches, but carrying the legend, "A little the worse for wear, but still in the ring." Each time, what had been built new was conspicuously better. The 1903 fire had purged from the Bowery the most disreputable of Coney's old haunts; the renovated Steeplechase had indeed been an improved park, bigger, offering more fun, and much of it housed within a great weather-proof glass pavilion. But despite the admirable tradition, despite the undeniable fact that fire had always resulted in more prodigious entertainments lodged in statelier mansions, Coney Island preferred, other things being equal, no fire.

Sympathy can be recruited for this point of view upon consideration of the materials with which the mansions of an amusement park are built. An entrepreneur concerned with a season lasting only fourteen weekends is not likely to think in terms of steel and concrete. To be sure, the City of New York had, on this Friday night, nearly completed construction of a Municipal Bathing House just to the east of Dreamland, and it was made of concrete, but the City of New York is not an entrepreneur. Your casual-venture capitalist, charged with building an amusement park, thinks in terms of lath and staff. Lath is thin wood, used in narrow strips. Staff is a composition of plaster of Paris and hemp fiber, molded into the desired shape and then nailed into place. It was first developed for the Paris Exposition of 1878 and the more charitable etymologists have concluded that the word *staff* is a genteel corruption of *stuff*. Certainly, like stuff, it burns wickedly and well. Fire underwriters look upon staff with, for pardonable reasons, a considerable loathing. Looking upon the great sea of staff that billowed over Dreamland in 1911, the fire underwriters had testily set an insurance rate of five and one-half per cent on the area; translated, this means that for the landlord to buy $100 worth of insurance for one year he would have had to pay a premium of $5.50. This is a high rate; it is a rate generally referred to pejoratively as prohibitive; how high it is may be reckoned by contrasting it with the rate obtaining today on a commercial office building. Admittedly conditions differ, but so does the value of the dollar: under ordinary conditions of safety, the premium for fire insurance on an office building today would be $0.03. Moreover, even at the rate of five and one-half per

cent many American underwriters had flatly refused to insure
the Coney Island buildings; it was left to that inveterate
gambler, Lloyd's of London, to carry the unappreciable load.

There was, however, one narrow gleam of hope, one salutary
side to the situation which had not existed in 1903 or in 1907.
The city's Department of Water Supply had constructed, at
considerable expense and with a considerable measure of com-
placency, a new and special high pressure pumping station,
precisely to assist in fighting the great conflagrations that
seemed periodically to overwhelm Coney Island. The station
was at Twelfth Street and Neptune Avenue, near Coney Island
Creek; it boasted five pumps; these could deliver 4,500 gallons
a minute, or enough to operate twelve lines of hose with a
pressure of at least 125 pounds at every nozzle. The Department of Water Supply set great store by this installation and for
its part the Fire Department was understandably delighted to
have it available. The merchants and concessionaires were more
than tickled; they had watched while the special high-pressure
Corey hydrants had been affixed to the high-pressure mains;
they had applauded, only the month before, when in rehearsal
the high-pressure system had responded to the demands made
upon it with disdainful efficiency. Never again, the Islanders
had thought, would fire ravage the community. In the pumping
station, the five pumps maintained a steady, confident pressure
of fifty pounds; they purred and they pounded; their tending
engineers had been awaiting the moment when they would be
called upon to perform, not in a rehearsal, but in a real emer-
gency. That moment was now at hand.

Down in the bowels of Hell Gate, where a fresh layer of tar
had been suddenly metamorphosed into a sheet of flame, at first
there was panic; two or three workmen scuttled up the steps
toward an exit and safety; the others shouted and scrambled

about in confusion, half-lit by the leaping tongues of fire. Englestein was momentarily frozen by fear. Through his mind flickered guilt, responsibility, blame, and other weighty considerations. He knew he must act, and act quickly, but he was, like so many of us when confronted with the menace of fire, the complete amateur. He made his decision, and it was wrong. He tried to put the fire out.

There were some hand extinguishers in Hell Gate, and a reel of hose. He and his workers wasted valuable minutes scrambling up the incline of the spillway in search of them; once equipped with these toys, they turned again, moved by a mad hope, and set themselves to fight the flames. Where all was lath and staff, where all had been freshly painted, this effort was doomed. The fire was already licking at the narrow rafters athwart the frame of the building. Englestein and his workmen ran for their lives.

Out on one of Dreamland's broad promenades, James Lillis, a night watchman, turned when he heard running steps. He shouted to the shadowy figures; then, from the corner of his eye, he caught a glimpse of darting orange. He wheeled and raced for Dreamland's administration building, twenty running steps away. "Fire!" he yelled, into the night, and "Fire!" he

The guardian imp furled his diabolic wings at approximately 1:30 a.m. on Saturday, May 27, 1911. Thereafter Hell broke wide open. COURTESY THE FRANCIS K. MOORE COLLECTION

yelled again, then dashed inside the building and yanked hard on the automatic alarm switch. It was then one fifty-eight a.m. The fire had been living and growing for at least ten minutes.

The variable breeze, earlier from the south, had shifted a few points. It was now from the southwest. In the course of nature, the breeze would carry the fire to the next building north. This was the building that housed the premature babies, each in its incubator.

The alarm bells set off by Lillis rang in the near-by engine houses. The nearest was on West Eighth Street, not a hundred yards from Dreamland. Next away was on West Fifteenth Street. After only moments, with a great clattering of horses' hooves, the steamers and engines and hook-and-ladders were tumbling through the streets.

The alarm bells rang, as well, in the high-pressure pumping station. At once the engineers went to work. At once a needle, streaking a line of ink across a paper drum, leaped from the line showing a routine and normal fifty pounds of pressure to the line showing one hundred and sixty pounds. The engineers exchanged confident smiles.

The bells rang in the police precinct station on West Eighth Street, right next to the fire house. At the desk, Lieutenant Matthew Kennedy pricked up his ears like an old fire-horse. His career as a cop had been congruent with Coney's conflagrations: he had joined the force as a patrolman just in time to be on hand for the fire that blazed in May, 1899 (this night was the twelfth anniversary of that occasion); during the fire in November, 1903, he had had the opportunity to be a hero, rescuing several persons, and winning a departmental commendation and a promotion to sergeant; when Steeplechase was destroyed, in July, 1907, he had again acted with such conspicuous gallantry as to win his lieutenancy. His reassignment two weeks before to the Coney Island precinct, after an absence of several years, seemed tonight to have been ordered, not by the commissioner, but by Fate. Lieutenant Kennedy, sitting at the desk, listening to the alarm bells, thought of his wife and her family, the Sangunittos, living two blocks away on Sheridan's Walk. Then he set about the task of alerting the several dozen people asleep, as he knew, in Dreamland, and the several hundred who might find themselves in the path of the flames, in the boarding-houses to either side of the park. Policemen raced out of the precinct station house, pelting along the side street into Surf Avenue and then fanning out to east and west. Telephone bells jangled, disturbing the sleep of police reserves.

Lillis' first cry of "Fire!" had been heard by Ernest Barnard, the night watchman of the Great Divide show, an entertainment near the West Eighth Street entrance to Dreamland. Barnard ran out of the park to Surf Avenue, taking up the cry. He was heard by two policemen, Fred Snyder, who ran to the fire house on West Eighth Street, and Fred Ehlers. Methodical was the word for Ehlers. He had been told, long since, that whatever happened on his beat he was to write down in his note book; that what was written in his note book would comprise a record of the important events occurring on his beat; that diligence and thoroughness were the qualities by which he would attain the stripes of a sergeant. Patrolman Ehlers listened to the shouts, observed Snyder hustling toward the fire station, took out his note book and pencil, glanced at his watch, and then wrote. "2.03 a.m.," he wrote, "Snyder turned in fire alarm on my post." Methodical, but late.

Not so the firemen. Battalion Chief William Rogers was the first to arrive, on the dead run from the engine house. He took one look at the flaming Hell Gate building and ordered a second alarm to be sent in. Here, bells clanging, came the first due engine and truck; Rogers ordered three lines stretched from the high-pressure hydrants into Hell Gate. It was done. The controlling nozzles were opened. There was a gratifying jet of water. The firemen began to play their hoses on the flames. But something was amiss. The streams of water fell short and ever shorter. Rogers, watching, felt anger mount in him. Time was running; the breeze, shifting now, was carrying the fire to either side of Hell Gate; what had happened? What had gone wrong? He ordered—it was now six minutes after two—a third alarm turned in. The flames, fanned by the breeze, crackled and roared and mounted higher; great flaring sparks, lifted on the updraft, danced up and off toward the incubators, toward the Dreamland power plant, toward the soaring tower. Desperate Rogers ordered steamers hooked up to the low-pressure mains, ordered additional lines to be taken from the pumpers to Hell Gate and the adjoining buildings, ordered a signal to be sent to telegraph headquarters commanding more pressure at once. And now, frustrated, the firemen began to fall back from the heat of the blaze. Furious, Chief Rogers saw that his men were holding their hands over the nozzles of their lines, as one might do with a garden hose, to get greater thrust.

In the incubator building, two o'clock was feeding-time for the premature babies. Miss Graf, the head nurse, had bestirred herself promptly and had summoned two of the wet nurses. Outside some men were shouting, she realized, and carrying on, but what could she expect? After all, she had known when she took this job at Coney Island that gangs of rowdies would be lallygagging outside in the streets till all hours. Miss Graf peered in at the most recent arrival, poor little mite (it weighed only one pound, fourteen ounces), red and wrinkled. She was about to assign the wet nurses to their tasks when suddenly she heard an outer door flung open, and steps pounding outside in the corridor. It was Dr. Fischel and, Miss Graf noticed with severity, he was in his nightshirt. His tone was urgent and im- perative; it brooked no argument; behind him loomed the un-

certain form of a police sergeant. Dr. Fischel himself took up
the littlest infant and one other; Miss Graf carried one; so did
each of the wet nurses. (But where could they go? thought Miss
Graf; where could they take the babies?) The sixth baby was
lying in its crib; a little girl, she was the child of Mrs. Anna
Duboid who, after her baby had been brought here to an incubator, had herself taken a job as wet nurse. She had been
wakened by the alarums and excursions outside and now here
she came, a dressing-gown about her shoulders; in a panic she
caught up her baby and rushed outside. Smoke billowed in
through the open door; Miss Graf heard for the first time the
ominous crackling. Through the door with the smoke came as
well a sense of confusion, of desperate hurry and urgent dismay
and disjointed tension. Dr. Fischel had started to order Mrs.
Duboid to—but to do what? To stop? To come back? Abruptly
he turned, as if forgetting all about her. He made sure the heads
of the infants in his arms were covered by blankets, to protect
them from the smoke; then, bidding his nurses follow after him,
he led the way out into the garish night, laden with his precious,
tiny, mortal burden.

When the bells of the first alarm had rung, they had sounded,
as usual, a code message that would describe, to any knowledgeable listener, the whereabouts of the fire. When three-
three-seven-nine was sounded, in fire stations, police precinct
stations, and newspaper city rooms, all over New York men
paused, harkened, then scrabbled through card-index files. The
most knowledgeable—such a man as Deputy Chief Thomas
Lally, in charge of the borough of Brooklyn, or Acting Chief of
Department John Kenlon, in his Manhattan home—recognized
the code instantly; they recognized, as well, trouble, for they
knew this was Dreamland's box and they were familiar with
the pattern of Coney Island conflagrations. These two did not
stand on the order of their going, they went. Each was in his

brand-new, sixty-horse-power red car, bell clanging, within moments, and bound for the Island. In the city rooms of New York's fifteen newspapers the responsible editors also cocked an ear; when six minutes later the second alarm sounded, from the box across from Dreamland at Surf Avenue and Arcade Walk, they were electrified; the third alarm, only two minutes later, prodded them into dispatching their best legmen even more summarily. The word spread into the late-night spots, the cafés and taverns; and the story grew in the telling: all Coney was burning. And indeed, when the curious hurried out into the streets they could see the southeastern sky already stained with red.

In Brooklyn, moreover, with each succeeding alarm there was a great rush of hoof-beats; sirens whined and bells clanged in the still night as fire-engines and hook-and-ladder trucks either raced for Coney or were temporarily assigned to fire houses which would otherwise have been stripped of equipment. Four engines and a truck at the first alarm; four more engines and two more trucks at the second alarm; three more engines and another truck at the third alarm; they made a brave show as the horses galloped, three and four abreast, through the quiet streets. And windows were flung open, heads peered out, lights went on, people struggled into topcoats, parties were made up to fill cars or carriages. There was a great sight to be seen: Coney would get its crowd of pleasure-seekers, certainly, but it would arrive eight or nine hours ahead of schedule.

Night watchmen and policemen meanwhile were racing through Dreamland, shouting to upstairs apartment windows, banging with nightsticks on doors. Another cop pounded along Sheridan's Walk. Upstairs in his sickroom, Julius Frosin, owner of the brand-new Frosin Hotel, listened to the shouts and the echoing footsteps. He made his way to the window. Yes; he could see it; there was a fire, all right. But—here he watched the

wind taking the sparks and blowing them east and north—there
was no reason for him to worry. Fire: a bad business. Still, it
might bring crowds down, the next day. Frosin went back to
his bed.

Mrs. Lena Schwartz woke up her grumbling husband. She
would take care of the baby, she told him, if he would only make
sure their new restaurant was safe. They dressed and left their
room, he, still grumbling, bound toward the Bowery, she, with
the baby in her arms, tagging along after him. Their money
was still in the wallet, still under the pillow.

The Sangunitto family tumbled out on to Sheridan's Walk.
Should they try to save anything from their photograph gallery?
What was the use? Wasn't the wind taking the fire in the op-
posite direction? They decided to walk up as far along Surf
Avenue as they could, and gawk. They locked their house be-
hind them.

Further down the walk, the gypsies had fallen to wrangling.
Who was to take care of the bears and the monkey? Could they
be safely escorted as far as the Brighton Beach Fair Grounds,
where some of their vast family had set up tents? If there really
was a fire, wouldn't it frighten their bears? And besides, when
there was such a rich commotion, wasn't it the business of every
gypsy, real or pretended, to be around and about, taking advantage of the confusion? At length two of the gypsies were
dispatched with the bears; the others scattered.

In Eileen Villa, the two McCullough youngsters had
awakened at the first alarm. The fire station at Fifteenth Street,
whose company answered the first call, was just across the
street from their bedroom; when the horses clattered out, they
were at their bedroom window, scrambling into their clothes.
The day had promised excitement, but nothing as wonderful as
this! But here came their uncle, Edward J. Tilyou, with a stern
injunction: they could get up, they could get dressed, but under

no circumstances were they to leave the front yard. They might go no further than the gate that swung at the foot of the garden on Surf Avenue. They were not, however, too disappointed. That garden gate was a splendid relay station for wild and frightful rumors, and they got them all, dutifully inflated them, and sent them on into the house to dismay their Aunt Emma. The fire had spread from Dreamland to Luna! Despite the most thrilling and heroic rescue efforts, all the incubator babies had fried to death! The fire had reached the shooting galleries and bullets were exploding as though from machine-guns! Three firemen had been shot! (In these last rumors they had a gleeful proprietary interest, for the idea of the modern shooting gallery had originated with their father, in whose Surf Avenue machine shop moving targets were manufactured for sale all over the world.) But the most hair-raising rumors had to do with the wild animals.

The animal arena was on the eastern side of Dreamland, a couple of hundred yards away from Hell Gate; the lagoon and the tower lay between. The first in the arena to waken were the beasts; fitful sleepers, they sniffed the acrid smoke, and an undercurrent of alarm swept through their cages. By the time policemen and night watchmen had managed to rout Ferrari and Bonavita out of bed, every animal was wide awake and pacing restlessly back and forth in his cage. (In the lagoon, a seal dodged about, surfacing every now and again to look toward the flames.) Ferrari's first concern was for his wife and small daughter, Louise. He was confident that the fire could be halted on the far side of the lagoon, but he knew that the animals might panic; to calm them he planned to let them out of their cages and into the main arena; under those circumstances he wanted his family safely away. He guided them through the steel-rimmed oval of the arena and out to one of Dreamland's promenades and beyond to Surf Avenue. He di

ected them to Henderson's Hotel, well beyond the area en-
dangered by the fire, and then turned back to care for his
menagerie. On the way back he broke into a run, for he noticed
that in just those very few minutes the tower had caught fire;
he could see now that the breeze was from the west, threaten-
ing to carry the flames closer to the arena. Dread began to ooze
into him, displacing his confidence. But still he had reason to
hope that the firemen would be able to quench the fire before
it could reach his charges.

Bonavita and a half-dozen keepers were on hand, attempting
to soothe the frightened beasts. Ferrari gave the order to free
them from their cages and herd them into the main oval. Most
of them cooperated smoothly enough, but one lioness, Victoria,
who was about to litter, balked, and a trainer, Gardo Revero,
was obliged to crawl into her cage barehanded and drag her
out backwards by the ears. Nor would Little Hip, the elephant,
stir from the block of concrete to which he was chained: he
would obey only Captain André, his bull man, who had not yet
returned from the farewell party in Manhattan.

Ferrari's notion—that the animals would be, by and large,
less restive out of their cages—was justified. He and Bonavita
and the staff of trainers kept the beasts on a steady, even,
rhythmic patrol of the oval; they made it seem like another
training period, conducted, to be sure, at an unlikely hour, and
with an uncomfortably acrid smell of smoke coming in on the
westerly breeze, but still something routine, if to a wild animal
such handling is ever routine. Whips cracked. Lions, pumas,
bears, wolves, leopards, hyena, anteater, antelopes, and deer
eyed their masters and followed the gentle, insistent commands.
It was an eerie performance, lighted by the several clusters of
bulbs overhead. All might have gone well, save for one tragic
mischance: the overhead lights flickered and then went out.
Now the terrified animals could see only by the red and flicker-

Bostock was lucky: he sold this concession and all his animal acts to Ferrari in the winter of 1910. Ferrari took the loss. COURTESY THE FRANCIS K. MOORE COLLECTION

ing glare of the fire outside. One of the great cats screamed, in an almost human voice. The others, panic-stricken, reacted. Hell broke loose.

The lights had been turned out on orders from a fireman. Chief Lally had arrived, on a screeching, record run from borough headquarters, at about two-fifteen; at once he had ordered a fourth alarm to be turned in. He next sent his aide at top speed to the high-pressure pumping station, laden with hot questions and searing oaths. He then rallied the firemen and set about to stop the fire in its tracks. There were two chief entrances opening into Dreamland from Surf Avenue. The firemen having been routed from the West Eighth Street entrance, Chief Lally proposed to send them in at the easterly entrance, which gave into the park through an elaborate display called Creation, where the first chapter of Genesis was dramatized, five times a day. The high-pressure system having signally failed, Chief Lally ordered lines from the steamers to be siamesed and deckpipes into position. The equipment was about to move toward the Creation entrance when it occurred to someone that, Dreamland being interlaced with electrical connections, a fireman could get hurt in there from something other than fire. As it happened, all the feedwires lighting the park's million lights passed through a main directly in front of the Creation entrance. Dreamland's Chief Electrician Caffer climbed down through a manhole and tore all the cables loose from their connections. All the electric light bulbs flickered and went out, for the last time.

But the park did not lack for illumination. Flames had shot up all three hundred and seventy-five feet of the great tower (the methodical cop, Ehlers, licked his pencil and wrote in his note book: "2.40. Tower burning. Fire progressing toward ocean"), writhing and weaving through its lattice-work and flaring into the sky. It was for several minutes a brilliant torch; it caught every eye; it was visible in Manhattan, and for miles out to sea. There were, indeed, two ocean liners lying at anchor off Ambrose Channel, the *Sant' Anna* of the Fabre Line and *La Lorraine* of the French Line. Aboard the latter was David Costello, who lived in Sheepshead Bay and who, moved by the quixotic idea that he might be able to descry his house, miles away, had come up on deck. He saw the fire break out; he saw the tower light up; he called out to others of the passengers; soon the starboard rail was packed. It was a magnificent spectacle to these casual sightseers; to the animal keepers in the arena it was baleful.

When the electricity failed them, Ferrari and Bonavita had determined to load as many of the beasts as they could into packing-cases and trundle them out of the park. Working with desperate speed, among fear-crazed animals, in flickering light, they nevertheless succeeded in crating five lionesses and four leopards. The boxes were dispatched to a nearby livery stable;

six Shetland ponies were blindfolded and led along as well
Marguerite, a lion cub, was entrusted to Bamboola's care. The;
were working against time; the fire had swept to their south.

In his note book, Patrolman Ehlers had duly recorded the
fact: "2.50; fire has reached east side of park and extends from
the Siege of Richmond to the ocean." There were still men
women, and children at the end of the two piers; the flames had
cut them off. Chief Lally had just ordered a fifth alarm turned
in. Outside the arena, the second-alarm companies were busy
with deckpipes and handlines, uneasily aware of the screaming
animals within. And still from the hoses there arched only weak
and ineffectual streams of water. Chief Lally, watching his men
hold their hands over the nozzles to get further reach, dashed
his white helmet to the ground in disgust. What had happened
over at the pumping station? The accepted rumor was that the
pumps had failed.

But when angry firemen burst into the pumping station, pro
fuse with bitter complaints, the engineers were able to point to
five hard-working pumps. The station's stated capacity was four
thousand, five hundred gallons a minute, but in fact five thou
sand gallons a minute were at that moment being fed into the
high-pressure system. This was enough for eighteen two
hundred-and-fifty-gallon streams at one hundred and fort
pounds of pressure, a fine firefighting pressure. The firemen
expostulated. Heatedly they insisted that the pressure at nozzle
back in Dreamland, was closer to twenty pounds. The engineer
nodded. They knew all about that. They pointed to the drum o
paper, still winding around, on which the needle still streaked
a line of ink. It told the whole story:

1.30 a.m.	50 pounds
1.58 a.m.	160 pounds
2.10 a.m.	20 pounds
2.50 a.m.	25 pounds

Why? The engineers shrugged. Clearly, too many connections had been made. Perhaps the firemen, when they retreated from Hell Gate, had left some connections bleeding? This was angrily denied. Then there was only one other answer possible: in the first panicky moments after the fire was discovered, Coney Island merchants all over the area had made improper connections so that they might hose their flimsy buildings against the possibility of another fire being started by flying sparks. There was nothing the firemen could say. Disgustedly, they sent a signal ordering the Department's three fireboats, the *eth Low, New Yorker,* and *Zophar Mills,* to come to the Coney Island Creek and hitch up to the pumping station in a belated effort to feed yet more water into the high-pressure system; disconsolately, they reported back to their superiors.

Sam Gumpertz, manager of Dreamland, stood on the north side of Surf Avenue, across from the main entrance to his park. It was fiercely hot where he stood; behind him already the facades of the buildings were beginning to blister; most of the other spectators had been content to withdraw into the side streets; but still Gumpertz lingered, somberly witnessing the destruction of his hopes. Here, approaching him, came Frederic Thompson, manager of Luna. All of Luna's employees were organized into a park fire department; all were busy wetting Luna's papier-mâché palaces; it was true that there had been connections made into a high-pressure system at Luna, fifteen of them; but Thompson had vigorously denied that these depleted the city's system. "We would be a nice crowd," he had said, "to be crippling our neighbor by stealing water needed to fight his fire;" Luna's water, he had insisted, was drawn from its own, separate main connected directly with the ocean. Now reporters saw him go up to Gumpertz, wring his hand and give him a consoling thump on the back. There were no words exchanged. The reporters gathered around

Gumpertz. Dreamland's manager was in the tradition. "T]
public may be sure," he said, "that a greater and finer Drean
land is going to rise from these ashes." Someone got the idea
telephoning Senator Reynolds, out in Long Beach. He was to
the news. The wire hummed for several moments. "Has ever
thing gone?" he asked, at length. He was informed that Drean
land, at least, was doomed. "Well, that's the toughest news
ever have had," he said. "Dreamland was worth $3,500,000, ar
there is only $500,000 insurance. I don't know what good
could do by going over there now, but I'll get dressed and g
there as soon as possible."

The fire raged on. Acting Chief of Department Kenlon w
on hand now, and he conferred with his aides about wir
direction, about the chances of the flames leaping Surf Avenu
about the danger to Luna Park. They noted how the fire w
backing up, actually spreading into the wind, and beginning
lick now at the boarding-houses along Sheridan's Walk. Kenlo
decided to put in the alarm that is the Department's last reso:
the double-nine. It was the first time in the history of t]
borough that this simultaneous alarm had been required. T]
signal "nine-nine" was rung in on the Surf Avenue box; to th
was added a third alarm on the box at the corner of Six
Avenue and Twenty-first Street in Brooklyn: it meant th
every company that would normally answer a third alarm
that box was to report to Coney Island; it meant further a gre
reshuffling of apparatus all over the city, with some Manhatt;
and Queens companies relocating in the far reaches of Broo
lyn. Thirty-three companies in all had by now responded to t]
alarms from Dreamland, some of them from as far as eight mil
away; the teams of fire-horses, on their journey down to t]
Island, had several times to be slowed to a walk to conser
their strength. The great throngs of curious that had gather
from Manhattan and Brooklyn to watch the blaze had be

stopped by the police lines at the edge of the fire zone, a mile and more away from Dreamland; these were now packed along either side of Ocean Parkway. There was no traffic on that six miles of straight speedway but fire apparatus—a long line of fire engines, each trailing its thin plume of fire and cinders. And each, as it thundered past, brought a cheer from the crowds.

At his post on Surf Avenue, Patrolman Ehlers kept a supervisory eye on the events taking place along his beat. Behind him, the fourth and fifth alarm companies were busy wetting down the facades of the buildings along the north side of the avenue; men scrambled over the rooftops, silhouetted by the glare, dousing the scraps of burning debris. In front of him, monstrous tongues of flame leaped into the sky; a ruby glow suffused the heavens. Dreamland's tower had been burning for thirty minutes. Now, with a spectacular crash, down it came, inward upon its foundations. Ehlers licked his pencil. "3.10," he wrote; "fire heading toward Surf Avenue. Tower collapses."

The crash of its fall, the cascade of sparks put an end to all further attempts to crate the wild animals in the arena. They had become utterly unmanageable. They were, indeed, fighting each other savagely, but for some merciful reason they did not attack their trainers. And now the arena itself began to burn. The keepers, alarmed, began to flee. In vain Ferrari ordered them back, imploring them to shoot as many of the animals as they could, to save them from burning to death. But there was no time. Ferrari himself, after firing one or two shots, was forced to retreat, leaving behind him the beginnings of a battle royal among the frantic beasts. As he came out of the blazing entrance to the ring, he ran into Captain André, Little Hip's bull man, his face grimed with smoke except where the tears had coursed down his cheeks. As soon as he had heard about the fire, André had sped for the Island; he knew that the elephant would obey him alone. He had lost valuable minutes

trying to force his way through the police lines and the
through the firemen. Ferrari had to restrain him. There was n
hope for Little Hip. André could hear the poor animal trumpet
ing as the waves of heat closed in on him. Sobbing, he per
mitted Ferrari to hustle him away.

The wind had now quartered and was blowing offshore. I
was the best turn conceivable for the beleaguered Island. Th
weary firemen rallied. They knew now that they would neve
be able to check the fire, but at least they hoped to control i
until it burned itself out. On the ocean side, out where Dream
land Pier and the Old Iron Pier jutted out into the water,
police launch, the *Patrol*, was engaged in rescuing those wh
had been trapped by the flames. First came the three fishermer
(One of them was named Reggie Boyd and it was inevitable
in view of the patois of Brooklyn, that this name would bree
confusion. One newspaper, to play on the safe side, announce
that both Reggie Boyd and George Bird were saved.) The
from Dreamland Pier the launch took off some frightene
waiters and the family of the pier's superintendent, Captai
Anderson. The police called to Atheer, the owner of the Shet
land pony concession. He refused to come aboard. He woul
stay with his ponies and his vision of the delight they ha
brought to children. The fire crept closer: the police raged a
Atheer, they waved imperatively, they ordered him aboard. Bu
Atheer turned away; he walked slowly off towards his ponie
stalls.

At the corner of Surf Avenue and Sheridan's Walk, temper
were as hot as the fire. Too late the roomers evicted from thei
boarding-houses had noticed that the flames had worked wes
They had left their homes with nothing except the clothes o
their backs; now they wrangled passionately with the firemer
demanding to be let through the lines to save their valuable
Money, cash money, their rent money for the rest of the season

couldn't these blockheads understand? Moreover, on the east and west side of Sheridan's Walk the houses were getting impartially drenched, for above them the employees of the Giant Roller Coaster were fighting to keep their newly installed railroad ties from catching fire, and the water from their hoses flooded down. The firemen, hard pressed by the insistent boarders, were in turn infuriated by the firefighting activity above them: they were convinced that it was precisely here that the high-pressure mains must have been tapped; these were the villains. First curses, then bricks flew through the air; they even turned their hoses on each other. But the men on the roller coaster contended they were drawing their water from the ocean via the big private fire engine owned by Charles Feltman, whose restaurant was down by the shore.

Suddenly, to the east, there arose a great shout from the crowd packed densely in the side streets and in the doorways and along the front of the buildings on the north side of Surf Avenue. Bursting out of the furnace that was Dreamland, straight through the entrance of Creation, came a thing calculated to tingle the scalp and chill the bone's marrow. It paused for a moment, ringed with flame. It screamed. Then it moved into the street toward the crowd, and the crowd scattered, aghast. It was a lion, a three-year-old, black-maned Nubian lion called Black Prince. His mane was a collar of fire; his flanks and his feet were torn and bleeding. He screamed again, piteously. To the four or five animal trainers in the crowd it was clear that Black Prince was hurt and wanted only to crawl away to a place where he could be alone and lick his wounds; but all others in the crowd were scared white. Cops moved in from either side of the lion, in gingerly fashion, guns drawn. Bullets began to whine through the streets. The trainers moved forward too. Black Prince, roaring once more in anguish, sprang across the street and into the entrance of the Rocky

Road to Dublin. This was an indoor scenic railway housed in
turreted, stuccoed eyesore alleged to be a representation o
Blarney Castle. (A principal owner was a Brooklyn politiciar
James Byrne, who was later to be borough president of Brook
lyn). As Black Prince streaked for the entrance, two men were
all unaware, coming out. One was Thomas Brophy, a fir
marshal, who had been attempting to telephone from a boot
in the lobby. What he saw sent him diving back into the tele
phone booth, where he broke his own personal record for sayin
a fast Hail Mary. The other was an elderly man, a Civil Wa
veteran named William Hyde, who was a professional weigh
guesser. He had just stashed his scales in, as he thought, a saf
place when he found himself faced with a lion while bullet
buzzed about his ears. Forgetting his age, Hyde sprinted to
telephone pole and shinned up. He was not alone. Every pol
on the north side of Surf Avenue was crowded. People ha
darted into the restaurants to either side of the Rocky Road t
Dublin and, still daunted, had permitted their impetus to carr
them up to the second floors, to the roofs. Here many leane
over, looking down, awaiting developments.

The trainers knew Black Prince at first hand. He had cut
deep gash on Harry Smith's nose only the Sunday before, an
scratched two long irregular furrows on Gardo Revero's scalp
These two now led the way into the Rocky Road to Dublin o
his trail. Behind them came another trainer, Doc Hastings
Ferrari; Bonavita; and two policemen, Patrolmen John Noona
and Henry Coots. The trainers had only whips and revolver
loaded with blank cartridges.

It was almost pitch dark inside the Rocky Road. The onl
lights were small naked bulbs set at intervals along the wall
Smith could make out Black Prince's bloody footprints and h
could hear the great cat's roars from somewhere ahead of him
the trainers kept firing their blanks to keep him on the move

Ie never stopped roaring, and his voice resounded terrifyingly
1 the gloomy darkness. The men climbed up the incline of the
ailway. To Smith, it seemed like climbing a steeple. Up and
p they went. Presently they could make out a dark shape
even or eight feet directly in front of them. It was Black
'rince. He was switching his tail from side to side and the noise
e made shook the gimcrack building. Smith fired his revolver
nd ran ahead to turn him just as he reached the second incline.
'he lion turned, saw his tormentor, and jumped right at him.
mith was hit and went down and into the space between the
racks and dropped his gun. By the time he had scrambled to
is feet, Black Prince was climbing again and the seven men
oiled after him. It seemed to Smith that they climbed for an
our. At length he felt a cool sweep of fresh air and realized
hey were out in the open, on top of the building. Black Prince
vas standing, outlined against the sky, a rumble in his throat,
vounded, but every inch a monarch. From the roofs to either
ide of the Rocky Road people scattered in a panic. Down in
he street another roar went up: the crowd had sighted the
on: they would witness the regal execution. The trainers kept
p a continuous fire of blank cartridges which served at least
o show them where Black Prince was standing. He made a
plendid target. Ferrari gave the cops the order to fire. They
red. They emptied their belts, shooting at the lion. He fell, but
till he twitched. Coots leaned over the parapet and shouted
own for an axe; someone tossed him one. He split the lion's
kull. The seven men crept closer and examined their prey.
'hey found twenty-four bullets in his head alone. "It had to be
one," thought Harry Smith. "And he was a fine lion, too. The
nest Nubian I ever saw." But he wondered whether it might
ot have been possible to catch him, even at the last minute to
atch him and save him and take him away to Fox's Livery
table, along with the six lionesses.

Below in the street the crowd roared. Black Prince's body was dragged back down the incline and into the street. Some one found a pair of pliers. His teeth were swiftly snatched for souvenirs.

Down on the ocean sands the only other animal to escape the arena was found and slain. She was a leopardess, singed and cringing, and she was dispatched by a bullet from Patrolman John Dooley's police special.

From his post, Patrolman Ehlers inspected the scene before him. "3.25," he wrote; "fire reaches main entrance and Stuben bord's restaurant." He closed his note book and looked up. At his elbow was Inspector Robert Emmet Dooley. "What the hell are you doing with that note book?" asked the inspector. "The fire," Ehlers answered stoutly, "is on my post, and I am making out a report." Dooley stared at him, speechless. "As per the instruction manual," said Ehlers, stolidly. "Well, cut it out," Dooley ordered. "Cut it out!" He shook his head and walked on. Ehlers, hurt, put his note book in his pocket.

By this time, the buildings to either side of Dreamland were catching; the task of the firemen was one of containment; and since the water pressure had not improved, they were losing. Steubenbord's restaurant (valued at $75,000) burned. Abe Lentz's dancing pavilion and hotel ($90,000) burned. Taunton's bathing pavilion ($50,000) burned. Johnson's carrousel and pavilion ($75,000) burned. The Whirlwind Ride ($75,000) burned. L. A. Thompson's Oriental Scenic Railway ($95,000) and his Pike's Peak Railway ($75,000) each caught fire, flamed up, shuddered, and at length collapsed. One hotel after another burned: Stratton's ($60,000), Jolly's ($50,000), and then Julius Frosin's ($50,000). Men came to carry Frosin from his sick bed. He was in a state of collapse. He forgot to tell his rescuers that he had several hundred dollars in cash, tucked away in his bureau drawer, along with two big diamond rings; these, and his hotel, were all he had in the world. On their way out, the men carrying him did think to save his cash register (still empty); it seemed to them a valuable item; they took it for safe keeping to the West Eighth Street police station; the floor of the precinct house was littered with typewriters and cash registers. To the east, Balmer's (formerly Vanderveer's) Bathing Pavilion, a Coney landmark for more than a quarter century, caught fire, blazed, and relapsed into ashes. It had netted $80,000 a year. Only the year before, Balmer, before he died, had rejected an offer of $600,000 for its purchase. There were forty thousand bathing suits in the pavilion, of which fifteen thousand were brand-new. Mournfully, Balmer's widow told reporters that she had insured the baths for only $67,000. Her net loss was $150,000.

When Balmer's Baths started burning, the end was in sight for all the shacks and cabins and rooming-houses that lined the New Iron Pier Walk. High above that walk stood the Observation Tower. It had been brought to Coney from the Phila-

First the Dreamland Tower (left) and then the Observation Tower flared up to light the whole sky, in Coney's greatest spectacular. COURTESY THE FRANCIS K. MOORE COLLECTION

delphia Centennial, in 1877; this was the tower from whic
for nearly an entire season, a trio of sharpies had made a killin
by spying through binoculars the colors of the winning horse a
the nearby Brighton Beach oval and thereafter signalling t
confederates so that they might place winning wagers with th
unwitting bookies. The tower's elevators had been shut dow
however, for years; ever since its acquisition by George Tilyo
its chief function had been to carry a great sign advertisin
Steeplechase Park. This sign now caught fire from the intens
heat. Once again every eye bugged at the sight of a might
flaming torch; once again the sky glared fiercely; once aga
great leaping orange daggers stabbed dizzily upward. But th
spectacle lasted only for a few minutes: like the Dreamlan
tower, this, too, collapsed and fell inward on its base.

At the junction of West Fifth Street and Surf Avenue the fi
was halted, chiefly by the offshore breeze. The Galveston Floo
building, where there was an exhibition of deep-sea divin
El Dorado, a triple-decked carrousel, and Chambers' all-nigh
drug store still stood, though scorched, at four o'clock; by fiv
the painted horses on El Dorado's carrousel were so blistere
and blackened as to seem to be so many Persian lambs, b
they were still unburned. The fire was contained between We
Fifth and West Tenth Streets. More than four hundred fireme
had fought the nightmare blaze; now, company by compan
they repaired to a restaurant on the north side of Surf Avenu
run by the Segall brothers, for mugs of steaming hot coffe
Here they commiserated with each other and roundly curse
the high-pressure pumping system (at six a.m. the pressure ha
climbed to sixty pounds; by six-thirty it would be at o
hundred and forty pounds). Company by company they bega
to head back to their stations.

The sun came up. It promised, ironically, to be a fine da
the sort of day that would have beckoned from Coney to at lea

two hundred thousand pleasure-seekers; but the sun stared down instead, through a great pall of smoke, on a scene of devastation, on a yawning vacancy. A handful of brick ovens along the south side of Surf Avenue told of former hotels; one or two gaunt, twisted arches were left of the bridge that had spanned the Dreamland lagoon; all else was leveled. In the lagoon, where the water had steamed and boiled, there floated the corpse of the performing seal. Dreamland's steel pier and the Iron Pier were almost entirely reduced to smoldering piles. Almost, but not quite entirely: the fire had burned itself out within fifteen feet of William Atheer's Shetland pony stalls; the ponies and their owner were safe.

And now the Islanders wearily got to their feet. Their economy had suffered a grievous blow: more than $5,200,000 worth of property had been wiped out, to which loss had to be added the incalculable flood of dollars that had been destined for their tills. More than two thousand, five hundred of them had lost their jobs, sixteen hundred wiped off Dreamland's pay sheet alone. In less than five hours their dream of Coney's most successful season ever had gone glimmering. They sighed and stretched and squared their shoulders and went to work.

Mrs. Lena Schwartz went back to her boarding-house on the west side of Sheridan's Walk. It was drenched and blistered but still standing. She climbed to her room and went straight to her bed and burrowed under her pillow. The wallet with the $110 was gone.

Frances Mensch, the twenty-year-old daughter of a family that owned several of these rooming houses, found her room water-soaked. A thief had stolen a large ostrich feather from one of her hats, she noted bitterly, but had left the hat behind.

Conrad Steubenbord found some chairs and tables somewhere; he set them out amidst the ashes of his restaurant; he strung some electric lights on poles; he broached a keg of beer.

He was open and ready to do business. Here came his first customer, Fred Thompson of Luna Park, and paid him ten dollars for a glass of beer.

Colonel Ferrari still had his ponies, the lionesses, four leopards. He spread some sawdust; he rigged a tent. Bamboola approached him, hangdog. Ferrari hadn't seen his wild man since the time, hours before, when he had entrusted Marguerite, his lion cub, to him. Mournfully Bamboola now reported. "Two souses," he said, "came along in an automobile and punched me in the jaw and took your lion cub away from me. I haven't seen it since." The police were notified; there was a flurry of excitement; but it was short-lived: Marguerite was found where she had been left by the two souses, fenced in behind some overturned chairs in Bristol's Restaurant, across from Luna Park.

The two young McCullough brothers, having gobbled down some oatmeal, were at last permitted to run loose. They raced down Surf Avenue for a look at the smoking ruins and came on their father, standing across from the spot where his principal shooting gallery had been. He was tugging at his black mustache and mentally adding up his losses and wondering how much of his machine shop in the rear might have been saved. (It would prove to be a total loss.) The two boys lingered for a moment, teetering from one foot to the other, wanting to express their sympathy, but at the same time anxious to see if they could find the body of the dead lion they had heard about. Their father was preoccupied. They went on.

Black Prince's carcass was already inside a small tent on the south side of Surf Avenue, on exhibition at ten cents a peek. A slack-wire artist named Melvin Howard, temporarily down on his luck, had gotten permission to skin and stuff the lion and exploit him for whatever he could get. A barker was working outside the tent; both the barker and the sign proclaimed that the dead animal within was Sultan. But Sultan had died in the animal arena; it was definitely Black Prince whose stuffed carcass was on display. The mild fraud had been considered necessary when it was learned that most of the newspaper stories had identified the lion in the streets as Sultan; when the morbid should start coming, in an hour or two, it was Sultan they would demand to see. Frank Wilstach, Dreamland's press agent, had his story all worked out. He proposed to say that Black Prince had been sick, hardly able to climb to his feet. "The fact is," he would say, "the poor brute had never seemed himself since he bit that Spaniard a few days ago. [The Spaniard was Revero, whom Black Prince had scratched.] I don't know how it was, but it didn't seem to agree with him, and it was just like Oliver Goldsmith's mad dog, 'The dog it was that died.' We hardly expected Black Prince to live through Friday night anyhow, and so he had no chance of escaping." Wilstach was, all things considered, in a fairly good humor. For many years he had been at work on a manuscript of inestimable value to a press agent, a dictionary of similes; it had been in his desk in Dreamland's publicity office. His assistant had broken into the desk and plucked it forth; in Wilstach's opinion, there was no more precious brand snatched from the burning.

In Manhattan, a civic-minded gentleman sat down to his breakfast and his *New York Times*. Almost at once he jumped again to his feet, aghast. This was John D. Lindsay, president of the New York Society for the Prevention of Cruelty to Children, and his eye had just fallen on a headline announcing that all the incubator babies had perished in the fire. Only after several telephone calls was he somewhat reassured. He satisfied himself that the babies had been temporarily lodged in safety at the home of a Coney Island physician and had been transported to the Infant Asylum at Amsterdam Avenue and Sixty-First Street only an hour or so ago. But he was still in a temper as he dashed off a letter to the editor of the *Times*. "I trust," he wrote, "that unfortunate infants will not again be permitted to be exhibited under similar gruesome conditions."

That the *Times* had erred was pardonable; its last edition was normally scheduled to close at about two a.m.; on this occasion they held their forms open until after three so that they might carry a few paragraphs on the fire, and an unverified rumor crept in among the otherwise unexceptionable facts reported. New York's afternoon papers, with ample time to be more scrupulous, were crammed with daft tales strung under giddy headlines; the *Evening World*, for example, proclaimed in its noon edition that one hundred and forty-six animals had perished in the flames, and the number had risen to one hundred and fifty in the city edition; by the end of the afternoon and the "latest extra," some degree of responsibility had been asserted, and the count was down to "nearly one hundred" which, if fifty-five can be said to be nearly one

Well, anyway, people still sing "Meet Me Tonight in Dreamland."

PHOTO BY EDWARD A. WATERMAN

undred, was not too wide of the mark. The effect of these
tories on the public was to make everyone want to go out to
Coney. All day Saturday and Sunday the crowds poured onto
he Island. They came by every possible means. To be sure, the
ron Pier had been gutted but George Tilyou, with his cus-
omary perspicacity, closed a deal first thing Saturday morning
with the Iron Steamboat Company whereby for $30,000 the
steamboats from Manhattan were permitted to dock at his Steeplechase pier. Every boat had a full load. So anxious, indeed,
were New Yorkers to come out to the island that the rubberneck
wagons in Longacre Square, which customarily went no further
south than Chinatown, were pressed into service for the long
haul to Coney. The chauffeurs, presented with this golden opportunity, went on strike for a raise from $21 to $25 a week.
The owners started to hold out but caved in when the shills
threatened to demand a raise from $1.50 to $1.75 a day for
just sitting in the wagons.

At Coney, the Islanders were ready with their makeshifts. All
day Sunday one enterprising pitchman did well selling the
rusty head of the hatchet with which "Captain Jack Bonavita
ran from cage to cage, driving this here hatchet through the
skulls of lions and tigers to end their suffering;" the pitchman
had some difficulty replenishing his stock of this item, properly
rusted, but for the evening trade he was back in business. Another man sold dogs. "The only dog saved from the fire—a little
Saint Bernard puppy, gents, bred by one of the wealthiest stock-
holders of Dreamland! Registered! Going for only five dollars!
Only this man's great financial losses have prompted him to let
this valuable animal go for a pitiful five dollars!" It was true
that there had been a Saint Bernard in Dreamland; it was true
that he had been saved. He was the property of Dr. Fischel, he
had been in the incubator building, and he had been rescued
by Sergeant Klinck shortly after the babies had been removed.

But at $5 the dog for sale did not move very fast. He sold fairly well at $4; toward the end of the day he sold very well indeed at $1 when the barker threw in a blue ribbon and his personal word of honor as to the puppy's registration. A third man did an excellent business with pictures of Little Hip, guaranteed to be souvenirs of the fire. In proof, they were slightly charred. A *Sun* reporter, idly investigating, found a small boy, hidden behind a packing-case, engaged in charring each picture with a candle.

Sam Gumpertz, ever the showman, had rigged a tent for "A Congress of Freaks." The Fat Lady, the Tattooed Wonder, the Biggest Giant in History, Zip, the What-Is-It—these were arrayed, not on their former velvet daises, but anyhow, on upended boxes; but they were there, and the crowds paid to see them and to put to them questions about their experiences during the spectacular conflagration.

The Coney folk put on a brave show but they were fiddling long after Rome had burned. The showmen had heart, but not the businessmen. One of the directors of Dreamland came out and eyed the ruins sourly. "We sought to appeal to a highly developed sense of the artistic," he intoned, reflecting on his losses, "but it did not take us long to discover that Coney Island was scarcely the place for that sort of thing. Architectural and decorative beauty were virtually lost upon the great majority of visitors, with the result that from year to year Dreamland was popularized, that is to say, the original design abandoned." Coming from a man who, as showman, had not been successful enough to draw the crowds to his bailiwick, this comment was redolent of sour grapes, but it was left to Senator Reynolds to give Dreamland's future the kiss of death. "This looks like a fine chance," said he, "for the city to increase its park space and water front."

To the knowing, no further comment was necessary. There

would be, they recognized, no attempt to rebuild. Dreamland's
board of directors would meet, but only for the purpose of
arranging to extricate their investments. (In this effort they
would succeed: the city was to pay $1,800,000 for Dreamland's
real estate.) Gone in smoke was the dream to make of Coney
the nation's most brilliantly sparkling seaside resort. When the
bucket of pitch toppled over in Hell Gate, an era closed. In
closing it down, Coney put on its most spectacular pageant: by
all odds the costliest, it employed a cast of thousands, it was
witnessed by an audience of hundreds of thousands, and, considered simply as fireworks, it had been unrivaled. As predicted, the season had been a smashing success. But it was over
before it had begun. Timing, in show business, is everything;
and on this occasion, as to timing, somebody had goofed.

An era had closed. Never again would the world of fashion
come to Coney except in small groups and those, indeed,
slumming. The great restaurants would close their doors. The
great amusement parks would become parking lots or city
parks. The crowds would change. Where once champagne was
standard tipple, instead it would be orange pop. Lobster
would give place to the hot dog.

An era had closed; a new era was about to begin; a new king
would be crowned. He would bear not a sceptre but a nickel
five-cent bit; he would travel not in a regal tally-ho but in the
subway.

The pall of smoke hung heavy over the Island.

DRAWING BY STEPHEN VOORHEES. COURTESY THE *Brooklyn Daily Eagle*

~*Illustrious*~

THERE was in 1867 a youth who drove a pie-wagon over the rutted country lanes south of Brooklyn, and at first glance this pieman seemed favored by fortune above all other piemen. His pies were excellent, their crusts soft and flaky; his clients, drawn from amongst the inns and lager-beer saloons that lined the beach of Coney Island, were many and daily growing in number. And yet this young pieman was dissatisfied. Along with his pies, everywhere he went he took with him a perplexing problem. Pies, his clients had made clear to him, were not enough. They wanted as well sandwiches, they had told him, and preferably hot sandwiches. But sandwiches meant loaves of bread and ham and cheeses and knives and nuisance, and as for hot sandwiches, how was he to manage, in a small wagon on a country road? Other piemen would have dismissed the problem and gone calling on a girl. This pieman was, however, made of sterner stuff. He had conceived an epochal idea, and he took it to the wheelwright who had built his pie-wagon.

The wheelwright listened. There were, he said, no technical difficulties involved. A tin-lined chest could be built to keep rolls fresh and a small charcoal stove could be rigged inside the

agon to boil sausages. What the wheelwright wanted to know
vas: What was so good about a sausage sandwich? The pieman
iffidently replied that he didn't know, he had just thought it
night be a good thing to try. Easy. Handy. Different, somehow.
Setter, maybe, than a ham sandwich or a cheese sandwich.
And so long as there was no problem about rigging the stove—

The wheelwright shrugged and installed the stove. Having
done so, and having lighted the charcoal for a test run, he asked
or a sample of the odd sandwich the pieman had suggested.
Apprehensively, the pieman set a kettle on to boil and readied
his sausages and rolls.

And now attend, for an historic moment is at hand. It is a
moment comparable to that when an apple plunked on the
pate of Isaac Newton, or to that when stout Cortez stood
silent, upon a peak in Darien. At this moment, astrologists in-
form us, Venus was in Taurus, a circumstance betokening
wondrous delight for all mankind; and, since Taurus is the Bull,
it was suggested that the delight would have something to do
with beef and that the epiphany of this prodigy would be at-
tended down through the years with a monstrous deal of fanci-
ul legend. Whatever the prodigy, the presence of Venus, of
course, insured that all would love it.

There was no scribe present on this momentous occasion.
But we are permitted to hazard a reconstruction of the scene.
When the sausages had been boiled and plucked from the
kettle, when they were, each of them, nestling within their rolls,
when the wheelwright had taken his first bite—

"Hey!"

"You mean . . . ?"

"This is all right!"

"Maybe a bit of mustard?"

"Good idea! A lot of mustard!"

"How about some sauerkraut?"

"Mmmm—optional. But have a kettle handy."

The pieman's voice trembled. "Then you think . . . ?"

"Feltman," said the wheelwright, "you have definitely g
something here."

The pieman, and let us all bow our heads to reverence hi
for a moment, was Charles Feltman. The wheelwright is know
to history only as Donovan; his first name has been lost, som
where along the dusty corridors of time. But surely he has gor
to his reward. Surely, on some nether cloud of eternal bliss l
is now couched in comfort, pridefully reflecting on the cruci
part he played in the discovery of the Coney Island red ho
Surely it is enough for him to know that he has been remem
bered. He will not care that his given name has been forgotte
Nor, as he daily waves aside his celestially allotted share
manna, choosing instead his daily hot dog, will he begrudg
Charles Feltman's greater fame.

Charles Lamb, in his celebrated "Dissertation Upon Roa
Pig," set it down as his carefully considered judgment that, "C
all the delicacies in the whole *mundus edibilis*, I will maintai
[roast pig] to be the most delicate—*princeps obsoniorum*," b
which he intended that we should believe crackling to be th
tastiest tidbit in the world. Alas! poor Charles Lamb! He die
in 1834: he never had a chance to taste a hot dog.

The name, of course, came later. But the prodigy itself mad
its first appearance in 1867. We are not concerned with th
various frightful monstrosities that have since been perpetrate
by unprincipled descendants of the Borgias. Men lost to sham
have skewered the dog and called it frank-kabob; they hav
stuffed it with spaghetti and called it frank-aroni; they hav
stifled it in chili sauce and called it a chihuahua; they hav
strangled it with fried onions and called it a poodle; in Cal
fornia (naturally) they have bloated it to twelve inches i
length and called it a Superfrank: there seems no limit to the

ightful malpractices. Sensibility demands that all these be re-
cted with a shudder. We are concerned only with the noble,
e unimpeached hot dog—a succulent, fragrant frankfurter,
rnished with mustard and clasped tenderly by an enfolding
ilk roll (sauerkraut optional)—an irresistible temptation to the
petite—today an institution dear to the palate, the digestive
chitecture, and the heart of every American—gobbled down
the rate of eight billion a year—firm cornerstone of a $500,-
0,000 industry—the pride of Coney Island. The place where
homas Jefferson wrote the Declaration of Independence is
own and it has been suitably memorialized. (It is not in-
ppropriate that for some years the site should have been
cupied by a hot dog stand.) But, incredibly, the hallowed
ot on which man took his first delicious bite of a hot dog—it
at the corner of East New York and Howard Avenues, in
rooklyn—is ignored. And Clio weeps.

When the hot dog first loomed on the horizon, the clam was
ng on Coney. Clams were easily raked up from the shores of

hen the Clam was still king on Coney. *Puck, 1878.* N. Y. PUBLIC LIBRARY

Sheepshead Bay, even from the ocean beach; they were fresh
they were plentiful, they were yummy. And they were serve
everywhere, the staple delicacy. Lucy Vanderveer offere
grilled clams, sleek with butter, for a penny apiece; Pete
Tilyou promised a bowl of his own special clam chowder fre
to each who rented, for twenty-five cents, a bathing-suit at h
Surf House; clambakes and clam roasts were at the heart o
every pic-nic and outing. Even later, when those who came t
Coney bared great naked wads of banknotes, and grew cor
tentious over dinner checks at the Manhattan Beach or Ville
pigue's or the Shelburne or Ravenhall's, even when the chan
pagne on draft at the Brighton Beach had soared from te
to fifteen cents a glass, the clam's crown was secure.

But its days were numbered. The succulent sausage was on i
way. By 1871 Feltman had subleased a tiny plot of ground o
one of the huge Coney Island shore lots: in his first season h
counted precisely 3,684 patrons, every one of them, after tas
ing, a true believer in, nay, an apostle for the hot dog. In th
next eight years Feltman was to desert his subleased shant
lease his own shore lot, build the first in an expanding series o
restaurants and beer gardens, and average eighty thousan
patrons a year, always in part thanks to the hot dog; by 188
a real estate dealer would advertise that there were availabl
on Coney more than a dozen choice locations for sausag
stands. The hot dog had arrived.

And now, as is the case with every notable success, there wa
set in operation an old, old process. When a man contrives
better mouse-trap or composes a livelier song or discovers
bigger continent or flies to a farther star, there will inevitabl
be those who, on the one hand, claim they got there first an
those who, on the other hand, sniff and maintain it was wrong
dangerous, and probably subversive to have gotten there at al

The hot dog's first opposition sprang up on Coney itself. Th ealous whisper went about: These sausages are made of dog-meat. John Y. McKane, making a great show of self-righteous-ness, protested, "Nobody knows what is inside these sausages." He plastered an excise tax of $200 on every sausage stand, a bountiful source of income, for there were even more sausage stands on Coney, by 1887, than there were houses of prostitu-tion, and almost as many as there were saloons. "We cannot dictate to a man what he must sell," said the Chief, sucking his teeth reflectively and mentally totting up his cash receipts, "but we can make it hard for him to carry on his business."

The scurrilous rumors spread. Politicians in Brooklyn made a great noise, alleging that they had found a rendering plant making sausages for the Coney Island trade out of dead horses, conjuring up a fictitious malefactor they called Jack the Skinner who, they claimed, was paid five dollars for every scrofulous old nag he delivered, if only he would personally dispose of the hide and the hoofs.

Humorists poked barbs into the hot dog. Both *Judge* and *Puck* printed cartoons showing butchers feeding puppies into the hopper of a machine and grinding sausages out of the other end. Playgrounds competing with Coney delightedly took up the slander. In Schuetzen Park, at Union Hill, New Jersey, as early as 1890 one of the amusement attractions was a device into the maw of which live poodles were tossed and, after a hideous clashing of gears, out of the end of which emerged a long string of sausages. But the noble hot dog persevered in its popularity; serenely it proceeded toward greater triumphs.

Since the hot dog's traducers were successively confounded, it remained only for the coattail riders and the bandwagon jumpers to materialize, each pretending that it was he who had invented the hot dog, each striving scurvily to wrest from Coney its greatest glory. The first of these claim-jumpers was a man named Anton Ludwig Feuchtwanger, who is variously

By 1874, with the assistance of the hot dog, Feltman had been able to mushroom from a shanty to a pretentious Ocean Pavilion. COURTESY THE FRANCIS K. MOORE COLLECTION

credited with having operated a concession at the Chicago Columbian Exposition of 1893 and the St. Louis Louisiana Purchase Exposition of 1904. According to the canard, Feuchtwanger peddled white cotton gloves along with his hot frankfurters so that his customers might hold them to nibble in comfort; he switched, it is alleged, from gloves to rolls because so many of his clients insisted on grabbing off the gloves as souvenirs. It is a pawky tale, but if there is any truth in it it proves only that Chicago lags a quarter-century behind New York in latching onto a good idea, and what news is there in that?

The same myth-mongers would have it that Harry Stevens, founder of the catering firm, introduced the frankfurter-in-roll to the East around the turn of the century, during a baseball game at the Polo Grounds. This fabrication would be laughable if, at its core, it were not possible to sniff out a sinister plot to permit the New York Giants, rather than the Brooklyn Dodgers, to bask in reflected glory. Quite probably Stevens did vend enrolled frankfurters at the Polo Grounds around 1900;

but they had tickled the palates of Dodger fans at Washington Park as far back as 1888.

Finally, there is the matter of the pungent name, hot dog. Not enough that rascals had impugned the ambrosial innards of the dog, not enough that johnny-come-latelies had tried to snatch credit for invention of the illustrious tidbit; now auslanders, cloaking themselves with spurious scholarship, undertook to stake a claim to having coined the name. Tad Dorgan, a New York sports cartoonist, is said to have been present at the Polo Grounds on the chilly day when Harry Stevens first served hot frankfurters in rolls; because, so runs the story, he did not know how to spell "dachshund," he came up with "hot dog." Dorgan is one of those who had the knack of coining slang phrases; he is credited, correctly or not, with "Yes, we have

and by the 1920's, thanks to the shrewd administration of his two sons, Feltman's was as pleasant a restaurant as you could want. COURTESY CHARLES A. FELTMAN

no bananas," "Dumb Dora," "cake-eater," "dumbbell," and "Twenty-three, skidoo." But very definitely he did not originate "hot dog." Within a year of the time Feltman had first put frankfurter inside roll, those living in the German quarter of old New York were buying them regularly from a man who cooked them in a three-compartment kettle at a stand on the corner of Grand Street and the Bowery; thereabouts they were affection ately known as *hundewurst* or *hündschen,* that is, little dogs and already they were being spoken of as hot dogs at Coney Island.*

In his sprawling Ocean Pavilion, between Surf Avenue and the sea, Charles Feltman could afford to ignore both the tra ducers of the hot dog and those who prated of prior claims to its invention. Having made history, he was now content to make money. The ocean had obligingly increased the size of his shorefront lot and with every succeeding year he continued to improve his property until at length he could fairly claim to having the finest and most successful restaurant on the Island Indeed, it was more than a restaurant: it was an interminable series of dining rooms and al fresco beer gardens, a vast ball room for dancing, and a collection of amusement devices a well. Around 1880 he installed one of Charles Looff's charming

---

* Etymologists pay scant attention to somebody's say-so about the first use of a word or phrase. They pinpoint its first occurrence in print as the only trustworthy indication of its provenance. The respected *Dictionary of Ameri canisms* is generally regarded as the most authoritative text available. According to this source, the first reference in print to the hot dog appeared in a *Saturday Evening Post* story, published in April, 1909. Dorgan's syndicators, King Features, can find no Dorgan cartoon which includes the magic phrase earlier than 1915. But there is at least one example earlier than either of these: the *New York Sun,* on Sunday, August 12, 1906, ran a feature article on Coney Island in which the reporter described how Fred Thompson, co-owner of Luna Park, "began to design stage settings with one hand, while he balanced a hot dog sandwich with the other." Undoubtedly a diligent researcher will be able to turn up still earlier references in print to the hot dog, but it is good bet that when they are found they will be in a Coney Island context.

carrousels in the beer garden facing on Surf Avenue; this was the second carrousel on Coney (the first, for which the horses had also been carved by Looff, was on the grounds of Lucy Vanderveer's pavilion). Later his sons added a roller coaster, the Ziz, which ran along Tenth Street from Surf Avenue to the sea. And there were German bands and Tyrolean singers. But always it was the food that brought the custom. There was no more delightful place to eat than in Feltman's gardens, under low-swinging boughs of maple, surrounded by a prospect of lawns and neatly trimmed hedges. Fat, comfortable women in velvet bodices, men wearing white stockings and a feather in their hats knew that at Feltman's they would be served good solid fare at reasonable prices. They came to eat and they came to sing and they came to drink Bavarian beer. The hot dog was all but forgotten. Now it was thick planked steaks and the shore dinner and, while the racetracks were at their height, the more important trainers and jockeys and gamblers also became regulars at Feltman's, gathering at a big table built around a maple tree, where they sat in chairs marked with their names on brass plates and ate dishes specially prepared in their honor. Two hundred thousand patrons a year during the 1880's, three hundred and seventy thousand a year during the 1890's, nine hundred thousand a year in the first decade of this century, and, in the second decade, more than two million a year. The endless dining rooms were geared to serve eight thousand at a time, and Feltman's was justified in taking for its slogan, "Caterers to the Millions."

But the hot dog was not utterly ignored. Scattered about the Feltman premises were seven sizeable grills, and they were all kept busy. And in 1920, when extension of the subway put Coney Island within a nickel of all New York City's millions, these grills began to work overtime. In 1921, Feltman's served more than 3,500,000 customers; in 1922 more than 4,100,000; in

1923 more than 5,230,000—and of this staggering total th
majority bought the hot dog, for a dime apiece. There was nov
no question but that the ten-cent hot dog was king. But alread
a palace revolution was brewing.

In the summer of 1915 a young man named Nathan Hand
werker took a Sunday off from his job as manager of a modes
restaurant in downtown Manhattan and went for a stroll o.
Coney Island. Outside Feltman's he paused. There was a help
wanted sign in the window. Ten minutes later Nathan wa
slicing hot-dog rolls for a living. Within a year, thanks to th
fatherly Feltman's practice of permitting employees to eat ho
dogs free, Nathan had saved $300, enough to rent the groun
floor of a building near the corner of Surf and Stillwell Avenue
He knocked out the weather-worn clapboard sidings and in
stalled counters; above them he nailed signs that shrieked lik
fire-engine sirens; the five-cent hot dog had been born.

It was almost stillborn. Nathan had anticipated the nicke
empire by two or three years. He nearly went broke. Even whe:
he offered root beer on the house, even when he threw in a fre
pickle with every hot dog, suspicious folk, loaded with dime:
ignored him to go on to Feltman's. Then came the subway an
the boardwalk.

Fortuitously, Nathan's stand had a strategic location, directl
between the brand-new subway terminal and the boardwall
Only the blind could debouch from the subway without bein
assailed by his garish billboard with its commanding pointe
finger and its exhortation, "Follow the Crowd to Nathan's."

But what crowd? At first, even those who had no dimes bu
only nickels in their pockets were mistrustful of Nathan's five
cent red hots; they were persuaded that anything so chea
must be inferior, maybe even dangerous. And so they passe
on, as before, and headed for Feltman's. Nathan decided tha
the time had come for Coney Island tactics. To gather a tip c

stomers, he hired a dozen or so of Coney's derelicts as shills, eeding them full of free frankfurters, lining them up in front of is counters to prove how popular were his dogs. But the crowd aw only bums, and hastily passed by on the other side of the reet. Nathan accepted the challenge. From a friend in the neatrical costume business he borrowed ten white jackets, ten airs of white trousers, and ten stethoscopes. In these he clad en fresh-shaven bums of lofty mien. Just as the first Sunday norning rush-hour throngs began to pour from the subway erminal, he disposed his character actors in front of his counter nd bade them start to gobble. Above them was a newly painted ign: "If doctors eat our hot dogs, you know they're good!" As allyhoo, it could not be faulted. From that day to this there as been a police problem, trying to clear the broad sidewalk n front of Nathan's.

Feltman's stood proudly pat. More splendid chefs were ummoned, more glamorous entertainments were introduced, nd, during the boom years just before the 1929 crash, affairs vere better than ever before. But the depression—and the in- istent pressure of the new nickel empire—ate away at the rand old restaurant's grosses. Indeed, it was coming clear by he 1930's that Coney's character had changed so radically as to reclude such a leisurely and ample restaurant as Feltman's had een. The business was sold in 1946; the new owners went ankrupt; in 1954 the restaurant disappeared forever, going lown under a great wave of concessions, penny arcades, ball ;ames, rides, and cheap-jack amusements.

But Nathan's was splendidly gaited for Coney's new era. Iere, surely, is the world's biggest small business man. Across iis hot dog counter, a scant twenty feet long, there are passed '5,000 frankfurters every summer weekend; once on Decora- ion Day, 1954, 55,000 hot dogs were sold in a single day. So nsistent is his clientele that Nathan's must stay open the year

At first, Nathan ignored the hot dog in his store-front signs, but not f
long. Here, he stands in back of the malted milk sign. COURTESY NATHAN
FAMOUS

round. Indeed, on the night of the great blizzard of 1947, whe
twenty-five inches of snow fell, Nathan himself, who no longe
surprises easily on any matter connected with hot dogs, wa
staggered to discover that he was obliged to keep open unt
long past midnight, to serve indomitable addicts 1,800 hot dog
Nathan's one hundred millionth hot dog was cooked and serve
with appropriate ceremony on July 6, 1955. His annual gro:
has now topped six million hot dogs, and there is no reason t
believe that it will not mount annually higher.

"From a Hot Dog," runs Nathan's most recent slogan, "to
National Habit." He lighted his torch from Feltman's candl
he holds it proudly high. His incredible hot dog stand ha
survived the Coney Island era dominated by the nickel empire
when subway fares rose to a dime, so did Nathan's hot do
today subway fares are fifteen cents, and Nathan's unflagging
popular dogs have kept pace. No one today is touchier on th
subject of the hot dog's quality, no one more dedicated to th

And so it goes, on every pleasant day from March through October. Today, of course, Nathan knows that the hot dog is the come-on.

proposition that there exists no more sublime delicacy. He has himself eaten at least one hot dog a day for the last thirty-nine years. Someone told him that President Eisenhower had remarked that there were many people eating caviar and champagne who would be better off on a diet of hot dogs and beer. Nathan Handwerker nodded. "And," he said, "I'll gladly wrassle anyone who's been living on caviar and champagne for thirty-nine years."

But still, in this enlightened modern day, the hot dog has its denigrators. Its adherents have learned that, if fifteen cents is the price of the best available dog, eternal vigilance is the price that must be paid to keep its good name unsullied. Not long ago, in the course of a debate in the Senate of the State of New York, on a bill of no importance, the minority leader declared, in a thoughtless moment, "This bill is as old and wrinkled as a warmed-over Coney Island frankfurter." The Senator who had the honor to represent, in that body, the great American play-

ground, was aghast. He turned pale, his hand trembled. For
moment, indeed, he could not credit his ears. Clutching at h
desk for support, he rose to his feet and demanded recognitio

"Mr. President," he said, his voice choked with emotion, '
rise to a point of high personal privilege. I cannot allow to pa
uncontested such an ignoble and unveracious slur on America
culinary ambassador to the world."

"I submit, Mr. President," he went on, in part, "that ther
exists no such entity as an old, a wrinkled, or a warmed-ov
Coney Island frankfurter. Coney Island frankfurters—we wh
know and love them call them [and here his listeners could tel
from his respectful and stately delivery, that he was usin
capital letters] Hot Dogs—are too eagerly consumed by a grate
ful public ever to have the chance to become even slightly coo
let alone cold enough to warm over.

"When, in earlier times, the recently deceased King of Eng
land and his Queen came to these United States to visit an
to observe our American customs and institutions, and whe
they were entertained by the President of these United State
what dish did he serve them, as the symbol and pinnacle o
American culinary art? The Hot Dog.*

"When, during the war, our young manhood was scattere
over the jungles and deserts of the earth, what dish did the
yearn for most, try hardest to create in a strange environment
The Hot Dog.

"When Rita Hayworth returned to this great country, afte
having lived in the pampered lap of oriental luxury abroad
what was the first thing she asked for, as her foot touche
American soil. A Hot Dog.

---

* Historians of the dog incline to agree that this encounter, King vis-à-v
Hot Dog, was the Coney Island red hot's proudest moment. The *New Yor
Times* hurled a headline across three columns, in type one-half inch high:
KING EATS HOT DOGS AT PICNIC
It should be noted that the King, having eaten one, came back for more.

"When an American wants to exclaim in enthusiasm, what xpression does he use? 'Hot Dog!'

"Other lands may have the dishes that represent them—their heasants under glass, their expensive delicacies intended only or the wealthy and powerful. We Americans express our demo-ratic genius in our choice of food as well as in our political astitutions. Our favored dish, relished alike by rich and poor, aale and female, ancient dodderer and diapered toddler, lamorous celebrity and obscure, humble citizen, is the Hot)og.

"And what is the relation of Coney Island to the Hot Dog? he same as the relation of the artist to his masterpiece, the armer to his prize crop, the fond and doting parent to his child. :oney Island *is* the Hot Dog, Mr. President, and the Hot Dog Coney Island!"

A pallid effort, it may be argued, too earthbound ever to rank rith the address by Patrick Henry to the Virginia House of urgesses, or Cicero's oration against Catiline before the enate of Rome, but it was on the right track. In any case, the enator was able to drive home his argument with a splendid xample. The entire Senate knocked off and, during a recess, nacked sumptuously off some of Nathan's Famous Hot Dogs.

Harper's Weekly, 1881. N. Y. PUBLIC LIBRARY

~Prodigious~

AFTER 1920, Coney Island changed from a resort that delighte
the eye to one that assaulted the ear. As soon as custome
could be numbered, on a pleasant day, by the million, a ca
culating glint showed in the eye of every carnival man in th
country and presently, on the slender sliver of land just bac
from the beach, there was jammed the greatest concentration c
small business enterprises on earth, with the owner of eac
enthusiastically engaged in a savage, ceaseless, and strider
competition with every other. Since the time-honored tools c
such a competitive effort were the ballyhoo and the barker, th
effect on the customer was staggering. Indeed, the sum total c
cacophonic blare created for Coney its own free ballyho
where so many were so aggressively vying for each pleasur
seeker's nickel or dime, all profited from the crowds of curiou
attracted by the thousand-throated hullabaloo. The change di
not, however, come overnight. Even as far back as 1913, befor
the extension of the subway had dumped New York City
millions on the beach, the Lord Mayor of London had bee
brought down for a quick peek. That worthy was stupende

250   "There is nothing in the world like Coney Island," he said. "

ten Lord Mayor's shows, twenty Earl's Courts, and thirty
rightons, all rolled into one." But when he was there, Coney
as still relatively placid. The decibel count was still on the
ax.

There is no accurate census of the number of attractions that
ere spread over Coney like a mulch, during the 1920's, but
rely there were more than one thousand. And each of them—
deshows, games and rides, animal acts, and spectacles—re-
uired for its health a barker who could inflame the cash cus-
mers with curiosity and thus keep steady the flow of nickels
d dimes. Additionally, as many showmen as could contrive
or afford it offered a ballyhoo,* the more ostentatious the
etter. It was one thing so long as the barkers depended only
n their lungs and perhaps a megaphone. But when public-
ddress systems, electrically amplified, came into general use,
was quite another thing. Moreover, besides the bewildering
rofusion of entertainments, there were the hundreds of restau-

---

* Ballyhoo is one of the most persistently misused words in the American
nguage, so misused, indeed, that its originally incorrect meaning has by now
perseded its correct meaning and successfully masquerades in many reputable
ctionaries. There is an impression that ballyhoo is what the barker utters.
rictly speaking, this is incorrect. Originally (and still today, with a few stub-
rn diehards) ballyhoo was the slice of free entertainment that might or
ight not be a preview of the show that lay beyond the admission gate, but
at was in any event designed to attract attention to that show. Ballyhoo
rformers usually shared the platform in front of the show with the barker.
he platform itself was usually raised. This was not so much to let a crowd
e the antics of the performers as to insure that they see the shillabers who,
the conclusion of the barker's spiel, would press forward and climb up the
eps to go through the motions of buying tickets, like so many judas-sheep.
1894, George Tilyou erected a Ferris wheel on Coney Island; in the change-
oth, as cashier, he installed his pretty blonde sister Kathryn; she was
wned in evening dress and resplendent with her mother's diamonds; two
efty citizens were engaged to flank her, as if they were her bodyguards. All
is ostentation was ballyhoo, although primitive in concept. Ideally, ballyhoo
akes noise, for noise attracts attention. Bagpipers make for good ballyhoo:
eir skirling can be heard for blocks.

rants, hot dog stands, ice cream parlors, and concessionair
selling everything from hot corn-on-the-cob to frozen custar
In self-defense, some of these merchants likewise resorted fir
to barkers and spielers, and later to electrically magnifi
talkers. There was even, for a few seasons, a group of dete
mined evangelists who set up their pitch in the Gospel-by-th
Sea Mission and, complete with a barker who was local
known as "The Bible Guy," vigorously hawked the Holy Bib.
There were other noises: the overhead clatter of roller coaste
and scenic railways, the crash of Dodgems, the crack of bulle
from the shooting galleries, and, underlying all else, the might
murmurous hum of a million people a day, laughing, cryin
shouting, squealing with delight; alive and having fun; as goo
a recipe for Bedlam as can be imagined. But above it all the
soared triumphant—hoarse symbol of the nickel empire—t
urgent, wheedling voice of the barker.

"Remember, remember, ladies and gentlemen, the cool of t
evening is the time to see the ostrich and mark his ma
pecu-li-ar-ities!"

As nearly as can be determined, the first barker to hit Con
arrived around 1880. He was a circus man who found hims
unexpectedly at liberty, one fine spring day, when his circ
lost the best two-out-of-three falls to a law suit. He and a gro
of the circus's sideshow freaks came down to the beach for
holiday. They had expected to find only bathhouses and be
stuben; they were mildly astonished to come upon a mitt jo
in West Brighton, with a gypsy fortune-teller busy at work. S
confirmed what their practiced eyes had told them: busine
was wonderful. At once the barker banged a fist into his pal
He and his freaks went into a huddle. Why not? They had th
canvas posters—they are called valentines, in the trade—a
besides, wouldn't it be simpler to stick to one place rather th
work a series of questionable one-night stands? The bark

arned that John Y. McKane would grant a license cheaply
nough; within a week he was strutting up and down on a plat-
orm in front of a tent complete with the outside flash, cracking
 buggy whip and intoning his ancient incantations. "It was,"
s he said later, "a go from the jump." His valentines luridly
ortrayed pits of jungle snakes, a Two-Headed Boy, a Wild Man
om Borneo shredding a tiger with his bare hands, a Fat
Voman, a Human Skeleton, and—that pe-cul-iar mon-ster-osity
-an ostrich. Crack! went his buggy-whip against the canvas.
That's the way she looks, gents. You'll find them on the inside
ıst as they are represented on the canvas! Step right up and
he gentlemanly usher will escort you to points of vantage!"

   That first Coney Island sideshow collapsed after one season,
ictim of a theft by a sharp competitor. But the pattern had
een set, and the word was beginning to get around in carnival
ircles. There were, no doubt about it, advantages to sitting on
 platform in one seaside place as opposed to scrambling about,
vorrying about train connections, losing sleep in ill-ventilated
ıppers, suffering rain-outs in barely civilized villages on the
ılains, having salaries swiped by company managers in the
tockies, being marooned in the Bible belt. Coney had crowds,
Joney was comfortable, Coney was cool, and Coney was close
o New York. But no matter how much a few errant performers
nay have enjoyed the primitive set-up, carnival owners, their
ninds moving in set grooves, continued to prefer the road. The
ideshow disappeared, briefly, from Coney.

   The barkers, however, having once been introduced, lingered.
'audeville entrepreneurs, engaged in feverish competition
long the Bowery and Surf Avenue, found them indispensable.
They crowed and crooned in front of Henderson's, the Imperial,
Wacke's Trocadero. They inflated the talents of some artists
vho, although far from the summits of their careers, were none-
heless causing respectful talk. Erich Weiss, who had already

changed his name to Harry Houdini, worked in a Coney Islar
sideshow as an escape artist in the early 1890's. Outside—

*"The greatest novelty mystery act in the world! How can yc
believe it, even when you see it happening before your eye
Just think this over, ladies and gentlemen, the time consume
in making the change from bag to trunk is one! two! only thre
seconds! We challenge the world to produce an attraction wii
greater Mystery, Speed, or Dexterity!"*

Inside, Houdini was working for $12 a week. Then one nig
he and his brother gave an exhibition of magic at a high schoc
his glance fell on a girl scarcely eighteen years old; he tumble
into love with her, and she with him. Within a week he ha
invited her to come to Coney Island with him. When he ke
her out too late, she wept; what would her parents think? "
you were my wife, they wouldn't dare punish you," he sai
fiercely, and guided her into a pawn-shop where, with h
money, he bought her a ring. They wondered how they mig
get married. She thought of a man with whom her father ha
once had some business—"John Y. McKane," she said, "I'm su
he can marry us!" She relates that the Pooh-Bah of Cone
Island in fact did marry them, after first urging them, "a coup
of foolish kids," to go home to their mothers, "or I'll be tempte
to have you both arrested." But, she said later, he relented an
himself presided over their nuptials. The date, as reported b
the bride, was June 22, 1894, which shows that even at the ou
set of his career Houdini was supremely capable of Myster
Speed, and Dexterity, for on that date McKane was secure
behind the bars of Sing Sing.

Barkers worked as well in front of such Bowery cabarets a
Inman's Casino and Perry's Glass Pavilion, but they were ke
busier using their canes to dislodge the urchins who used t
gather nightly in front of the slatted windows, hoping for a fre
peek at the girly shows within. And in 1895 Little Egy

rived, fairly fresh from her triumphs on the Midway of the
olumbian Exposition at Chicago.

*"This way for the Streets of Cairo! One hundred and fifty
Oriental beauties! The warmest spectacle on earth! Pre-sen-ting
Little Egypt! See her prance, see her wriggle! See her dance the
Hootchy-Kootchy! Anywhere else but in the ocean breezes of
Coney Island she would be consumed by her own fire! Don't
rush! Don't crowd! Plenty of seats for all!"*

Little Egypt was a sensation; imitators sprang up all over
Coney Island, churning their umbilici. But tastes changed.
Presently there was no crowd, no rush whatever. Little Egypt
herself decamped; by the end of the season of 1903 there was
only one imitator left, still disconsolately wriggling; a journalist
overheard the show's manager bidding his barker rise to a
supreme effort, against the imminent arrival of an excursion
steamer loaded with pleasure-seekers from New York; valiantly

LEFT. Antic ballyhoo at Coney. COURTESY THE FRANCIS K. MOORE COLLECTION
RIGHT. Little Egypt hits the beach. MUSEUM OF THE CITY OF NEW YORK

The original Streets of Cairo, as presented at the corner of Surf Avenue and West Tenth Street (1897). A BYRON PHOTOGRAPH, COURTESY THE FRANCIS K. MOORE COLLECTION

the barker launched into a stirring spiel; his voice, lyric and passionate, brought the crowd off the boat expectantly toward his change-booth; beside him on the platform the pseudo-Little Egypt, demurely veiled for the ballyhoo, langorously stirred her tummy, winked, and slipped within, her very departure an exotic promise of hidden Oriental delights for all who followed; the barker's voice now was hushed, charged with allure, a caress; every man in the crowd reached for his pocket and moved toward the change-booth. Then, all of a sudden, from a half-block away there came another sound. A baby elephant trumpeted. Heads in the crowd turned. The elephant squealed again. The crowd wavered, considered, and then broke away enraptured. Not a single soul paid his dime to watch the belly dancer. The show's manager glared at his barker. The barker shrugged. "I'm good," he said, "I admit it. But when they get an elephant to do their spiel, who can compete?"

Meantime, at Surf Avenue and West Tenth Street where Little Egypt had danced in the Streets of Cairo, a barker was still at work, but now the attraction was the most thrilling of all outdoor rides. This was the Loop-the-Loop, a device so daring that people paid admissions just to watch others, less timorous, take the ride. The first experimental centrifugal coasters had included circular loops; passengers' heads would snap on their necks as the car came down to complete its circle. But thanks to E. W. Green, a Brooklyn engineer, Edward Prescott was able to iron out the painful wrinkles. His loop was an ellipse, thirty feet high: a four-passenger car rolled down a graduated slope, picking up speed enough to whirl into the loop, pause breathtakingly at the top, and then swoop down and out of the loop and come gently to rest at the top of a second slope. The ride was a triumph of engineering and perfectly safe: a glass of

This fiendish gadget, a predecessor of the Loop-the-Loop, was called the Flip-Flap and was housed for a time in Sea Lion Park, Coney Island's (and the world's) first outdoor amusement park. COURTESY KINGS COUNTY CLERK'S OFFICE

water, carried as a test, would never spill a drop. Yet, when people watched, fascinated, they wondered. Boy would look at girl, quizzically, and they would turn away to find some less reckless amusement. There were, to be sure, always enough daredevils in the crowd, over a summer weekend, to keep the Loop-the-Loop busy, but in time another flaw was revealed: it couldn't earn money fast enough to justify its favored position on Surf Avenue. For four passengers to experience their unrivaled thrill took nearly five minutes, but a roller coaster car can carry two dozen passengers around its course in half the time. So the Loop-the-Loop disappeared, but it is likely that the crowds never missed it. There were too many new voices barking at them, urging their attention, this way, over here, step right up!

"Yes, look well upon this group of savages, ladies and gentlemen! They are the dread Igorots, fierce head-hunters from the Philippine Islands! And what you see before you is but a miserable tithe of the vast anthropological, educational, thrilling, and altogether unimaginable sights that will unfold before you as you pass through the Igorot Village!"

The man responsible for transporting a tribe of tractable, friendly, non-head-hunting Igorots halfway around the world to Coney Island was Samuel W. Gumpertz. It was 1905 when he whisked them past an astonished immigration official; in the next quarter-century the number of freaks, oddities, and outlandish human beings he similarly escorted was to rise above three thousand; his traffic made Coney into the acknowledged world's capital of the eccentric and the bizarre; and, in the course of peddling his queer wares, he developed the sideshow spiel to a flamboyant art. Gumpertz was constantly on the prowl for new grotesques. Five times he went to Asia, with side trips to Java and the Philippines; five times he went to Africa and twice into the unexplored heart of the dark continent; his

xpeditions to Europe he never counted. For any adult human
ess than three feet or more than seven feet tall, he would drop
verything and cross an ocean. He learned to chaffer in German,
rench, Spanish, and Italian; he even picked up a patois of the
yrenees, to aid him in contracting for the services of the
warfs with which that region was said to abound. Barnum's
itiful frauds, foisted on a gullible citizenry, were kissed off
nd frozen against the cushion. Barnum had exhibited, as a
Vild Man from Borneo, a colored citizen of the United States
hom he had taught to snarl ferociously and hurl himself
gainst the bars of a cage. Gumpertz went himself to Borneo
nd leased nineteen Wild Men from a local tribal chieftain for
vo hundred bags of salt. If they were not legitimately wild, at
ast they were unquestionably from Borneo. From Algeria he
nported a troop of fierce Berber horsemen; he paid the govern-
ent of French Equatorial Africa $3,000 a week for two years
> show Americans how a dozen women from the banks of the
bangi River had stretched their lips over wooden platters up
> ten inches wide; from Burma he brought to Coney women
ho had lengthened their necks fourteen inches by gradually
lding brass rings; from French Somaliland came a platoon of
arriors who had decorated themselves, in accordance with
ibal custom, by smearing blue clay into self-inflicted wounds.

By the time Gumpertz arrived on Coney, at the behest of
enator William Reynolds, to organize and manage a midget
deshow called the Lilliputian Village, he had already had an
xtensive career in show business, ranging from child acro-
atics to performing in Colonel Buffalo Bill Cody's Wild West
ircus to exploiting the talents of Sandow the Strong Man and
arry Houdini to producing road shows of Shakespearean
pertory. His success with Lilliputia, however, was such that
e decided to settle down. He became manager of Dreamland
r Senator Reynolds, and at once began to conceive new enter-

tainments, often calling on old friends to make sure that th
new would also be good. Thus he deputized George Hamid,
young Lebanese tumbler whom he had met when they wer
both youngsters on Buffalo Bill's payroll, to break in the pe
formers for a new kind of "Streets of Cairo," sword-dancer
jugglers, and acrobats; and Hamid did so well that Freder
Thompson, across the street in Luna Park, promptly engage
him to duplicate his triumph on Luna's Midway. (Gumper
never complained. His association with Hamid was to last, o
and on, for decades: when, in the 1930's, Gumpertz was direc
ing the Ringling Brothers and Barnum & Bailey Circus, Hami
booked many of his acts; still later the two were partners o
the Million Dollar Pier at Atlantic City.) Gumpertz also pr
vailed on Omar Sami to quit the road and settle down with
concession or two in Dreamland, and this was a moment o
weighty consequence for Coney Island, for Omar Sami was th
generally acknowledged King of Ballyhoo Spielers.

Omar's origins and antecedents are cloaked in shadow
Walter Pritchard Eaton, the prospective dean of America
theatre criticism, came to review Omar's performance as h
might have that of Forrest or Booth or Mansfield or Barr
more; he wrote a glowing tribute to the spieler's histrion
powers; but he set it down as his belief that Omar was
Vermont Hindu. Frank J. Wilstach, Dreamland's press agen
was outraged. "Irreverence," he cried, "desecration, blasphem
Omar of the honey tongue, the captivating smile, the hypnot
glance, and the unshatterable larynx to be dubbed a Vermo
Hindu? Oh, horrible!" Omar, Wilstach insisted, his tongue r
doubt thrust well into his cheek, "is a topnotch Englishman, a
Oxford graduate, and a spieler who, in an oratorical contes
could put Elbert Hubbard and William Jennings Bryan at th
foot of the class." Omar's friends, he added, called him Clarenc

There was, however, no doubt as to Omar's ability nor as

is experience. He had spieled the world over, from, as he used
to say, India to Indiana, from Hoboken to Hindustan, from
amchatka to Kalamazoo, from Yakima to Yucatan. At gathering a push, at turning a tip, he had no peer. Gumpertz was
understandably anxious to lasso this champion of chatter and
get him to settle permanently in Dreamland so that his other
spielers might model their efforts on his. And indeed there was
need for such a model. Spielers were, by 1910, getting out of
hand, whether because the wells of their inspiration were beginning to dry up or from sheer hysteria it was difficult to say.
Irvin S. Cobb, for example, swore that one day he came upon a
Coney Island barker whose technique was, quite literally, to
bark. This man did nothing, Cobb claimed, except to yap like
a fox terrier, interminably. He strode back and forth upon his
platform, pointing with his cane at the canvas valentines behind
him, but nothing came from his mouth from eleven in the
morning until twelve at night save yips, yelps, and yaps. Cobb
also deposed that, on another occasion at Coney Island, he had
seen a reedy youth with a prominent Adam's apple take the
platform in front of a concession, cross his eyes, waggle his
Adam's apple alarmingly, give voice to three harrowing shrieks,
and forthwith commence writhing and jerking, apparently in
the grip of a most convincing fit. A crowd gathered, of course,
and when it was big enough the youth all at once miraculously
pulled himself together. Eyes, Adam's apple, and behavior returned to normal. Without a word he turned and passed through
the admission gate and, Cobb reported, the entire crowd
followed after him, apparently under the impression that he
would put on a repeat performance inside. To a conscientious
showman like Gumpertz, such antics were anathema. He
summoned all the boosters, shillabers, spielers, and ballyhoo
talkers over whom he had authority and required that they sit
at Omar Sami's feet and heed his instructions.

Omar was an early advocate of the relaxed sell. He listene
dreamily as a few of his pupils went through their paces, d
claiming with all the oratorical fervor of a corn-country ho;
caller, only with the difference that their accents marked mo.
of them as stemming from Brooklyn or, at the extremest, fro
Manhattan's lower East Side. At length the docent raised h
hand to hush the spiel. They were, he told them, without th
art, the system, the brainwork required of a good barker, wh
he reminded them, is called on to perform every bit as much ;
an actor playing the most exacting role. "The first principle (
a good ballyhoo spiel," he urged his pupils, "is to talk naturall;
The aim of the old spieler was to make a noise. That sort (
thing won't go nowadays. New Yorkers," he reminded then
noticing that a reporter was present, making notes on th
lecture, "are the hardest people in the world to talk to. Whe
you have a crowd of educated people you must address the
as such, and not as you would a bunch of simps. And," he we
on, more cheerfully, "when you have a mob of roughnecks
interest and move inside, talk to them in their own lingo."

Unfortunately, only two examples of the master's style hav
been preserved for us. In the first he presented himself,
silence, clad in an Arabian Nights get-up, turban, sash, an
brilliant loose red bloomers. "See! See the great Hindu hy
notist!" bellowed an apprentice spieler. And then, after a fe
people had gathered to see, a Japanese juggler appeared, t
attract a still larger crowd. Faster and faster the juggler twirle
his sticks and paper balloons. When once the crowd was larg
enough, Omar, the Hindu hypnotist, locked the Japanese in
coffin on the platform. Only then did he speak. He spok
quietly, and the crowd obediently craned forward to listen t
him. "You do not beleef me," Omar would say, "when I tell yo
of what a greatness this show is. And why do you not bele
me? Because it is tolt to you at Coney Islant, and in your hear

ou say—what is the word?—humbug." Now since this was
xactly what most of the crowd was at that moment thinking,
iey all nodded, mesmerized. The master proceeded. "But I ask
ou, why shoult we bring these great entertainments over the
cean at a cost of many thousands of money, far from our own
int where the sun is hot all the year and the sacred Ganges
ow to the sea from the great hills that wear white turbans of
ternal snow and whisper secrets in the ears of the stars—why
hoult we do this if our entertainments is humbug?" His voice
aving by now dropped to a huge whisper, Omar would step
ack with a flourish and open the coffin in which he had locked
ie Japanese. It would, of course, be empty. At the same
ioment the Japanese would appear from behind a screen.
pplause from the crowd while Omar, with a wily smile and a
uileful gesture toward the ticket-seller, would bow low and
ad the way inside. And after him the crowd would rush.

In 1910 Omar owned a show called "Alias Kid Allen," a highly
ioral entertainment having to do with celebrated contemporary
riminals. He hired as his ticket-seller one Harry Collins, a man
/ho could contort his features into a splendidly desperate and
illainous expression. He was clad in convict's stripes. Having

gathered a crowd, Omar would point to him. "Here, ladies and gentlemen," he would say, "we have one of the most desperate criminals known to the annals of crime. This heretofore irreclaimable culprit, wrongdoer, scoundrel, caitiff, wretch, reprobate, recreant, and ruffian came to me the early part of the season and told me he thought he could be an honest man if given the chance. I have trusted him, as you see, ladies and gentlemen. This man, with a deplorable past, is being kept under my constant surveillance. I think he'll make good." On Decoration Day, 1910, "Alias Kid Allen" did a fabulous business. All day the dimes flooded in; all day Harry Collins leered and glowered at the crowds; all day, as Omar concluded his spiel, Collins turned on him a look of dumb and pious gratitude. At the close of business, when Omar came around to collect the dimes that Collins had taken in, he found only a note: "Dear Omar," it read, "I have made good." But apparently Omar's seeds had not been sown on hopelessly barren ground, for on Friday, May 26, 1911, a penitent Collins returned to Dreamland and to Omar. He proffered him a fifty-dollar bill to make restitution. Omar looked at him. This time Collins' expression was beatific: it shone: it bespoke contrition: the absconder looked like a remorseful monk. As it happened, Omar had been casting about for an actor to play the part of a venerable religious devotee in the new entertainment he was producing that year; he engaged Collins on the spot. Have we not here a truly moral tale? And unflawed: for had Collins been a lazier man, had his guardian angel relaxed even for an instant his vigilance, restitution would never have been made. Remorse gnawed at Collins in time's nick. He came with his fifty dollars on a Friday morning; if he had waited till Saturday he might never have come at all, for it was Friday night when Dreamland burned.

When Dreamland burned, it whisked away from off Gum

pertz's shoulders the collection of politicians and investors who had ordered him about, bidding him paint the park this color, expand the walks by that width, go to the other place to find new concessions. The fire severely scorched their interest in show business, but he was in it to stay. He put together the Dreamland Circus Sideshow while the embers of the park were still smoldering: presently it was flanked by a dozen concessions either owned or leased by him, each complete with a barker and a clamorous ballyhoo, and each coining money. It was this Surf Avenue array of concessions that guaranteed to Samuel Gumpertz his permanent niche in show business as godfather of the sideshow and more particularly of the freak. While Dreamland existed, the emphasis at Coney was still on splendor and visual magnificence. But once the real estate was available, the sideshows crept in and took over. Economically, there was no choice. Nor was there any difficulty in persuading the performers themselves that Coney was their best permanent roost. They had suspected as much for twenty years or more; they had been awaiting only the entrepreneur who would wave them front and center. Gumpertz was their man. To one side of them was the Eden Musée, to the other was Underground Chinatown, but the freaks at last had a place of honor at Coney.

The Eden Musée had for years been P. T. Barnum's original museum and had later doubled as a cameo theatre where singers and dancers could stage recitals. At its home in West Twenty-third Street, in Manhattan, it had won international renown for its waxworks, second only, perhaps, to the Tussaud collection in London. Gumpertz bought the waxworks and the name, and brought them to Coney. He had a gallery of waxen American presidents, a waxen Chamber of Horrors, and an extremely realistic waxen cop standing just inside the door, so lifelike that visitors used often to pause to ask him the way. He added new figures, of course, to keep in step with the times:

Lindbergh; Gerald Chapman, the murderer; Leopold and Loeb; and a fancy assemblage of Hollywood stars gathered around a dinner-table, Charlie Chaplin, Douglas Fairbanks, Mary Pickford, Bebe Daniels, Milton Sills, and Dorothy Gish, all in opulent evening dress. It was a careless match, dropped near this dinner party, that started a ruinous fire, in 1928. Charlie Chaplin was the first to sag, limp and liquid, but presently, as it was reported in the *New York Herald Tribune,* "Marat slumped in his bathtub, Charlotte Corday dropped her knife and melted at his feet . . . Ex-President Taft ran out over his shoetops . . . and Leopold and Loeb ran out through a crack in the floor." Only Heywood Broun, the columnist for the *New York World,* was not saddened by the calamity. For Broun recalled how, when he was a small boy, he had been taken to the Chamber of Horrors and had paused, fascinated and aghast, by the figure of a trapped hunter being burned at the stake by Indians. He recalled how the hunter's head had rolled, uncannily, from side to side. Adult hands had urged him on, promising him a look at different Indians, real Indians from India. And sure enough, he had come upon another tableau: an elephant, its foot raised, poised to plunge down on a child's head. Just beyond *that,* he recalled, was the waxwork figure of a drowned damsel, lying on the bottom of the sea. He hoped the Eden Musée was gone for good. But it wasn't. Sam Gumpertz saw to it that it rose again from its ashes; only this time, for good measure, he added a waxwork figure of Broun himself.

Underground Chinatown was a waxwork libel on what goes on in the Chinese quarter of a big city, complete with murky dens where opium smokers lay in their bunks and scenes of terrified maidens being hauled away to a life of white slavery. All was in a dim light, to heighten the illusion. And there must still be folk who, walking through present-day Chinatowns on their way to unexceptionable meals, experience a dim, queasy unease, a distant echo of the time when they were taken, as children, through this exhibit. There were displayed, as well, some horrifying tableaux of medieval torture instruments; only after vigorous protests from Chinese officials were notices put up acknowledging that such punishments were no longer part of Chinese legal procedure.

But while both these waxwork shows did a respectable business, it was the Congress of Curious People that fairly packed them in. By 1920, as many as thirty thousand slow-moving spectators, eyes a-goggle and jaws slack, would take the twenty-minute tour through the Dreamland Circus Sideshow.

"Now, ladies and gentlemen, if you please, step over here and see the world's tiniest people. Note the yardstick—an accurate, an exact, a perfectly calibrated instrument against which to measure the height of these miniscule humans, some of them members of the foreign titled aristocracy! (Step forward, Count, and you too, Baron, and stand by the yardstick.) Each and every one of these little people, ladies and gentlemen, is a full-grown human being! (Thank you, Count. Thank you, Baron.)"

Ever since his early Coney Island days with the Lilliputian Village, Gumpertz had a soft spot in his heart for midgets. Then his star performers had been Mercy Lavinia Warren Bump Stratton, the thirty-two inch widow of Charles (General Tom Thumb) Stratton, and her second husband, an Italian dwarf named Count Primo Magri (his title had been conferred on him by the Pope). Lavinia, who was a Massachusetts Yankee, a member of the Eastern Star, and a D.A.R. proud of her *May-flower* ancestors, had thought twice before agreeing to come to Coney Island. After all, during her marriage to the General she had been a friend to President Ulysses S. Grant; she had consorted with the crowned heads of Europe, Napoleon III,

Mr. and Mrs. Charles
(General Tom Thumb)
Stratton.

Victoria, Victor Emmanuel, Franz Josef; she had stayed at Marlborough House with the Prince and Princess of Wales; the Khedive of Egypt had pressed on her $2,500, an apartment in his palace, and the use of his private train; she had owned yachts, horses, jewels. Should she then appear at Coney? But she had needed the money.

Later, after Lavinia had retired to Middleboro, Gumpertz adopted a French midget, paying her parents $4,000 for the privilege. He called her Lady Little, and she was a long-time resident of Coney. But even better known was Baron Paucci, an Italian who was advertised as only twenty-four inches tall but was in fact a few inches bigger. The Baron was a fast stepper, always ready for wine, women, and good horseraces. He was likewise swift to take offense from any remark passed about him, by a spectator passing by. And why not?

"And now, ladies and gentlemen, the most remarkable curiosity ever seen by man—a Freak of Giant Strength—Eats and Enjoys Humans—More Ferocious than the Wild Man of Borneo! What is it? Scientists cannot name it—part human, part animal —growls like a dog, barks like a dog, bites like a dog! In his native haunts in the far distant island of Neaceo he protects

himself from capture by wielding his enormous feet with tell-ing effect! If you miss seeing this Wild Man you will regret it for the rest of your life!"

Zip, the first What-Is-It, was one of Barnum's discoveries, and the great showman made a mint by exhibiting him as an outlandish monster from some vague and distant land. He was in fact an American Negro microcephalus, that is, a dark-com-plexioned citizen with an abnormally small skull. The impres-sion crept abroad that Zip was an idiot, but on this point there is evidence to give the prudent pause. "Every library," wrote Oliver Wendell Holmes, in his *Autocrat of the Breakfast Table,* "should try to be complete on something, if it were only the history of pinheads." But the long, happy career of Zip makes it clear that Holmes held out an easier goal than might have seemed to be the case at first sight. Zip was, to be sure, a pin-head; indeed, all the hair on his head save for a tuft on the very pate was shaved to carry the beholder's eye up to the head of the pin; but it is very unlikely that he was an idiot. When, after surviving Barnum, he came to Coney Island, to be sure he used to envelope himself in a white cotton garment and swirl it about him, all the while going through a kind of Swedish drill, for all the world as though he had not a brain in his pointy

Zip

head. And yet, it may be argued, this was a living. Indeed it was an excellent living: no sideshow performer in all Coney's history grossed better than Zip. One story designed to discredit his intelligence would have it that the Broadway producer, David Belasco, was convinced that Zip had brains up to the moment when he tossed the pinhead a half-dollar. Zip, according to the legend, tossed it right back, persuading Belasco that he must be crazy. Crazy like a fox: for what better drumbeater could a sideshow performer have than a successful Broadway producer? The record shows that Zip's real name was William Henry Johnson; that he once saved a child from drowning, at Coney Island; that his income was unparalleled, among all the Congress of Curious People; and that he lived a long and happy life. He was eighty-four when he died, in 1926, and among the honorary pallbearers were the Fat Girl, the Tattooed Lady, the Human Skeleton, and Cliko the Bushman.

Cliko succeeded Zip as a Wild Man. He was a friendly little chap, about three-and-a-half feet tall, a native of Africa. The keeper who first brought him to America was a scoundrel who imprisoned him in an animal cage, fed him on scraps from a garbage can, clothed him in old and greasy rags, and convinced his associates that Cliko was indeed a savage and wicked monster. Fortunately, this vile man was taken to a hospital with influenza and at once it developed that Cliko was as amiable and sociable as anyone could wish. His only failing was a very ordinary one: he loved to get roaring drunk. He took to Coney like a sandpiper, turning up every summer during his declining years.

By 1929, there being no American citizen gullible enough to credit the existence of a Wild Man, Professor Sam Wagner, who had assumed Gumpertz's position as Coney's foremost impresario of the odd, was constrained to present Zip's successors simply as pinheads. He had, however, not one, but two, count them, two of them. They were members of an otherwise normal family of Georgia crackers and Professor Sam personally signed them up, thanks only to a letter of introduction from the mayor of New York to the mayor of Hartwell, Georgia. And they became, during the depression years and into the 1930's, Coney's greatest sideshow drawing-cards. Professor Sam called them Pipo and Zipo, and paid them $75 a week, a landfall for their Southern family. In 1940, at twenty-eight, Pipo had the intelligence of an eighteen-months-old baby; his sister Zipo was forty and rather brighter, with a mental age of about five. Professor Sam used to be quite fond of them, and they of him. "They have nothing to worry about," he used to say, truthfully, "and, as a matter of fact, nothing to worry with."

"Here, ladies and gentlemen, sits the Fattest of all the Fat Girls since the Dawn of History! Special girders are required beneath her platform, and special girdles must be constructed to contain her fabulous avoirdupois. Six hundred and seventy pounds of golden good nature! No one else can make this claim!"

There have been a succession of Fat Women at Coney: Singing Lottie De Meyer ("Oh Boy, Some Entertainer") and Princess La La ("Tahiti's Largest Hula Dancer") are the most recent: but nothing can dim the memory of the fattest and friendliest of all, Mrs. Amanda Siebert, known as Jolly Irene. Her vast bulk was sufficiently remarkable—she tipped the scales at 689 pounds when she was in her prime—but even more exceptional was her unflaggingly sunny disposition in the face of what must have been a personal tragedy. In 1901, when she was twenty-one, she weighed a pleasing 120 pounds; she had been married a year or so; soon she became a mother. Childbirth, for some obscure reason, kicked her endocrine balance out of whack, and she began to pack it on. But she was indomitably cheerful. For a time she traveled with Ringling Brothers Circus;

she quit when she got too fat to negotiate her bulk into ordinary railroad cars; press agents put it out that she was insulted when the circus people suggested she ride in the baggage car. But it took more than that to insult Jolly Irene. She simply preferred the more stable life of a Coney performer. She lived in Coney, at the Hotel Clement; she worked in Coney; when she married a second time, it was to a Coney Islander. If she rued the occasional difficulties in which she found herself—like the time when she fell painfully from her bed, and the assistance of the Fire Department was required to lift her back again—she never complained. The hundreds of thousands who passed by her platform were infected by her gaiety. She had hundreds of friends, and with good reason. When she died, in 1940, sickness had whittled her weight down to some 500 pounds; her double-size coffin could not be carried into the Church of Our Lady of Solace; her grave was also double the usual size. But then, so was the number of mourners who came to the solemn requiem mass.

"He bends horseshoes straight and crowbars crooked! He picks his teeth with railroad spikes and clips his nails with garden shears! Ladies and gentlemen! The mightiest mortal since the days of the Biblical Samson!"

One of Coney's earliest strong men doubled as janitor in a Surf Avenue sideshow for $5 a week. His name was Angelo Siciliano, and he would hoist a man in each hand, tear two telephone books at once apart, break tenpenny nails in two, and run through the rest of the strong man's routine. But he was destined for more aesthetic pursuits. One day an artist happened to be one of the gawking crowd, and he bore Siciliano away to a career as a sculptor's model. Presently, as Charles Atlas, he had won the title of "The World's Most Perfectly Developed Man" and had gone into business for himself as the nation's foremost muscle-builder. Atlas was scarcely at Coney

ong enough to get acquainted, but his successor, William
Lincoln Travis, stayed on for years in Professor Sam Wagner's
World Circus Sideshow, and he, too, won the wholehearted
affection of the regulars at the resort. Travis was an easy mark,
both for children and for barkers and ballyhoo talkers down
on their luck. "My policy," he said, "is to give as much as possible for as little as I can take in return." He used to moralize
from his platform. After lifting ten big men, weighing an aggre-
gate 1,800 pounds, he would tell the crowd around him: "Walk
erect, head up, chest out, shoulders back. Sit the same way.
Be just in all your dealings, and see that you get justice in return." Travis amazed Dr. Moses Bluestone, a Coney Island
physician who for years took care of Coney's freaks. The doctor's sphygmomanometer told him that the strong man's blood
pressure was 250; on every visit he would warn Travis that he
should slow down or, preferably, quit entirely. Travis would
answer by lifting the doctor's desk four feet off the floor and
setting it back in place hindside to. "I could never convince
him," said Dr. Bluestone, "that he was in delicate health." But
Travis was still demonstrating feats of strength at the age of
sixty-seven. One Saturday night in the middle of the 1941 season, as usual Travis went through a half-dozen performances.
An hour later he was dead. It took only four men to carry his
casket to the crematory.

Other Coney sideshow performers did themselves damage to
make a living. Captain Fred Walters, the Blue Man, began his
career when he found that the silver nitrate he had taken as
therapy for a nervous complaint gave his skin a bluish cast. He
increased the dosage, turned blue, and stayed that way until
he had eventually done himself irreparable harm. On the other
hand, there were some who delighted the press agents by dis-
covering that true love lay behind the valentines. Percilla, the
Monkey Girl, victim of a freak hirsutism that caused hair to

grow thickly over her face and body, set her cap for Emmitt
Bejano, the Alligator Boy, who has ichthyosis, a skin disease
that covers him with tough, gray, quadrangular scales, and
their marriage has been a happy one. And just before the 1953
season, the Tattooed Lady who was to appear at David Rosen's
Surf Avenue Palace of Wonders was married to one of Rosen's
outside talkers. The Tattooed Lady, Jean Carroll, came by her
vivid decorations in an unusual way. She was born with an
authentic beard; by the time she was ten her beard was six
inches long and she was already traveling with the Hagenbeck
and Wallace Circus. But she fell in love with a contortionist; he
wanted to marry her, but shied at her whiskers. It was a grave
dilemma. She liked the carnival life, but what would she do,
without a beard? A sword-swallower pointed out that if she
liked, while a physician was removing her beard with an elec-
trolytic needle in front, she could engage a tattoo artist to etch
a few of his masterpieces in back. And so she did. It was after
her first husband died that she married Larry Rapp, the spieler,
and they threw their wedding party at Hubert's Museum and
Flea Circus in Manhattan. After they had tossed their coats
and hats on the penny peepshow machines, the guests—who
included a midget clown; Fifi, the Sheep-headed Girl; Alzoria,
the Turtle Girl; Jackie Donahue, the Human Auto Tire; Sam
Smith, the Human Ostrich; Lola, the Leopard Girl; Princess
Sahloo, the Snake Dancer; and Albert-Alberta, half man, half
woman—had a fine time. At four a.m. festivities wound up
when Miss Carroll modestly raised the diaphanous pink skirts
of her wedding gown to show her guests the Crown of Thorns
tattooed on her right leg and the Rock of Ages on her left—two
of the seven hundred designs and pictures she carries with her
wherever she goes. "My new hubby's one guy who'll never get
bored," she said. "When things get dull at home, I'll go into a
shimmy, and what'll he see? Free motion pictures!"

But at times the loss of her whiskers saddened Miss Carroll. "Only by falling for a guy," she would say, "would I have shed that silky foliage of mine." One Coney Island Bearded Lady who never shed her whiskers through four marriages was Jane Barnell, perhaps the most celebrated of her kind and certainly the most widely traveled and persevering of her kind in the history of show business. Miss Barnell, whose beard, at its most splendidly luxuriant, measured better than thirteen inches, began her career when she was only four years old and she was still appearing more than sixty-eight years later. Talkers used to introduce her in a variety of ways and under a variety of names but her own favorite ran:

"It gives me the greatest pleasure at this time to introduce a little woman who comes to us from an aristocratic plantation in the Old South and who is recognized by our finest doctors, physicians, and medical men as the foremost unquestioned and authentic female Bearded Lady in medical history. Ladies and gentlemen, Lady Olga!"

Miss Barnell made Coney her summer headquarters starting with the 1939 season, after she had quit the Ringling Brothers and Barnum & Bailey because of the union. She feared she might be required to join. At Coney she found that while she could never come to love the audiences—they have for forty years been the most persistently prying in the country—there were nevertheless compensations. For one, she was convinced that the ocean air was good for her asthma. For another, she was fond of the roasted corn-on-the-cob that is a favorite delicacy at Coney. (Once, in the early years of the Second Great War, a couple of young French sailors found their way down to the beach. In the course of mousing around, they came upon a pair of cute blondes nibbling away at some corn-on-the-cob. The French sailors stared. At last, "Formidable!" said one. C'est comme les chevaux!") On her sideshow platform, Miss

Barnell stared out blankly at nothing, as do many such performers who have learned that pity is a distasteful emotion under any circumstances. She had a short temper and thought nothing of unleashing it when questions got too personal. Off the platform was when she most enjoyed the beach. She became a familiar figure along the boardwalk, veiled, a Paisley scarf wrapped around her neck to conceal her beard, striding along briskly and taking in great gulps of the salt air, against her asthma. After a few seasons at Coney, she made the definitive comment on those who sit on the sideshow platforms and those who gather below, to gawk. "If the truth was known," said Miss Barnell, "we're all freaks together."

"You may talk, ladies and gentlemen, you may cough. They will not hear you. They do not even know you are here. And now, suppose you all follow me. Just come this way, if you will, and we will meet the first of our temporary visitors."

No sideshow in Coney's history had as extended a run as the Premature Baby Incubators. At no other sideshow was the spiel so restrained, so lacking in boastful polysyllables, or so scientifically correct. The very fact that they were there at all was an anomaly, and one that many people were never able to resolve. They could never have existed at all, and they most certainly would never have lasted—as they did—from 1903 to 1943, if it had not been for the unremitting scientific integrity of their founder, Dr. Martin Arthur Couney.

Dr. Couney was an Alsatian who came to Paris in the 1890's to study under a celebrated pediatrician, and he early showed his special concern for premature babies, that is, those born at least three weeks before their normal forty-week term. In those days, medical men had no routine procedure for maintaining life in a premature baby; Dr. Couney assisted in the first fumbling efforts. A fair was to be held in Berlin, in 1896; most of the exhibits were to be medical and scientific; his chief urged

Dr. Couney to conduct a demonstration of their methods at this fair. The exhibit was called the *Kinderbrutanstalt,* literally, the child hatchery, and it was a sensation. At the behest of an English promotor, Dr. Couney traveled the next year to Earl's Court, but it is difficult to teach the English, their doctors refused to send premature babies to his Earl's Court cradle, he was obliged to get his supply from Paris. The next year he was in Omaha, for the Trans-Mississippi Exposition; in 1900 he opened his incubators for the Paris World's Fair; but in 1901 he was back in this country, at Buffalo, for the Pan-American Exposition. He decided to stay, for in those days it seemed that there was to be a World's Fair or Exposition of some sort in some American city in each succeeding year; but in 1903 he was persuaded to come to Coney and exhibit his premature babies at Luna Park. With the exception of one two-year period, 1939-1940, when he was at the New York World's Fair, he never left Coney save to retire, in 1943. During that time, of 8,500 premature babies, he saved 7,500, a record that could not be matched by the rest of organized medicine throughout the world. It is, indeed, difficult too highly to praise Dr. Couney's efforts. At a time when, because of a combination of factors that included lack of interest, lack of specialized training, and lack of funds, the medical profession was skirting the problem of the premature baby, Dr. Couney's incubators were almost alone in the country.

When first he arrived on Coney Island there was a flurry of indignation. The Brooklyn Society for the Prevention of Cruelty to Children inquired. Had he a medical license? What did he mean by exhibiting infants for a fee? Wasn't there something vaguely improper about his procedures? The fact was that he had not had time to take out a practitioner's license when he first arrived in this country, but that was soon remedied. As for the fees he collected (twenty-five cents at first; after 1937 this was reduced to twenty cents) they were manifestly necessary. To care for premature infants costs a lot of money: for wet nurses, for trained nurses, both around the clock; for special formulae; for oxygen; and, as technology advanced, for air-conditioning and soundproofing and all the other perquisites of a modern hospital. To be sure, Dr. Couney made a living from his exhibits, but on the other hand he would have made far more had he chosen to close them down and go into private practice. In 1939, he reckoned his daily overhead at $140, which meant that he needed seven hundred customers on a daily average, to break even; in turn this meant that he had to do a land-office business on the weekends for, unlike the other sideshows, his incubators' daily overhead was urgent and incessant. Nor was there anything even vaguely improper about his procedures. They were, indeed, the best in the country for his specialized work. American Medical Association spokesmen were always notably respectful when it came to discussing Dr. Couney's methods and results.

The doctor was under no illusions as to the fact that he was running a sideshow, but he was nevertheless very careful to make his a very different sideshow. It was a scientific exhibit, and while he delighted in being fatherly to all the nurses and lecturers (never spielers or talkers) and others who staffed his enterprise he could be a very stern father when crossed. Rules were rules. Wet nurses were strictly forbidden to eat in local restaurants or to buy food from any of the perambulant peddlers. Lecturers were fired if they permitted jokes to creep into their spiel—oops, their scientific explanations. With the years, Coney came to be peppered with graduates of his incubators. Two of them worked for a time at Luna Park; there was another in a local five-and-ten; a fourth, who was an electrician for a number of years at Steeplechase Park, used to come back so often to visit (on the house, professional courtesy) that at

ength he ended up married to one of the registered nurses.
And, the doctor noticed, many of his visitors came back again
and again. They would identify with one or another baby and
return regularly to see how it was doing. One Coney Island
resident turned up once a week for thirty-seven seasons.

The smallest infant in Dr. Couney's Coney Island experience
weighed 705 grams, about one and one-half pounds. (The
smallest survivor recorded in medical history weighed 600
grams, or about one and one-quarter pounds, but, as Dr.
Couney pointed out, in each of these cases the weight was
measured some time after birth. A baby loses weight as soon as
t has been born; it is doubtful that any baby weighing less
han two pounds at birth could survive.) His own daughter
Hildegarde was prematurely born and completed her term in
his incubators, surviving to be a healthy young woman who
became one of his principal assistants toward the end of his
career.

*"Now this little baby came in nine days ago. It weighed only
one pound eleven ounces and we were afraid we might be too
late. It was even bluer than that little fellow over there in the
other incubator . . . Yes, ma'am, it was a premature birth
. . A little over six months . . ."*

By the 1930's, Dr. Couney's were the only soft-spoken barkers left on Coney. The gentle, hypnotic art of Omar Sami was
as dead as the dodo. No longer did the spieler call on psychological cunning; his only resource was racket. The blare pur-
ued the visitors to Coney from the moment they debouched
rom the subways; it pursued them all along Surf Avenue; it
acketed off the walls of the Bowery; it resounded along the
boardwalk. Every few steps there was another microphone,
and back of it an amplifier turned up full volume. The high-
triker:

"Heavy and hard, ladies and gents, heavy and hard. Send it

up, send it up, send it up to the top! Heavy on the soak-em,
men, heavy on the soak-em!"

A man standing beside a tray of kewpie dolls:

"Guess your weight or occupation or age! Which one? Winn
prize! Only ten cents! Guess the make of your car! Guess you
weight, guess your age, hell, I'll even guess your sex!"

A woman at a custard stand:

"How many more here? How many more? Oh, it's creamy
it's delicious, and when we sell 'em all, we go home! So ste
up! What kind? What kind?"

The voices were frenetic, for the small businessman had fel
the pinch. At least half the games and rides and sideshows tha
had packed the resort during the 1920's had closed down whei
the flood of dimes became a trickle of nickels and was then cu
off almost entirely. Lean days fell, too, on the freak shows. Th
fact was that the entrepreneurs were finding it more difficult t
find bona fide freaks, were obliged to depend more on gaffec
or phony, freaks. To a considerable extent, this was the resul
of medical progress. The skin diseases and disfiguring birth
marks that had made so many unhappy folk take to a life o:
the carny circuit were proving susceptible of treatment; endoc
rinologists had probed further into the mysteries of the pitui
tary and were increasingly able to cope with acromegal
(which causes giantism) and adiposogenitalism (which cause
Fat Boys and Girls) and pituitary dwarfism. Siamese twins, i
was learned, could be carved apart. As for the unfortunate wit
withered legs, or with no arms, like Harry Bulson, the Spide
Boy, and Forrest Sayman, the Armless Wonder, the time wa
approaching when folk would wonder why they did not undei
take, as would the badly wounded soldiers, to be outfitted wit
artificial limbs. And so on every hand the barkers grew mor
desperate and the ballyhoo more blatant. Even in front of suc
esteemed Coney entertainments as the Cyclone, the lofty 50(

ot roller coaster run by two veteran amusement experts, Chris
eucht and George Kister, a weary voice sounded in a depress-
g chant:

*"Hey, hey, hey! Roller coaster going up! Allaway up, allaway
, hey, hey, hey!"*

Now the Cyclone was (and is) probably the best example of
roller coaster in the world. It had cost $175,000 to build; its
ghest peak was eighty-six feet; it was swift and smooth-rid-
g; for years it had been a top-notch money-maker. It had
rilled its riders by the hundreds of thousands; it was later to
ve at least one rider, Emilio Franco, a West Virginia coal
iner, the superthrill of his life. Franco suffered from aphonia,
hysterical affliction that had made him speechless. When he
imbed into the Cyclone he was skeptical, but when he was
unched into its screaming eighty-six-foot dive he screamed
o. And when, a moment later, he stepped out of the car at
ie end he announced, "I feel sick." Then he almost fainted,
; he realized what had happened.

For the Cyclone, in 1938, to be forced to slash prices of ad-

hris Feucht, who operates the Cyclone in partnership with George
ister, has owned roller coasters on Coney for more than 50 years.
)URTESY CONEY ISLAND CHAMBER OF COMMERCE. PHOTO BY MAUREY GARBER

mission, for the Cyclone to have to depend on the monstrously amplified voice of a bored talker, said much for the qualitative decline of barking and ballyhoo and for the simultaneous quantitative crescendo.

And then, quite suddenly, there came a change. In 1938, a law was passed. The beach and the boardwalk were put under the jurisdiction of the Park Department, the commissioner of which, Robert Moses, promptly outlawed the ballyhoo and indicated that the spieler would henceforth have to mute his voice or likewise face outlawry. Moreover, the License Commissioner, Paul Moss, announced that the same would apply on Surf Avenue and the Bowery.

Well! Such a wailing and caterwauling from Coney's sideshow promotors! Jimmy Sullivan, 65, a three-foot midget who for five years had ballyhooed a ride called the Motordrome by engaging in a boxing-match with another midget, announced that he was going back on relief. "Commissioner Moses has forced me to," said Sullivan. "He won't let me earn an honest living. He doesn't think ballyhoo is dignified." Professor Sam Wagner, David Rosen, and Fred Sindel—the three ranking freak show entrepreneurs—were all arrested for ballyhooing their sideshows. They pleaded that the whole history of the Island had been woven around the mastery of the ballyhoo artist. They invoked the shade of Omar Sami. Ballyhoo, they insisted, was "traditional," it was "inseparable," it was "ancient," it was "customary." "Custom and usage, even though of long standing, cannot be used to override the plain provisions of the penal statutes," ruled the judge. Thereafter he flipped the pages of the statute books, seeking a plain provision. He sighed. The court reporter heard him mutter something about "the most intricate set of statutes ever devised" and "maze of violations." The court thereupon dismissed the charges for want of a punishment to fit the crime.

But the ballyhoo on Coney was dead. Professor Sam Wagner
eened over the injustice of it, but he bit the bullet. With
ostalgia, he recalled the seasons when thirty thousand people
day had filed through Sam Gumpertz's Dreamland Circus
ideshow. In 1938, he moaned, he was lucky if he could draw
pitiful eight thousand.

Dr. Couney was only slightly more hopeful. "Look," he said,
ointing toward the boardwalk. "See all those rubbish cans
ning the rail? Moses put them there. Why, you used to come
ut here in the morning and find the boardwalk cluttered with
ll sorts of junk. Now look at it. It's clean." Moses, the doctor
sisted, might just possibly save the Island. "I have been here
or thirty-five years," he said, "and I have known Coney Island
rhen it was truly great. But the Island has gone backward and
ow it has reached the end. Maybe Mr. Moses can restore it,
ut I don't know how. Maybe by force."

But these bleak premonitions did not endure. Amusement
en on Coney discovered that the crowds still came; the sea
ill rolled up on the white sand; there was still fun for all. But
rith a difference. Things had quieted down. The jangle and
e clatter were gone, gone with the demise of the nickel
mpire.

Something new was in gestation: none could be quite sure
rhat; but maybe this time it would not be a squalling monster.
urely it would be big and bouncing: all hands hoped it might
rove, as well, more decorous.

Harper's Weekly, 1881. N. Y. PUBLIC LIBRARY

~*Frolicsome*~

On every warm summer weekend on Coney Island a gr[e]
swarm of people may be found heading for a slow-moving li[ne]
that leads always to the same entertainment device. Typical[ly]
they will wait nearly an hour to enjoy a ride that lasts for p[er]
haps one mildly exhilarating minute. Judged as a thrill, the ri[de]
packs about as much punch as a cup of cambric tea. Nor [is]
there anything novel about it; on the contrary, there is on[ly]
one ride more ancient in the entire country. It is a safe bet th[at]
at any given moment, there are youngsters standing in this li[ne]
whose fathers and mothers stood here a generation ago, and t[he]
odds would not be too high that there are even some who[se]
grandfathers and grandmothers pressed patiently forwa[rd]
toward the same admission gate. Nevertheless, this ride is, ye[ar]
in and year out, the most popular entertainment device in a[ny]
amusement park in the world. On Broadway, smash hits ha[ve]
opened and had their laughably brief runs of four or five yea[rs]
and closed, but still this ride unceasingly packs them in. Movi[es,]
radio, and television have each mounted their threats but t[he]
ride has met them with only the most minor concessions [to]
change. Something like one hundred million admissions ha[ve]

een checked through its turnstiles and the end of its success
nowhere in sight. Most perplexing of all, perhaps four out of
ve of those who wait patiently in line nearly an hour for their
rief, tepid ride know that when it is over they will be obliged
» pass through a tunnel only to emerge blinking onto a small
age where they will be teased, tripped up, tickled, prodded,
1d submitted to various adolescent indignities at the hands of
olicsome strangers, such as having their hats whisked off or
1eir skirts blown up about their faces, while all the time an
1dience of four or five hundred persons rocks in helpless
1ughter at their confusion and dismay. This abiding phenome-
on is called the Steeplechase Horses; it is the premier enter-
1inment offered at Steeplechase Park, the last and only endur-
1g amusement park at Coney Island, the park that is today,
»r all intents and purposes, synonomous and very nearly co-
•rminous with the entertainment area that is summoned up in
1e imagination of the millions whenever they hear the magic
ords, "Coney Island." The Steeplechase Horses are, addi-
onally, a lasting monument to Coney's greatest showman, the
an who in 1897 installed them as the principal attraction of
1s prototypal carnival grounds. This was George Cornelius
ilyou, whose formula, to lapse into the alliterations of the
deshow spiel, was a matchless mixture of sentimentality,
1rewd psychology, a sound sense of civic expansion, and a
1ffusion of sophomoric sex.

To claim that Tilyou was Coney's greatest showman will
art an argument. He hit the road to scout out attractions for
s park, but he never ransacked the world, as did a Sam Gum-
ertz, nor were the attractions Tilyou brought back to Coney
. eye-catching as Gumpertz's. Tilyou patented a couple of
»zen features and mechanical devices, but he had nothing like
1e inventive ingenuity of a William Mangels, whose rides,
1ch as the Whip, have been features of amusement parks in

In 1900, when this picture was taken, George C. Tilyou dressed the part of a successful showman. It was still partly just front.

a score of countries all over the world. Tilyou's creative imagi nation was a pale and paltry thing beside that of Frederi Thompson, the co-founder of Luna Park on Coney and th Hippodrome in Manhattan. But apart from the fact that Ti you's Steeplechase Park triumphantly survives where all th others are only fond memories, there is good reason to ced him the palm as Coney's greatest showman. In one respect, h stood alone. No one in the outdoor amusement field, not eve Phineas T. Barnum, had Tilyou's sure psychological insigh into what people wanted, when they sought entertainmen and into what would make them come back again and agai He was not himself wholly aware of his gift. In 1909, whe Coney was at its glittering height as a center of popular enter tainment, with three vast parks all going full swing and a sky line bristling for a mile or more with rides, dips, chutes, wheel giant see-saws, and roller coasters, a journalist asked the suze

ains of Luna, Dreamland, and Steeplechase to explain why
heir resorts had appeal. The others were offhand and gave
whatever answer occurred to them at the moment, but Tilyou
ad been genuinely puzzling over the matter. "Generally
peaking," he said, "I would think that any success in the
musement business is unaccountable. But from particular in-
tances I've come to the broad conclusion that what attracts
he crowd is the wearied mind's demand for relief in uncon-
idered muscular action." This is a very limited appreciation
f his own discovery. Barnum is credited with the judgment
hat there is a sucker born every minute, and it is a useful
phorism; but Tilyou, mining this rich lode further, brought
p an even more priceless nugget. He showed that people will
ay good money over and over again for the privilege of them-
elves supplying the entertainment. During the season the
teeplechase pavilion resounds day and night with the merri-
nent of those who have shelled out to make themselves look
idiculous and to watch others in the same foolish predicament.
t Steeplechase, the paying patron is the show. It is the apogee
f canny showmanship.

George C. Tilyou was born in New York City in 1862. When
e was three years old his parents, Peter and Ellen Mahoney
Tilyou, leased one of the huge 300-foot ocean-front lots then
vailable on Coney, for $35 a year, and on it they built the
urf House. Peter's father had been a recorder in New York;
hanks to this political background the Surf House over the
ears became a favorite resort for New York and Brooklyn city
fficials and their families. Young George may have read some
f Horatio Alger's earliest books and absorbed their virtuous
omilies; in any event, there was about his boyhood something
f "Eric, or Little By Little"—but with a difference. Alger's
eroes were dimwitted youths who won their way to good
ortune by relentless piety and the occasional sweat of their

brow. Young Tilyou was pious and he never shirked work, bu
he was far from dimwitted. Indeed, by the time he was fou
teen he had already displayed a precocious insight into th
psychology of the holiday pleasure-seeker.

Coney, in the summer of 1876, was crowded with touris
from the Midwest who, drawn east by the Philadelphia Cer
tennial Exhibition, had wandered down for their first glimps
of a real, live ocean. George showed the true Coney Islan
instinct. Correctly guessing that these simple folk would be
lieve that an article had value if only it had a price upon i
he filled medicine bottles with salt water and cigar boxes wit
sand and sold them by the score at a quarter apiece. Yea
later he told an interviewer, "For my first day's labor, I realize
$13.45, which seemed to me a fortune, so I immediately retire
Having heard of the great exhibition in Philadelphia, I starte
alone for that place with the full intention of purchasing th
main building, but after arriving on the grounds I change
my plans and bought pink lemonade and pop-corn instead.
Such a course could not better describe the behavior of a goof
Alger hero, but of course young Tilyou—his quoted statemen
to the contrary notwithstanding—did no such thing. Instea
he very sensibly spent his profits on the purchase of a horse
then borrowed another; from driftwood he contrived a stage
coach; the following season he started transporting tripper
from the boat landing at Norton's Point on the west end o
Coney to Culver Plaza in the middle of the Island, and he wa
always ready to encourage his passengers to stop off at hi
father's Surf House on the way, if they were so minded. By th
end of the season he owned six horses and two stages; this wa
an enterprise successful enough to attract the attention o
John Y. McKane, then riding high as political boss of the Island
McKane promptly got ideas about selling a franchise for th
route; even more promptly young Tilyou, as yet loath to buc

McKane, sold all his assets and looked around for further opportunities. In 1879, when he was seventeen, the real estate business beckoned. At that time land could not be sold; title was firmly held by the town of Gravesend; but there was a brisk and piratical traffic in leases and sub-leases. What had happened to one lot on Ocean Parkway was common gossip. One of the more venal of the town's commissioners of common lands had leased the lot for $41 a year; one-eighth of it he sub-leased for $1,000 a year to a woman who in turn leased a modest fraction of her one-eighth for $4,000 a year. Where pyramids like these were a-building, there was room for a man of seventeen with vision. Presently young Tilyou was netting $250 a month, operating out of an office he had constructed by cleating two bathhouses together. His younger brother Edward became his partner.

The Steeplechase Park of 1898 featured, then as now, the Steeplechase Horses, which careened over the track in the background.   MUSEUM OF THE CITY OF NEW YORK

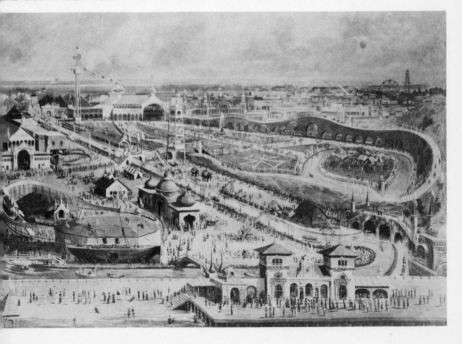

But this was just money, and it bored him. He thirsted to be a showman. Here were all these people, down from New York and Brooklyn for the sun and the sea breezes: was it enough that they had a splendid beach and an ocean? Didn't they want entertainment as well? Tilyou bet that they did. When he was twenty, he and his father Peter put up the Island's first theatre: Tilyou's Surf Theatre; Pat Rooney, Sam Bernard, and Weber & Fields are among those who appeared on its stage; and to make sure that audiences would be able to find their way easily, through the cluster of clam bars and bathhouses and lager-beer saloons, the Tilyous cut a rude alley that bisected the walks from Surf Avenue to the ocean, and paved it with planks. They called it Ocean View Walk, but the name didn't stick. A Mrs. Newton, the mother of the Dick Newton who was already McKane's chief lieutenant, came by one day and saw the throngs of people heading down the plank walk toward the Surf Theatre. She sniffed. "What are you trying to do, George?" she asked. "If you're not careful, this place will get to be a regular Bowery!" In New York the Bowery, as she knew, had already become synonomous with sin and theatrical bright lights and immoral gaiety; the same would soon be true of this narrow alley a block away from the Atlantic; and hers was the name that stuck.

A successful real estate operator, the manager of a profitable theatre, Tilyou was in his twenties already a man of substance. When the law was passed permitting the sale of Gravesend's common lands, he shelved his dream of becoming an entertainment magnate in favor of an expanding bank balance. He rented his theatre and concentrated on real estate. In the spring of 1886 he published the first (and last) issue of a four-page newspaper, *Tilyou's Real Estate Telephone*, a revealing document on several counts. For one, it shows that its editor and publisher had left his heart on the same shelf with his dream of show business. He could not help himself: he gave his most preferred space to a burst of his own doggerel: if he was corny he was also carny: and he perceived that then, as now, Coney's greatest razzle-dazzle and hoop-la was the sand and the sea. Those who wince at puns should avert their gaze:

SEA SONABLE

"Ocean me not," the lover cried,
"I am your surf—to you I'm tide;
Don't breaker heart, fair one, but wave
Objections thine, this sand I crave."

"Oh billow Bill," she blushed, "I sea
You would beach ozen shore by me,
But I'm mermaid not yet in seine,
And shell for years that way remain."

He was less an editor than a sideshow barker, and he was convinced that enticing though the ballyhoo might be the show inside was even more resplendent. The voice was stentorian yet seductive; we can see the outflung arm and the brandished cane directing our gaze to the ballyhoo: "If Paris is France," he wrote, "then Coney Island, between June and September, is the world. English dukes and earls, French viscomtes, German barons, senators and even presidents and vice-presidents, railroad kings, merchant princes, society queens—every human being of eminence or note in the American Continent can be found promenading the enormous hotel corridors, dining in the vast saloons or wandering on the beach." With the greatest difficulty he restrained himself from the use of exclamation points, but occasionally they burst out like nettlerash. "Westward, Ho!" he called, intending merely the western half of Coney Island, "Westward is the way to look! For employ-

ment and business you may now look towards the East, if you
will, but for enterprise, mirth and recreation keep your eye
on the West!" And indeed it was George Tilyou who gave the
name West Brighton to the community in the center of the
Island, where in the next twenty years all the great amusement
parks would arise.

His journal also affords a picture of Coney in 1886. Nearly
two pages were given over to announcements of the properties
available for lease or purchase: lots, cottages, apartments,
hotels and pavilions, boarding houses, and concession stands
for everything from pails and shovels to sausages and weighing
scales and ball games and shooting galleries—anything, as he
said, "from a Railroad to a Lemonade Stand," priced from as
little as $25 for a vacant lot to $4,000 for rental of a hotel to
$30,000 for sale of seven three-story houses on the Boulevard
near the Brighton Beach racetrack. And there were

CONEY ISLAND NOTES

The Hotel Brighton is being repaired where the heavy
tides of the past winter damaged the brick foundation.

Feltman is getting his large Hotel and Dancing Pavilion
in readiness for business, as he anticipates an early opening
for the season.

Boats will land at the Old Iron Pier the coming season.

Stratton & Henderson will open their "Sea Side Hotel" with
a company of first class artists about May 1st.

De Verna, it is rumored, intends building a large theatre
at the Island, somewhat after the plans of the Metropolitan
Opera House, New York.

It is said that the Brighton will introduce American fireworks the coming summer on their grounds.

Racing will be inaugurated at Brighton Beach Fair Grounds
about May 20th.

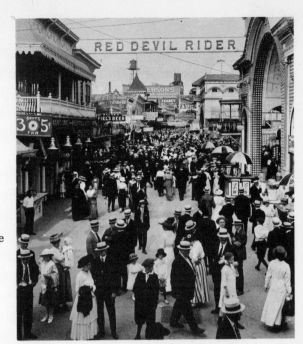

The Tilyous built it; Mrs. Newton named it; from the start it was Coney Island's midway. This was the Bowery, in 1909.
COURTESY THE FRANCIS K. MOORE COLLECTION

But the most notable aspect of his paper was what was missing. He had advertisements, including one for his father's New Sea Beach Bathing Pavilion, where "1,000 new Fancy Flannel Bathing Suits" were on hand against the coming season, and another for one of the first rides to be established on Coney ("Visitors should not fail to ride on the great Flying Boat Coaster in front of Feltman's Ocean Pavilion"); he had articles on local history, editorials on local politics; but nowhere was there so much as a mention of the name of Coney's most important citizen, John Y. McKane. The omission was not inadvertent. Indeed, affairs had been building to a climax for some time between the Tilyous and the Pooh-Bah of Coney Island. Father and son both quite openly opposed McKane. There is a tradition on Coney to the effect that, at least in the case of the son, the opposition to McKane was moral. George Tilyou, so runs the story, was a reformer, and because Coney Islanders have always been tolerably free and easy in their ways, the word *reformer* is more often sneered than spoken.

But it was not the idealism of a reformer that set Tilyou's teeth on edge when he thought about McKane; rather it was the stubborn realism of a businessman. McKane, to Tilyou's way of thinking, jeopardized grosses. By appointing ruffians and rogues as his justices of the peace, by winking at prostitution, by plundering the community, he was making Coney a stench in the nostrils of decent folk everywhere; and Tilyou wanted those decent folk as his customers. When in 1887 the investigating committee of the State Assembly was unable to loosen McKane's grip on the resort, Tilyou accepted the inevitable. His real estate office was on land owned by Lucy Vanderveer, and so was McKane's police headquarters. His landlady, with some embarrassment, explained to him that McKane had instructed her to give him the boot. He nodded. He had expected it. He was, as they say in show business, at liberty.

His capital dwindled. His father had been stripped of his property and forced off the island; only the intervention of a friend, Theodore Kramer, had enabled his mother to hang on to a bit of land. Kramer was a milkman and the father of a big family. He was one of those—the family trade—who had been welcomed at the Surf House and encouraged to come back again. When he heard how McKane's guile and strong arm had wrested from the Tilyous their property and their livelihood, he came to Ellen, George's mother, and offered her his life savings so that she might save Eileen Villa, the family home. She hesitated, but he insisted. In the meantime, she had opened the Mikado Baths, taking the name from the Mikado Bathing Club, a group of Brooklyn politicians who had for years held their clambakes at the Surf House. (One of them was Charley Ebbets, the sportsman who owned a big share of the Brooklyn Dodgers.) George kept his mouth shut. He helped his mother run the Mikado; he amused himself by inventing a primitive ride, the Aerial Racing Slide; but he chafed. It never, however, occurred to him to move away from Coney: he had sand in his shoes, and there is a saying on Coney that you never shake it loose.

In 1893 he married Mary O'Donnell, borrowed some money from his mother, and took off on his honeymoon to see the Chicago World's Columbian Exposition of 1893. There, on the Midway Plaisance, he was captivated by the wondrous invention of G. W. G. Ferris. He looked about, noting how jaws dropped and eyes popped as people looked on this first Ferris Wheel, and he coveted it. The time was propitious: McKane, as he knew, was in trouble, back on Coney, perhaps at last on the skids. He was too late to buy the monstrous toy; it was already promised to the St. Louis Fair for delivery in 1904; but he could have a more modest wheel built. The Ferris Wheel was two hundred and fifty feet in diameter; each of its thirty-six cars accommodated sixty passengers. Tilyou borrowed more money and ordered, for delivery in the spring of 1894, a wheel one hundred and twenty-five feet in diameter, with twelve cars carrying eighteen passengers apiece. He rented some land between Surf Avenue and the ocean and put up a sign that unblushingly announced: "On This Site Will Be Erected the World's Largest Ferris Wheel"; on the strength of this whopper he sold enough concession space to make payment on delivery. He studded his plaything with hundreds of incandescent lamps; it was the Island's first, big, glittering attraction, and its owner was off the nut before it had been in operation half-a-hundred days.

And now, with McKane in Sing Sing and Coney Island part of Brooklyn and decent folk once again flocking to the beach by the scores of thousands on every summer weekend, Tilyou was able to branch out. He had his Aerial Slide, he had his Ferris wheel, he imported a something called the Intramural

Bicycle Railway, he built another ride called the Double Dip Chutes; but they were scattered all over West Brighton. It might never have occurred to him to group them all in one place and assist them to multiply had it not been for the arrival on Coney of Captain Paul Boyton.

Boyton was almost as much a world-wide celebrity eighty years ago as Lindbergh was thirty years ago. Lindbergh was the first to fly solo across the Atlantic; Boyton did not, to be sure, swim the entire distance but there was as much fooferaw over his exploits as if he had. His apprentice years were spent in sedentary pursuits: at fifteen he joined the Union Navy, to fight in the Civil War; for a month or so he fought in a Mexican revolution; he was a franc-tireur in the Franco-Prussian War and participated briefly in the French Commune; he wanted to help the Cubans throw off their Spanish yoke, but when his vessel was captured off Sandy Hook he reluctantly headed for South Africa to dig up diamonds. By 1873 he was captain of the first life-saving service, at Atlantic City; in that year and the next he singlehandedly saved seventy-one lives. He was then twenty-six years old and on the threshold of fame. It came in an unlikely guise. A Pittsburgh manufacturer, C. S. Merriman, had invented a rubber suit as a life-saving device for transatlantic steamship passengers; he wondered if Boyton would care to demonstrate it. The suit was very supple and perfectly water-tight. Behind the head, on the back, on the chest, and along each thigh were compartments filled with air. Only the face was exposed. It weighed thirty-five pounds. Boyton climbed in. He found that he could float standing up, leaving his chest and shoulders well out of water; with a small, double-bladed paddle he could lie on his back and shoot through the water feet first at the rate of one hundred strokes a minute. He was enchanted. In the summer of 1874 he paddled miles out to sea off the Jersey coast, but this was child's play:

he determined to make his way back to shore from a ship two
hundred miles at sea. The journals of the time handled his
proposal as they would have that of any other nut, as a one-day
joke. Boyton found it impossible to buy passage on any ship
bound out of New York harbor. In the face of this unanimous
skepticism, he bade his friends farewell, urged them to keep
the coffee warm on the back of the stove, and stowed away
aboard the steamer *Queen,* bound for Queenstown and Liverpool. Two hundred miles out to sea, the *Queen's* master,
Captain Bragg, saw that a group of passengers had gathered on
the forward deck and here, from their midst, came a man clad
in rubber from head to foot, and headed for the rail. Bragg
dashed down and got a grip on Boyton just before he could
plunge into the drink. Boyton claimed that he was a penitent
stowaway, so ashamed of his behavior that he proposed forthwith to head home. But it was no use: Bragg yanked off his
rubber suit and insisted Boyton stay as his guest.

Bragg was, however, reckoning without Boyton's gift of gab.
Ten days out of New York, a day off the coast of Ireland,

If Boyton's exploits had been
performed in the glare of
modern journalism, his name
would still be a household
word. As it was, he and his
rubber suit caused quite a
rumpus.
COURTESY PAUL BOYTON, JR.

and Boyton had persuaded him that he could land in Ireland unaided. On the night of October 21, 1874, Boyton went over side of a ship rolling in heavy seas. The *Queen* paused, her motors stilled, until he had kicked his way clear. Then he was alone, in the darkness.

Boyton was water-borne at nine p.m. At eleven the sea was being pounded by a westerly gale, and during that night fifty-six craft, from skiffs to Channel packets, were to be wrecked on the shores of the British Isles; but Boyton paddled on. After seven hours in the water he passed the Cape Clear Light and came wearily up Roaringwater Bay past Baltimore toward Skibbereen. There the folk thought he must have paddled all the way from New York. By the time he got to Cork, by stage, he was a full-fledged celebrity. In Dublin, he paddled down the Liffey and across the bay from Howth Head to Dalkey; in London, Queen Victoria presented him with a gold chronometer, and in February he floated down the Thames; after one fruitless attempt, he paddled his way across the Channel from Cap Gris Nez to Fan Bay, eating comfortably and puffing on a cigar as he went. He was greeted by an eleven-gun salute and a telegram from President Grant. From then on, it was a succession of triumphs: swimming 450 miles down the Rhine, negotiating the Rhone, the Seine, the Po, the Loire, the Tiber, the Danube, and the Tagus. He rigged up a tiny boat, the *Baby Mine*, loaded it with food and gear, and towed it after him from Naples to Capri, across the Straits of Gibraltar and of Messina. New York accorded him a hero's welcome and its newspapers devoted hundreds of columns to his conquests of the Mississippi, the Missouri, the Ohio, the Hudson. The president of Peru gave him a captaincy for, as was commonly believed, the feat of swimming by night to a Chilean man-of-war and blowing it up. In 1885 he took a party of reporters down New York Bay to show them how he could, undetected, clamp a dummy torpedo on the hull of a British Royal Navy cruiser; after he had done so and roused the watch, he and the reporters were pursued, captured, and held for a few minutes under arrest, but the exploit guaranteed him gorgeous publicity for his aquatic circus. He roadshowed this attraction for a number of years but at length decided to settle down. He bought a great plot of land back of the Elephant Hotel on Coney and opened his Sea Lion Park—the first outdoor amusement park in the world—in time for the Fourth of July weekend in 1895.

The captain was his own headline attraction, but there were as well a broad lagoon, and forty sea lions trained to juggle, and water races, and an old-mill water ride—and there was the Shoot-the-Chutes, an aquatic toboggan slide in flat-bottomed boats. This was so successful that presently the captain was able to launch similar watery thrills in Boston, Chicago, Washington, and San Francisco, but it was the idea of a park enclosed by a fence with admission charged at the gate that

Boyton's Shoot-the-Chutes, "The King of All Amusements," was the compelling magnet to the world's first outdoor amusement park. COURTESY KINGS COUNTY CLERK'S OFFICE

impressed George Tilyou. He cast about for the one sure-pop device that would do for him what the Shoot-the-Chutes had done for Boyton. The most popular sport of the times was, by all odds, horseracing; for six months a year Coney was crowded with people who had spent the afternoon at the races at Gravesend or Sheepshead Bay or Brighton Beach; when Tilyou heard of a British invention—a mechanical racecourse—he knew he had found what he needed. The device was imperfect, but Tilyou was able to develop and improve it beyond recognition. In time for the season of 1897 he opened Steeplechase Park on a plot slightly larger than fifteen acres. (Tilyou never said fifteen acres; he preferred to say 655,000 square feet. His sons, or their press agents, have gradually increased the size of the park. In 1922 his oldest son, the late Edward Tilyou, admitted that the claim of twenty-one acres was an exaggeration. "But who," he asked reasonably, "would ever think that the number twenty-one had been made up?" Today the same plot measures twenty-five acres, at least in the park's promotion material. As Milton Berger, the park's current press agent, says: "I inherited the figure, and I never did learn how to count acres." The premier attraction at the park, then as now, was the Steeplechase Horses: an undulant, curving, metal track over which large wooden (they are now metal) horses ran on wheels, coursing down by gravity and soaring up by momentum, in tolerable imitation of a real horse race. In addition, there was the Ferris wheel, a Grand Canal with naphtha launches, a miniature steam railroad, the biggest ballroom in the state of New York with four bands playing intermittently, and a variety of other rides. Keeping a firm check-rein on his addiction to inflated adjectives, "This stupendous amusement," Tilyou wrote, in 1901, "forms the most enchanting and magnetic fun-making resort in the world. An enchanting evening sight at the Steeplechase," he added, losing his grip on his

For sentimental reasons, the Tilyou family keeps its 64-year-old Ferris wheel rolling, season after season. And it's still fun.   COURTESY STEEPLE-
CHASE PARK

syntax, "is the numerous handsomely gowned ladies accompanied by gentlemen in full dress. The elite of the cities make
the Steeplechase their rendezvous while in town."

The statement was, in 1901, more wistful than accurate. In

their home across Surf Avenue, his wife Mary knew better. If business was poor at Steeplechase, there were plenty of chairs for her guests; if business was booming, her guests sat on the floor. Her guests were uncomfortable less often than she would have liked. Nineteen hundred and one was the year of the Pan-American Exposition at Buffalo and Tilyou went on a scouting trip. As eight years before the Ferris Wheel had dominated the Chicago fair, at Buffalo the eye-catcher was a cyclorama, A Trip to the Moon. It was a spectacular illusion, the creation of a young architectural student, Frederic W. Thompson. He had designed it late one night when hunger kept him awake. He had subsequently formed a partnership with Elmer (Skip) Dundy, and by 1901 it appeared that he would never be hungry again. Formerly bitter competitors in

A Trip to the Moon had the place of honor, just left of the entrance, in Luna Park's fantastic fairyland of soaring minarets. COURTESY THE FRANCIS K. MOORE COLLECTION

the business of supplying fairs with entertainments, they had
joined forces at Buffalo and were coining money faster than a
machine could have done. Besides their Trip to the Moon, they
had another cyclorama called Darkness and Dawn, a con-
trivance called the Old Plantation, a Giant See-Saw, and a half-
dozen other lucrative concessions. If they had a problem, it
was how they would fill their time from 1901 in Buffalo to 1904
in St. Louis. Tilyou solved it for them. He offered them a minimum guarantee against sixty per cent of the net if they would
bring their Trip to the Moon to Steeplechase. They came and
they brought the Giant See-Saw as well. The season of 1902 was
one of the wettest in Coney's history. Old-timers claim that of
the ninety-two days in June, July, and August, rain fell on
seventy. Business at Boyton's Sea Lion Park was macabre.
But despite the gruesome weather, Steeplechase, thanks to A
Trip to the Moon, did handsomely. That fall, Tilyou considered.
He knew that Boyton was in difficulty; he knew, moreover,
that Thompson and Dundy were aggressive, imaginative partners, men who could raise money and spend it in showmanlike
fashion. Coney, he concluded, would gain if Thompson and
Dundy were permanent residents. Perhaps they could be
maneuvered into the position of building their own park.
Having so reasoned, Tilyou offered them a renewal of their
contract in which their share of the net was sliced from sixty
to forty per cent. They glared at him. He grinned pleasantly.
They said they would let him know in a few days. When they
came back, it was to tell him that they had taken an option
on Paul Boyton's park and that they proposed to build a park
of their own that would drive Steeplechase right out of business. As soon as they could find the horses to do the job, they
added, they would move their Trip to the Moon out of Steeplechase and down Surf Avenue to Sea Lion Park. As for their
Giant See-Saw—but now there came a pause. The See-Saw did

not fit into Thompson's vision of their new park. Dundy mentioned that it had cost them $40,000, but of course, he added witheringly, Tilyou was too close-fisted to pay such a price. Tilyou smiled. "Let's toss for it," he offered, "double or nothing." Dundy tossed a coin toward a crack between two boards. It landed within an inch of the crack. Tilyou hefted a half-dollar, measured, and tossed. His coin landed, rolled in a curve, and settled—on the crack. Dundy whistled thoughtfully. "The See-Saw," said he, "is yours. Mind if I take your half-dollar, just to remember you by?" He and his partner, Thompson, left, on their way to build Luna Park. Tilyou winked to his brother-in-law, Fred Erzinger, who had witnessed the transaction. "Coney wins," he said.

Thompson and Dundy not only raised scads of money—John W. (Bet-a-Million) Gates put up a large share of the nearly $1,000,000 they borrowed—they also spent with a free hand. Indeed, they just about came out even. Dundy spent the last day before their grand opening raising $22 in change for use by their ticket-sellers that night; at that, some thousands of persons were admitted free because the change had run out. More than 43,000 persons passed through the gates to look upon what was unquestionably the most attractive park that had been built up to that time. The partners had bought more than Boyton's old Sea Lion Park; they had bought, as well, the land up to Surf Avenue where, until the fire of 1896, the Elephant had stood. (They found the remains of one of the Elephant's front legs when they were clearing ground; Thompson, for obscure reasons, regarded it as an omen of good luck and was ever afterwards partial to elephant acts.) And on it they had strewed a profusion of entertainments, a magic fairyland of spires and minarets and towers. "Straight lines," Thompson insisted, "are necessarily severe and dead." The Trip to the Moon was still a stellar attraction (the name of the park, however, came not from this illusion but from Skip Dundy's sister, Luna Dundy, back in Des Moines) but they had also added a Trip to the North Pole, a War of the Worlds, a Dragon's Gorge, bands, theatres, ballrooms, animal acts, railroads, rides, free vaudeville acts on a platform built out into the lagoon, and a hundred smaller concessions. And they had retained the Shoot-the-Chutes, on which for years Captain Paul Boyton would receive a handsome royalty. By day Luna was sufficiently captivating but by night it was breathtaking, with every building and its architectural ornaments picked out against the black velvet sky by hundreds of thousands of lights. "Ah, God," murmured one enraptured visitor, "what might the prophet have written in Revelation, if only he had first beheld a spectacle like this!"

Luna was an immediate and stupendous success, just as in Paris and London and Berlin and Buenos Aires and Rio de Janeiro parks with the same name have been successful, but Thompson and Dundy were not the men to stand still. If an attraction failed to pay for itself in a single season, it was in danger of being scrapped. They experimented constantly with rides: The Tickler, the Bump-the-Bumps, the Virginia Reel: as Thompson said of them, they were "nothing more than improved cellar doors"; his more static entertainments, like the Witching Waves or the Lost Girl, were "only elaborations of the doll-house stunts of childhood." He wanted movement, excitement, action. There were benches along the midway at Luna, but if Thompson saw too many people sitting on them he was provoked. He would summon one of his six bands and set the musicians to marching about, blaring lustily. Once, during a torrential summer thunder shower, all his customers sought shelter. Thompson was shocked. He ordered his biggest orchestra, sixty musicians, front and center and bade them play and play while he scurried about, chivvying the smaller bands into sullen activity. But no sooner was the last fretful tuba-player poomping amidst the downpour than Thompson heard his sixty-piece orchestra swing plaintively into a popular ditty of the day:

> Ain't it a shame, a measly shame,
> To keep me standing, out in the rain!

The others all joined in, in one massive, mournful chorus, and Thompson capitulated.

Thompson and Dundy parlayed their success with Luna into the great Hippodrome, in New York City, at a cost of $4,000,000. There was never a more glamorous arena for vaudeville acts: more than 6,000 persons crowded their way in for the opening performance to see elephants slide down the Shoot-

the-Chutes, and a battalion of chorus girls march unblinkingly
down a series of shallow steps to vanish into a tank of water,
and lissome divers plunge from seventy-foot platforms into the
same shallow pool. The partners were on the crest of the wave.
If their net receipts were not a constant reminder, their success
was attested by the fact that Dreamland, a frank imitation, had
opened across Surf Avenue from Luna with all possible dispatch, ready to compete with them after a single season. By
1905 a child who went to Coney Island could, thanks to Luna
and Dreamland and the other spectacular exhibits, arrive at a
fairly approximate idea of the universe around him and, in
the bargain, be magnificently entertained. He could visit an
Indian durbar, an Eskimo village, an island in the Philippines
complete with fifty-one allegedly head-hunting Igorots, a
garden in Japan, the Alps of Switzerland, or the canals of
Venice; he could watch Mount Pelée erupt, killing forty thousand, or sit enthralled while in front of him the dam burst and
the rivers engulfed Johnstown; he could be taken through the
Great Deep Rift Coal Mine of Pennsylvania, he could see the
huge tidal wave destroy Galveston; he could go under the sea
in a submarine or whirl giddily aloft in an airplane; he could
crawl into a tepee or an igloo or a Lilliputian village; he could
see a petrified whale or a performing flea; he could ride on a
camel or feed an elephant; it would take him a week to absorb
all the marvels proffered him and a lifetime to remember them.

But all these delights had by no means crowded Steeplechase
into the ocean. George Tilyou enthusiastically welcomed the
competition. The more that came to the Island, the better all
around. Indeed, he even invited further rivals. There was, for
example, LaMarcus A. Thompson. This man—he was not related to Fred Thompson—had put up a gravity railway on
Coney as far back as 1884; it was called the Switchback and,
although it was a relatively crude device, it was popular enough

Thanks to this ride, the first of its kind (1884), LaMarcus A. Thompson is known, among outdoor amusement men, as the "father of gravity."

to gross some $500 a day at five cents per passenger. Later in the same summer Charles Alcoke had opened an oval gravity ride, described in *Frank Leslie's Weekly*, in 1886, as "a contrivance designed to give passengers, for the insignificant expenditure of five cents, all the sensation of being carried away by a cyclone"; down went Thompson's grosses. The next summer there appeared a third primitive roller coaster on Coney, developed by Phillip Hinckle, and also superior to the Switchback; down still further went Thompson's grosses. Discouraged, he retreated from Coney to Atlantic City where he contrived the first scenic railway. This was an improvement on all the others, for the passengers were whirled through dark tunnels and grottoes; inside some, the cars tripped a switch that flooded the scenery with light; moreover, Thompson's Atlantic City ride no longer depended on gravity but rather on cable and steam power.

But despite the fact that Tilyou had himself opened a Steeplechase Pier at Atlantic City, his heart was still in Coney; he grieved that LaMarcus Thompson had deserted the beach. He tendered him a $40,000 guarantee if he would only bring back his scenic railway to Coney, and put it inside Steeplechase. Thompson did: and once more the cycle of success was repeated: so lucrative was the Scenic Railway that Thompson removed it from Steeplechase and established it just off Surf Avenue; moreover, he contrived a second amusement, the Pike's Peak Railway, an even more prosperous enterprise.

Tilyou's logic was irrefutable: the more attractions installed on Coney, the bigger the crowds, the greater the gaiety, the higher the profits. Nor did he fret over the fact that at Luna and Dreamland the diversions were more expensive and far more spectacular. His intuition had equipped him with a different formula, and he was beginning to ride it hard. A Trip to the Moon, he seemed to say to the public, is all very well, but after you have seen it once you have seen it for all time. True, he seemed to add, it is exhilarating to watch elephants slide down the Shoot-the-Chutes, but even elephants pall. There is only one creation, his formula insisted, endowed with infinite variety; this is the amusement devised by the Peerless Showman; it is people. All that Tilyou needed to do was contrive the most appropriate backgrounds for his star performers. By 1905 he had invented five of these and adapted a sixth. His inventions were:

The Wedding Ring, later called the Razzle Dazzle and still later the Hoop-La. This was a great circle of laminated wood suspended by wires from a center pole; as many as seventy persons at a time could perch insecurely upon it while four muscular and acrobatic attendants rocked it back and forth. When a girl lost her balance, in 1905, her ankles would show and she would have a reason to clutch at her escort. Hoop-la!

The Barrel of Love. This was a modest adaptation of the Switchback Railway. Passengers were strapped into seats in a revolving drum that rolled gently down one incline and up another. A nearby sign read: "Talk about love in a cottage! This has it beat a mile."

The Dew Drop. Its patrons climbed by leisurely stages to the top of a tower perhaps fifty feet high, climbed in, sat down, and were whirled feet first down and around and around and around again and out, upon a billowy platform. Once again, did you see those ankles?

The Whichaway, a swing that whirled its passengers eccentrically in any of four directions, but invariably catapulted a girl into her escort's lap.

The Earthquake Stairway. A flight of steps split down the middle so that one half could be jerked suddenly up while the other half was jerked a few inches down. A practical joke on the same level as the pail of water that tumbles down when a door is opened, this aberration was described at the time as "the most unique and side-splitting fun maker in existence."

Tilyou's adaptation was the feature of his main lobby. It was a system of compressed-air jets, to blow hats off the unwary and to send even the long, heavy skirts of the day swirling a few inches upward. As long before as 1876 such jets had been installed in the Philadelphia Exposition; they are used today at Steeplechase; they will, apparently, never lose their charm for a considerable section of humanity.

Remarkable as it may seem, each of these simple entertainments was notably popular in the early years of the century; around each of them thronged scores of people eager to see their fellows make fools of themselves; summer after summer they drew the same throngs back. In 1905, Steeplechase boasted twenty-five attractions, "every one of them original, up-to-date, and snappy," and since most of them were owned and con-

trolled by Tilyou they could all be sampled by buying a combination ticket for twenty-five cents. In those days the tendency
was to credit Tilyou's combination ticket for the undoubted
success of his park, and unquestionably it was shrewd mer-
chandising; but the main factor was his formula. Already by
1905 the celebrated Steeplechase Funny Face, the huge, grinning trade-mark described by at least one purist as "the most
incredibly vulgar insignia [sic]" he had ever seen, was causing
sensitive folk to wince as they passed by, along Surf Avenue.
(The frightful Face flaunts forty-four teeth, which is twelve
over par for the course, even presuming that any human smile
could reveal a complete set.) Behind that Face there were
wares quite different from those on display at Luna or Dreamland, but wares the public was quite as anxious to buy.

In a sense, although it could not have seemed so at the time,
the fire that razed Steeplechase in 1907 was a boon, for it
served to prove to Tilyou how popular his entertainments had
been. From all over the country hundreds of letters poured in
from former patrons, mourning the demise of the park and
exhorting him to rebuild. Here was an astonishing testimonial
to the merits of his formula. People had gone to Luna and to
Dreamland to ooh and aah, to be edified or amazed, but they
had come to Steeplechase to have fun. If Tilyou had hesitated,
if he had reflected that his comparable enterprises at Rockaway
Beach, Atlantic City, and Bridgeport were enough to keep him
busy and in funds, these letters changed his mind. Moreover,
he had the opportunity, in rebuilding from scratch, to design
a park expressly to fit his formula.

He organized a stock company and sold shares to the public
in lots of twenty at $5 a share. (Shareholders had a good
investment: their stock rarely paid less than a ten per cent
dividend, and for lagniappe they were given season passes to
the new park.) George C. Tilyou was president; his younger

brother Edward J. Tilyou, who had been general manager of the park since its inception, was secretary; Theodore W. Kramer, the Tilyous' old friend, was vice-president; and Tilyou's brother-in-law, James J. McCullough, was treasurer.

Up went a pavilion of steel and glass over a five-acre hardwood floor. This enabled him to operate an all-weather park; no longer did he need to pray for sunny weather, nor sweat and fret when clouds gathered over the beach. Outside there was still his Ferris wheel and his Giant See-Saw and a variety of carrousels and rides and coasters and swings; outside, too, was a vast swimming-pool; he lengthened the Steeplechase Pier so that steamboats from New York might find mooring. But it was inside, under the soaring, vaulted glass roof, that he really warmed to his task. This was the Pavilion of Fun, and here he concentrated all his earlier devices, improved now, and added still others. Once, the story goes, he had seen a baby mouse trying to escape from a deep soup-bowl: every attempt straight up the side was futile, and not until the mouse started racing around in a circle, gathering momentum, and always climbing a bit higher, was it able to escape. From this brief drama, Tilyou evolved what was first called the Human Roulette Wheel and later the Whirlpool, a whirling concave disc of polished wood, a melting-pot in which the ingredients were laughter, exhibitionism, and sex. When one or two dozen youngsters lay sprawling and scrambling on the sides of this disc, there would always be two or three dozen others, standing outside at the rim, laughing, pointing, clutching each other to point out some particularly ludicrous mishap inside, and gradually growing sufficiently fascinated with the tangle of arms and legs so that ("Come on, let's try it!" "You wanna?" "Sure! Where's the guy punches the ticket?") at the first opportunity they too would be sliding and scrambling and sprawling with the others. Another story runs that once, while

Rumps, bellies, legs, and breasts delighted Reginald Marsh's painter's eye; therefore he doted on Steeplechase. In this painting he focused on the Human Whirlpool and the Chair-o-plane. COURTESY REHN GALLERY, COLLECTION JOSEPH HIRSHHORN

he was strolling along the Coney Island beach, Tilyou came upon a group of youngsters at play. They had found a wheel somewhere, still on its axle; they had clapped a rude platform of boards on top of the wheel; one of their number would climb atop the platform and attempt to clutch on while the others spun the wheel. This incident inspired the Human Pool Table, a set of sixteen flat spinning discs, and with fiendish cunning Tilyou rigged these up at the foot of his old Dew Drop. Now, when a girl came whirling down and around and around the polished slide, she came dizzily to split-second rest on one disc, was flung to a second, a third, a fourth, now whirled this way, now that, her skirts flying, her squeals rising to the roof, her friends doubled up with laughter as they watched, and the entire company inside the pavilion infected with her mirth, the laughter spreading, rowdy, spirited, adolescent, uncontrollable, sensual, irresistible. And the Barrel of Love was now a great revolving drum of highly polished wood, ten feet in diameter and perhaps thirty feet long, slyly placed at the main entrance to the park so that two or three girls coming giggling in together might enter the Barrel without escorts but find, before they had negotiated the sliding, slippery, treacherous thirty feet that they had had the chance to twirl off-balance, clutching at air, so that every line of their young figures was shown to best advantage, or to slip and embrace the nearest male, the excited laughter again rising high—but in any event to emerge from the Barrel complete with escorts. Steeplechase—bigger, brighter, merrier than ever—by 1908 was back doing better business than ever at the old stand.

Never had there been such crowds at Coney. The resort had become an international phenomenon: every magazine of the era was obliged to dispatch writers and artists down to Coney to examine and assess. This hegira engendered its own remarkable competition. Each journalist vied with his fellows as to who could pen the most rhapsodic dithyramb. "Coney Island," wrote Richard LeGallienne, "is the Tom-Tom of America. Every nation has, and needs—and loves—its Tom-Tom. It has its needs of orgiastic escape from responsibility—that is, from the world of what-we-have-to-do into the world of what-we-would-like-to-do . . . Coney Island is the most human thing that God ever made, or permitted the devil to make." "Here it is," said Albert Bigelow Paine, "that the cup of gaiety and diversion overflows." To Lindsay Denison, Coney was "the magically realized dream of a poet or a painter." Guy Wetmore Carryl, who was so adept at graceful light verse, burst into song:

They used to talk of Bedlam and they used to talk of Babel,
In allusion to confusion of exaggerated style,
But in all of fact and fable, since the days of Cain and Abel,
No metaphor is better for the same than is an isle
That I wot of, that I got of late so generous a lot of,
That I recollect the style and charivari of that island
With a smile, and still shall do so for a while! . . .

Oh, the voice of Coney Island, as, alighting from a trolley,
You find her, and remind her that your deed should be excused!
With what bombilation jolly she replies to this, your folly!
She reckons you, she beckons you! Your suit is not refused!
She's a siren that a Byron might have lavished all his fire on,
She's a sorceress that spells you, that attracts you, that repels you,
And ah me! what things she tells you, when you want to be amused!

And Maxim Gorky came upon the Island by night, from the sea: "With the advent of night a fantastic city all of fire suddenly rises from the ocean into the sky. Thousands of ruddy sparks glimmer in the darkness, limning in fine, sensitive outline on the black background of the sky shapely towers of miraculous castles, palaces, and temples. Golden gossamer threads tremble in the air. They intertwine in transparent flaming patterns, which flutter and melt away, in love with their own beauty mirrored in the waters. Fabulous beyond conceiving, ineffably beautiful, is this fiery scintillation."

Fire, sparks, flaming patterns, fiery scintillation. The phrases were prophetic, for all three of Coney's great parks were to be ripped by fires in the following half-century. But only at Steeplechase would there be a disposition to repair, rebuild; only George Tilyou, and later his sons, insisted on maintaining their park. When Dreamland burned in 1911 and its politician-owners threw in the towel, Tilyou was able indeed to capitalize, however regretfully, on the circumstances. He purchased the blistered and soot-blackened El Dorado Carrousel and had it moved from West Fifth Street, where it had narrowly escaped destruction, down Surf Avenue to his pavilion, where he established it in the place of honor, centered amidst all his own inventions. It is, very likely, the most magnificent carrousel in the world. Bedecked with handsomely carved horses, pigs, ducks, cupids, and gondolas, it was originally built for William II, emperor of Germany; his imperial seal still adorns one of the chariots. When it was imported early in 1911 it was valued at $139,000; today it is insured for more than twice that sum, but its insurance does not accurately describe its value, for it is irreplaceable, a museum piece. There is no braver sight in any amusement park in the world than this imperial merry-go-round as it inscribes its stately circles, while the eye, carried up and around, rejoices in the ornate carvings and gay, rococo, colored statues with which the Tilyous have decorated their pavilion. The prospect is one of vigorous, unabashed, turn-of-century design; such artists as Reginald Marsh have long delighted to use it as background for their paintings.

Fire, when it came to Luna, brought merciful euthanasia. The park was launched on a long, gradual decline that commenced in the same year that Steeplechase first burned. Both Skip Dundy and Fred Thompson were sick men; the tension under which they had lived had cost them dearly. Dundy, who had suffered from heart trouble, died of pneumonia early in 1907. Without his business partner, Thompson was lost. The Hippodrome fell into the hands of the Shuberts and Luna opened year after year with never a single new attraction, for Thompson was caught up in the symptom of his sickness, alcoholism. Moreover, after his marriage to the young actress, Mabel Taliaferro, he was more concerned with producing plays, like *Polly of the Circus,* in which she could star, than in devising new spectacular illusions for his Coney Island park.

By 1912 he was bankrupt, and the business men crept in. A syndicate headed by Barron Collier, the advertising man, took over; within seven years Thompson had tragically succeeded in drinking himself to death. Without showmen at the helm, Luna drifted dowdily down the scale. Collier used sometimes to sail his yacht up Gravesend Bay and as far up Coney Island Creek toward the park as he could; then he and his party would disembark and take over Luna for the evening, while all the paying customers were shunted away. The spectacles grew frowsy and were dismantled; where once elephants had slid down the Shoot-the-Chutes now it was pigs. The park had its ups and downs in bankruptcy courts almost as giddy as the rides of its patrons on the Mile Sky Chaser. At length, in 1940, another syndicate bravely took over with a 21-year lease. The new manager promptly struck several of the old, beloved exhibits. "Coney," he announced, "is too conservative. Needs to be torn down and rebuilt." He put in new concessions, such as tanks in which daredevils fought sharks. "People," he said, "want blood for ten cents." But custom steadily declined, and new owners moved in to try their hand in 1944. That summer half of Luna burned; in 1947 another fire razed the old Trip to the Moon building; a third, in 1949, dealt the park its coup-de-grâce. The land became a parking lot and then the site for a housing development, and now only Steeplechase survives.

Steeplechase is still with us, a gay reminder of past excitements. George Tilyou died in 1914, but he had builded surely. His oldest son, the late Edward F. Tilyou, was eighteen when his father died; at once he assumed active management of the park. He and a pair of lively, irrepressible press agents, Matt and Eddie Dowden, had their hands full contriving to keep the park steadily in the public eye. For there was a brand-new audience to cajole. Patrons were no longer to be counted in

the hundreds of thousands, but in the millions, as first the
subway disgorged upon Coney all the hot and harassed masses
of Manhattan and the Bronx and later the Coney Island boardwalk offered them the tonic of ocean breezes. These were the
citizens of the nickel empire; and while the attractions at
Steeplechase could never be offered them for a nickel there
was a danger, unless their attention could somehow be attracted, they might continue so preoccupied with coupling or
changing diapers on the beach that they would never realize
those attractions were close at hand. Many of these newcomers
had never even heard of Steeplechase. Space in the newspapers
had to be hijacked. Thus, when General John J. Pershing returned from overseas, a garlanded hero, at the end of the first
Great War, and the newspapers were filled with long lists of
the honors being conferred on him and the gifts thrust upon
him, the Dowdens quite naturally sent him a gold lifetime pass
to the park. Miffed when no space was accorded this handsome
offering, they summoned a Western Union messenger and
gave him another pass, with instructions to deliver it in person
to the general at his hotel. Having notified all editors of the
upcoming ceremonial presentation, they thereupon engaged a
competent pickpocket to relieve the messenger of his gift en
route. That the general's present had been stolen by some
ingrate, perhaps even a subversive element, made headlines in
every paper in town.

Japes like these, however, were small potatoes in the park's
continuing popularity. More important was the fact that George
Tilyou's children, first Edward and since his death George and
Marie and Frank, have faithfully adhered to their father's un-
exampled formula. (Another daughter, Eileen Tilyou Mc-
Allister, administers the Steeplechase Pier at Atlantic City.)
That the formula is viable is attested by the way it has with-
stood the shock of three wars, a major depression, and Coney

Island's transition from the most fashionable seaside resort in the country, to the nickel empire of the 1920's and 1930's, to its uncertain status of today. The prevalent character of the Island seems to make no difference to Tilyou's formula. Whether Coney is glittering or dowdy, cheap or expensive, raffish or respectable, secure or facing a questionable future, Steeplechase packs them in. Season after season the crowds flock into the park, as many as fifteen thousand at a time, from the boardwalk, from Surf Avenue, and most of all from the Bowery.

It is appropriate that most of the patrons should approach George Tilyou's Steeplechase Park along the narrow street he first laid out seventy-odd years ago. Then, the young couples strolled along this Bowery headed for his Surf Theatre. Sixty years ago for the first time they walked down the Bowery for a look at the brand-new Steeplechase Horses, and among them were jockeys, come to Coney from the racetracks, who used to ride those horses in dead earnest, wagering on the outcome of the gravity ride. (It took them a while to learn that the horse with the heaviest rider had the best chance of winning.) At that time the Bowery was lined with dance pavilions and music halls and cabarets—Inman's Casino, Connor's Imperial Music Hall, the Trocadero, the West End Casino, Perry's Glass Pavilion—advertising "high class vaudeville artists in continuous performance," which was something less than the truth, and the Bowery restaurant beginning to get the biggest play was Louis Stauch's Newark House.

When Stauch came to the beach in 1877 he was sixteen years old. He had been hired to play piano at a wedding in nearby Bath Beach and promised a bed when the party was over; but his host reneged, and Stauch slept on Coney's sand. The next day he got a job with Paul Bauer, but he soon left to take a job in Daniel Welch's saloon. By day he was dishwasher and potato peeler; by night he was waiter, busboy, barkeep, and piano player—all for $15 a month and the privilege of sleeping on the kitchen floor. It was hard work, but Stauch had fallen in love with Coney Island. In two years he had saved $310. He leased Welch's place for $700 a year, and did so well that he renewed the lease for ten years at $2,000 a year. When a storm wrecked his first restaurant, he appealed to McKane. "I want to put up a building 60 by 120 feet," he said. "All right," said McKane, "I'll send my brother Jim to see you." McKane's brother came with a foreman. He scratched a small rectangle in the sand with the toe of his boot. "Make it 120 feet this way," he ordered, "and 60 feet that." Such, on the Coney Island of the 1880's, was a blueprint. Stauch, a silent, hardworking, humorless, goodhearted little man, won a reputation for serving a good, well-cooked meal at a reasonable price; his reputation spread across the nation. A few years later those who stopped in at Stauch's for a glass of Loewer's

The Bowery, back in the days when Jimmy Durante and Eddie Cantor and Vincent Lopez were singing and playing for $15 or $20 a week. COURTESY THE FRANCIS K. MOORE COLLECTION

Gambrinus beer on their way to Steeplechase might have heard a song sung by a skinny, intense, black-haired youngster. This was Israel Baline, who had not yet started writing his own songs under the name of Irving Berlin. And if the waiter who served their beer was a trifle slapdash, likely he was Frank Erickson who, having become impatient with the insecurity of his way of life, had already started a small handbook for the benefit of his fellow-waiters and was thereby launched on the career that would carry him to the summit of the nation's gambling business and, eventually, land him in jail.

Let a few years more pass, and the throngs on their way to Steeplechase would find this narrow street even more beguiling, for it had become the magnet for every song-plugger in the country, and in Carey Walsh's cabaret the perfesser at the piano was an exuberant youth named Jimmy Durante, and Eddie Cantor was one of the singing waiters, and down the street at Perry's the orchestra was a five-man combination with Vincent Lopez at the piano, and the cop on the beat was Jack West, Mae West's father, who liked to boast that he had been the first to introduce Van to Schenck. (But this was not quite true. Van & Schenck first worked together as motorman and conductor of a Brooklyn Rapid Transit trolley in Ridgewood, and their first professional engagement as a team was at Whiting's Cabaret on Surf Avenue—the same joint that was later called the College Inn.)

And there was bloody excitement on this narrow street, too, for it was here that a Coney Island strong man, Cyclone Lewis, hired himself out to an East Side gangster from New York named Kid Twist, to murder a gambler known only as The Bottler. Kid Twist was a Bowery regular, for he was enamored of one of Perry's girl singers, a marshmallow named Carroll Terry, to whom he used to pay court nearly every night. There was, however, competition for her favors. One night in 1911 a car was drawn up, waiting for Miss Terry just around the corner from the Bowery, when the rival thug, Louis (The Lump) Poggi, drew two beads, and (Bang!) there went Kid Twist and (Bang!) there went Cyclone Lewis. For any who cared to linger, the entertainment in those Bowery cabarets was excellent but, as Jimmy Durante remarked later, "You couldn't build a Sunday School out of those night spots."

The Bowery burned and burned again, and there were preachers who said it was a judgment. The times changed, and the cabarets disappeared, but at his end of the street Louis Stauch patiently rebuilt his restaurant after each conflagration, at length erecting an immense building that housed the biggest dance floor in the world. Certainly it was as big as a regulation football field; indeed, one winter night a semi-pro team, the Mohawks, did play an outfit representing a Jersey City athletic club, and the winning touchdown carried the referee right through the front door and out into the snow on the Bowery. Another who rebuilt each time was Paddy Shea, the Old Reliable, the Original, who first called his saloon the St. Dennis and later changed its name to the Gilsey House, in a frank attempt to snare the custom of the sports who for years had patronized the old Gilsey House in Manhattan. Paddy was a dour little man who watched the shifting crowds on the Bowery for more than four decades. Every morning, promptly at ten, he came out to sit in the sun in front of his saloon, like a reflective old turtle. He watched the cabarets and dance pavilions disappear, and the carnival concessions take their place; he heard the voice of the barker, hideously magnified by electricity, replace the voice of the singing waiter; he noted how the people walking west toward Steeplechase changed when the subways reached out to Coney. And he was intransigent: change, he insisted, was no improvement. Prohibition proved his point. Stauch sold his restaurant, Shea moved away from the Bowery, and the speakeasies crept in. A swart, squat young man, with a baleful eye, walked along the Bowery: he earned his pay as a bouncer for one of the speakeasies: his name was Al Capone. And flanking the shadowy saloons on every side there were the carnival concessions. By 1925 the Bowery was the epitome of every midway of every carnival in the country—penny arcades, waxwork museums, freak shows, ball games ("Here y'are! Everybody wins! Three balls for a dime!"), weight-guessers, ring-tosses, high strikers, fortune-tellers, roller coasters, fun houses, and shooting galleries. The crowds were bigger, and that man on stilts, stalking his way through the throngs, a walking advertisement for Steeplechase, that was a brash, likeable young Cockney named Archie Leach, an acrobat by trade but temporarily down on his luck, but we need not be sorry for him for presently he will have found his way to Hollywood and have changed his name to Cary Grant.

And the Bowery became a cacophony of sound, compounded of voices and the unceasing blare of a hundred radios and a score of barkers and the rhythmic crash of roller coasters and voices, the sudden unexpected snatch of conversation overheard: "You wanna drink, baby?" "With you, Ugly? You're so ugly, you must take ugly pills"—and the smell, a rich, cloying mixture of corn-on-the-cob and dime-store perfume and salt air and frying knishes and frozen custard and gunpowder and Shetland ponies' dung—and the crowds grew steadily bigger, and they shifted and eddied back and forth and paused here and there to encircle a barker or were diverted by this ride or that ball game but sooner or later they moved west and came to Steeplechase. Since 1940 they may have been drawn by the sight of the parachute jump, a 250-foot tower that was brought to Coney from Flushing Meadows after the New York World's Fair of 1939. Whatever attracted them, sooner or later they ended up standing in line to ride on the Steeplechase Horses, as people have done now for two generations. For the horse-play that follows this ride is a distillate of the hoary Steeple-chase formula.

It is the founder's formula, unchanged. It is the abiding proof that George C. Tilyou was a master showman.

The ride begins inside the pavilion: a girl and her boy friend can both ride the same horse, he sitting behind her with his arms pleasantly around her waist. The course will take them outside the pavilion, a long gliding rise and a swoop around two graceful curves in the cool evening air and then a race down the home stretch and back into the pavilion again. When they dismount, they may start down either of two ramps but in any event they will fetch up on a small, brightly lighted stage where their only companions are a clown and a dwarf, both of whom eye them beadily. The girl and her boy friend are self-conscious; they are dimly aware that beyond the bright

Don't laugh, she may be someone's grandmother. These carefree flappers are aboard Steeplechase's Racing Derby. The year? 1928.   COURTESY STEEPLECHASE PARK

lights there are people; they can sense the hush and hear expectant giggles. They look about. They see that they must pass through a narrow gate to reach an exit off to their right which seems to be guarded by an enormous papier-mâché elephant. Cautiously—ladies first—the girl takes a step into the narrow passage. A sudden spurt of compressed air from a jet in the floor whips her skirt above her waist; she shrieks and whirls about into her boy friend's arms; the clown at the same time touches him with a rod, giving him a sharp electric shock; he leaps, and as he clutches at his buttocks the floor gives way beneath him. She reaches out a hand, and promptly the air jet sends her skirt soaring again. Thoroughly flustered, she scurries through the narrow passage, her boy friend on her heels; as he passes, the dwarf swats him with a slapstick. Again the floor moves madly under them; piles of barrels near the elephant suddenly buckle and appear to be tumbling down on top of

The horses used to be made of wood, now they are made of iron, but otherwise it is the same ride that captivated people in 1897.   COURTESY STEEPLECHASE PARK. PHOTO BY MAUREY GARBER

them; they can hear an appreciative crowd howling with mirth as they stumble off through the exit into the merciful wide spaces of the pavilion.

If they choose—and very often they do—they may take seats, if they can find them, in the small theatre and linger to watch others go through the same routine. Presently, like all those around them, they will be aching with laughter. There is undeniably something irresistibly comic about this sophomoric procedure. There may be those who are skeptical, but a brief visit will convince even the most determined sourpuss. Some who watch the routine for the first time are astonished at how seldom the victims complain. But in fact the clown, the dwarf, and the man who, from the howdah of the elephant, controls the compressed-air jets are a very smoothly functioning team. Years of experience have taught them which woman with the severe and pinched expression will not relish any monkeyshines, and which litigious man is spoiling for trouble; these are invariably passed through with no nonsense. The audience is, curiously, predominantly feminine, so it cannot be said that the show's attraction is exclusively sexual. Indeed, at a time when bathing suits display all but an individual's most private parts, there can be little allure in watching a dress whirled up. No, the charm is the ancient one of the man slipping head-over-heels on a banana skin, of the pratfall, of self-conscious dignity finding itself in a ludicrously undignified predicament. And how it works! And, no doubt, will forever.

Jimmy Onorato, Coney-born and Coney-bred, has for many years been employed by the Tilyou family to manage Steeplechase. Although the park is open only some five months a year, his is a full-time job of care and maintenance, annually cleaning up after one season and annually getting ready for the next. On one cold, raw January evening he happened to be in an office of the park near Surf Avenue and his attention was arrested by something common to the people who were passing by outside. The hour was after five in the afternoon, a chilling breeze off the ocean was whipping sleet over the sidewalks; altogether it was a time when—as Onorato considered—sensible folk would be thinking exclusively of home and warmth. Yet, he noticed, time after time these shivering people hurrying along Surf Avenue would notice where they were, would pause to look up at the glass-and-steel pavilion, would, some of them, even stop for a moment to smile or chuckle out loud before they hurried on again. Onorato at first was puzzled. He even stepped outside into the street to look back at the park, frowning, trying to figure what made these others laugh. Since that night he has noticed the same phenomenon, year after year. He has decided that their chuckles are wholly reminiscent. In a bleak, wintry moment of misery, they are cheered just to see the pavilion, and to remember the fun they have had there. And, Onorato hopes, cheered to think of the fun they will have there once again. It is what Coney at its best has always offered, and what it still offers.

COURTESY STEEPLECHASE PARK

~~Island on Earth

CONEY ISLAND has a disconcerting habit of confounding its critics. Like the leading character at the Irish wake, it delights in coming to life just as the obsequies are about to begin. One after another the pundits have announced the resort's imminent demise, but each time the old girl has merely kicked her heels the higher. Most recently, the combination of the decline of the nickel empire and the advent of the Second Great War spelled, it was widely supposed, Coney's ultimate finis. And then an extraordinary thing happened. The *New York Daily Mirror,* in cooperation with the United States Army Air Force, promoted an air show and a fireworks display at Coney, on July 3, 1947. The number of people to show up for the doings exceeded 2,500,000.

Now 2,500,000 people is a lot of people. It is more people than lived at the time in St. Louis or Cleveland or Baltimore or Detroit or Los Angeles or Philadelphia. Indeed, only Chicago and New York City contained more souls than were packed on Coney's beach and boardwalk at one time on that day. Never before, surely, in all history have so many people turned out for a single show. They were lined up solidly along the boardwalk;

they spilled out on the beach and, as the day wore on, the beach itself got so crowded that there was only standing room on the sand, people couldn't even sit down, and those in the very front rows found that as the tide came in they were obliged to take off their shoes and stockings and stand in the water. There simply was no space for them to push back to. Poor old Coney! Nobody goes there any more!

In fact, a lot of people still come to Coney, and they come from all over the country. It may be confidently set down that there will be, counting repeaters, fifty million visitors to Coney this summer, and next, and next. For while the resort may have changed—and indeed it has, often and violently—while today it may have lost some of its quondam glamor, while the space in which folks can play may today be more cramped than it was in, say, 1900 or 1910, Coney is still the nation's foremost amusement area. And, for very sufficient reasons, it is likely to maintain a firm grip on this claim for some years to come.

Today what is connoted by the term Coney Island is an enclave eighteen blocks long and two blocks wide. From West Fifth Street to West Twenty-third Street is zoned as an amusement area. It is, to those with long memories, a pathetically cramped space. Our fathers and grandfathers, of course, wag their heads condescendingly, for they recall a Coney Island that stretched from Oriental Point on the east to Norton's Point on the west, the whole sweep given over to amusement and entertainment of one kind or another. There can be no doubt that those days are forever vanished. To the east the great wooden hotels of Brighton Beach and Manhattan Beach are long since gone; today, in their stead, twenty-story apartment buildings march in serried ranks almost to the water's edge. What was once a playground for the nation's most fashionable is today a staid middle-class residential neighborhood, rather overcrowded as is most of New York City, and, apparently, daily growing more so. To the west all that remains of Norton's Point, once one of the liveliest and most disreputable holiday spots on the Atlantic coast, is the name, and likely even that will soon be forgotten. There is one trace left: those who take the subway to the Stillwell Avenue terminal will see, as they descend the stairs to the street, a sign telling them where they may find busses to Norton's Point. All else has been swallowed up by Sea Gate, a restricted, upper-middle-class residential area of unremitting respectability whose inhabitants would be mortified if they were accused of being Coney Islanders. They have set up a fence, from ocean to bay, to close off their tip of the Island, but they are separated from their neighbors in the garish entertainment district by more than a fence. As well from the north Coney feels the implacable pressures of change. Year by year more residential housing units have gone up, creeping each year closer to the ocean. But it does not seem possible that they will ever push any farther than the north side of Surf Avenue.

For we can hear the insistent voices: Thus far and no farther. They are not unanimous. Every now and again there proceeds

It was still wintertime, but on a Sunday these were the crowds that turned out to stroll along Coney's brand-new boardwalk, 1923.   COURTESY STEEPLECHASE PARK

from the offices of the Park Commissioner an ominous growl, indicative that Robert Moses is engrossed in another dream of lawn-flanked parkways and trim tennis courts. More and more people, the Commissioner has insisted, want healthy, outdoor recreation; fewer and fewer care for a "mechanical gadget" resort like Coney Island. But in the next breath, because he is a realistic man, Moses added: "Maybe we're kidding ourselves." And indeed, surely somebody is kidding himself if he believes, in the teeth of an annual congregation of fifty million pleasure-seekers, that such a "mechanical gadget" resort as Coney Island is not still very popular.

The mechanical resources of Coney are unique in America. They have appreciably dwindled, in the last couple of decades, but they still outnumber what can be offered by any other amusement park in the country. Besides the thirty-odd different rides and swings in Steeplechase, Coney affords three roller coasters—the Cyclone, the Thunderbolt, and the Tornado; it boasts what is surely the biggest Ferris wheel, the Wonder Wheel; it offers forty bathhouse establishments, seventy "ball" games, a dozen carrousels, five tunnel rides, three fun houses, a waxworks museum, six penny arcades, a score of shooting galleries, two freak shows, a variety of other games, rides, entertainments, and souvenir shops, thirty-two frozen dessert stands, and 330 food and drink establishments. And always there is the boardwalk, and always there is the beach, and always there is the sea.

And the expanding national economy of the past two decades has made many of these mechanical devices so valuable as to be, for all intents and purposes, unique. Certainly they cannot at the present time be duplicated, or at least would not be duplicated by any sane businessman. As an example of this truism, there is the case of a ride that cost, before the war, $80,000. It was insured for its replacement cost and, when it

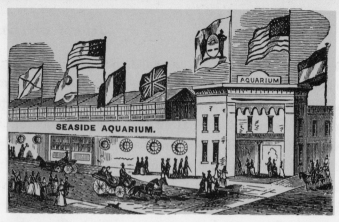

Back in the 1880's there was a primitive Aquarium on Coney Island, and folk complained that it raised a fierce stench.   SOUVENIR BOOKLET, HOTEL BRIGHTON C. 1880. N. Y. PUBLIC LIBRARY

burned in 1939, this cost was estimated at $130,000. It was decided, however, not to rebuild; the owners felt that they might as well wait until after the war and judge conditions at that time. In 1945 the replacement cost had soared to $250,000. Ten years later it was astronomical, and no one bothered to estimate it. What this means, quite simply, is that as matters now stand outdoor amusement park "mechanical gadgets" are prohibitively expensive; they cost so much that their operators cannot hope to amortize their investment at ten or even at twenty-five cents an admission. And this in turn means that Coney's position, as the nation's ranking amusement area, will be unchallenged for some time to come.

That the character of the resort will continue to change, of course, nobody can doubt. When Commissioner Moses extended one tentacle toward Coney, back in 1938, and clutched for his dominion the beach and the boardwalk, it was a portent. The Commissioner's tastes are urbane, civilized, and upper-middle-class. He likes a recreation area to be spruce and neat; he likes expanse, light, air; he prefers that the pleasure-seeker should have on every side prospects of delight. Coney has not been any of these things for something like forty years. But if the Commissioner can get his hands on the needed money, it will be again. Indeed, the shape of its future is already beginning to emerge. On the plot of land where Dreamland stood there is now New York City's new Aquarium; it delights the eye, it is set back against a sweep of lawn, its lines are trim and clean: it is typical of the Commissioner's taste. And he has made it clear that he hopes to plan other such exhibits. He is a patient man, as befits a long-range planner. Over the years, whenever one of Coney's absentee landlords, having decided he has milked a property sufficiently dry, lets a plot of real estate on or near the boardwalk go at a foreclosure sale, Moses is always on hand to bid the property in. He is, so to say, playing Monopoly, the parlor game that was so popular a few years ago. Already he has a number of choice sites along Surf Avenue, and still he bides his time. "I wouldn't want to sink Surf Avenue," he has said, somewhat wistfully, "but just get rid of about a third of it." There can be no question but what the Commissioner's vigorous hand would do Surf Avenue a lot of good.

Meantime, the entertainment entrepreneurs at Coney have themselves by no means been idle. There have been other changes at the resort, not of a dramatic kind, to be sure, but

In the spring of 1957, a modern Aquarium was opened as a year-round exhibit, a portent of further changes by Commissioner Moses.   COURTESY NEW YORK ZOOLOGICAL SOCIETY

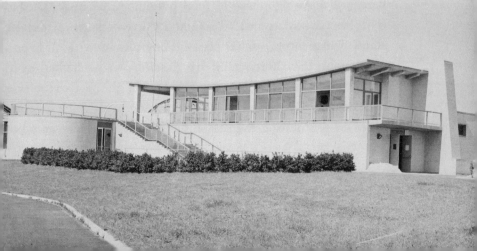

nonetheless very meaningful. In the declining days of the
nickel empire, the carnival midway games were, like as not, as
crooked as a corkscrew. Every other game was gaffed. Prizes
of any worth at all gathered dust from May to September; the
public took away only slum. Nor was the food of a standard to
satisfy the squeamish. And the rides, too, came in for their
share of bitter criticism, especially when, in 1937, a high school
student and a middle-aged man were killed when, in two
different accidents, they were thrown from roller coasters. But
in recent years, on all these scores, Coney's record has been
impressive.

The games are as honest as games of chance ever are. In
part this is due to the vigilance of the License Commission,
but an even more scrupulous control is exercised by the games'
operators themselves. These folk, veterans at slipping the gaff
into anything, have learned that at Coney the honest game
is good business. When one of their number begins, as they
say, to get a little of the best of it, they are the first to sense
the chicane and, by social pressure, to eliminate it.

As to the food and drink served at Coney, here the record
is, in its negative fashion, truly startling. The city's Health
Department began an intensive campaign, back in 1936, to
end food poisoning at the country's busiest beach. Since that
time, despite the fact that something like three-quarters of a
billion visitors have gobbled hot dogs, hamburgers, frozen
custards, roasted corn, clams, ice cream, and the like, there has
been not one single case of food poisoning at Coney. During
the resort's most recent season, the thirty-two frozen dessert
stands had a record of 100 per cent compliance with all health
regulations; the 330 food and drink establishments had a record
of 97 per cent compliance, and none of the violations was
major. Every Coney food and drink place gets a rigid inspection
at least twice during the season and the owners have come to

expect, in addition, at least one spot check by inspectors assigned to the area. They have learned, too, how to be good businessmen.

Since 1940 one man, William Olsen, tough, conscientious, and incorruptible, has been responsible for checking the safety of the rides at Coney. Technically, he is an elevator inspector for the city's Department of Buildings, but he has come to be a ranking expert on every kind of ride. His ear is attuned to the sound that each should make if it is operating at proper rhythm. When something sounds wrong, he does not hesitate to slap on a violation and close the ride down until it has been fixed. In 1956, indeed, he closed down one ride at the outset of the big Labor Day weekend—and its owner knew better than to complain. Olsen is justifiably proud of his record: there has been, during his tour of duty, no major accident due to mechanical failure of any Coney ride, and only one minor accident which did not involve serious injury. This safety record is unparalleled. The ride operators at Coney only wish that amusement parks elsewhere in the country had regulations as stringent as those that obtain at Coney, for they know that an accident anywhere can injure a ride's reputation everywhere. And they take satisfaction in the reflection that no Coney ride is responsible for any black eyes to the amusement industry.

These negative achievements, however valuable, yet leave the more important Coney Island businessmen discontented. They yearn for more positive, more glittering kudos. Some of them, remembering the banner day when 2,500,000 people packed their resort, hanker for spectacular theatricals, extravaganzas with the mammoth touch. The beach, they argue, can be the amphitheatre, and for their pageants they would convert

the sky and the sea into one vast stage. Prodded by their press-agent, Milton Berger, they dream of two-day Armed Forces Celebrations, of whopping fireworks displays, of theatrical and operatic presentations staged on vast platforms moored offshore, with the words and music broadcast by means of a network of loudspeakers spotted along the boardwalk. They envision aquatic carnivals to rival the most magnificent spectacles of the Roman Colosseum. And, one of these days, their dreams may come true.

The path on which the new Coney has been launched leads to a more decorous, a cleaner, a quieter, a more fashionable future, an upper-middle-class future. Today, with its large permanent population, the resort is already considerably more staid than it has been for many years. The old harridan still needs to have her face washed; her figure displays a regrettable tendency to slip out of its stays; her finery is patched and indeed she needs a whole new outfit. But her spirit is still contagious. You can see the twinkle in her eye for blocks away. When she laughs, you cannot help but laugh with her. And she knows her good points, and dwells on them.

For always there will be the salt sea and the sand, and always there will be the fun.

ᴛ has been convenient, in telling this history, to have occasional
ᴇcourse to obsolete or obsolescent slang, to carnival jargon, and to
ᴜnderworld cant. Usually the context makes the meaning of such
ᴡords or phrases clear. As additional assistance, however: ˙

blister: a woman of loose morals.

caper: a thieving or fraudulent exploit.

capper: an assistant in a confidence game.

carny: a carnival; the carnival world; also, a carnival worker.

chalk-eater: a horserace gambler whose preference is to bet on the favorite,
especially when the favorite is odds-on.

chutzpeh: a Yiddish phrase meaning colossal gall.

claw: one of a gang of pickpockets.

con: as a noun, this word refers to a confidence game. As a verb, *to con* means
to win the chump's confidence so that he may the more easily be defrauded.
A *short con* is a fraudulent scheme that requires only a brief time for
success, a matter of hours.

double-banker: a double-crosser; especially, one who physically muscles in on
an assault on an unsuspecting victim.

flat-joint: a carnival concession where gambling is the lure.

gaff: as a noun, a dishonest device that controls the play of a *flat-joint;* as a
verb, to install such a device.

grift: dishonest practice, and more especially of the less violent types. A *grifter*
is usually a cardsharp, a pickpocket, a *con* man, or a petty swindler.

gun: a pickpocket. The term has widened, in latter-day parlance, to include
any thief; but precisely a *gun* is a *dip* is a *claw* is a skilled pickpocket.

heeler: a political henchman.

high striker: the carnival device, perhaps thirty feet high, in which a wire
runs up to a noisy brass gong on top, and a contestant attempts to ring the
gong by striking a teeter-board in such a way as to send a small cylinder
of tough rubber up the wire.

jug: as a verb, to send to jail.

mitt-joint: a palm-reader's tent.

moll-buzzer: a thief, usually youthful, who specializes in snatching women's purses from baby carriages. *Moll-buzzers* work in pairs: one to distract the woman's attention, the other to grab the purse and run, after which the first blocks, while feigning to assist, the second's capture.

monte: a three-card variation of the three-shell game, in turn a descendant of thimble-rig, played with three thimbles weighted in the top with solder. The three-shell game requires of the chump that he guess under which of the shells is the pea; *three-card monte* requires that he guess which of the three rapidly-shuffled cards is (usually) the ace of spades. Sleight-of-hand is less important to a monte dealer than his running chatter, calculated to distract the chump's attention. David W. Maurer, the expert on various underworld argots, has said that Colonel Weaver, dean of shell-men, once grossed $4,000 in one day at the three-shell game.

outside flash: the gallery of garish posters, called valentines, in front of which works the barker for a freak show, or other sideshow attraction.

panel-girl: the chief distraction in that ancient swindle, the badger game. The *panel-girl*, using whichever wiles were hers to command, distracted the attention of the chump whilst valuables were extracted from his clothing through the panel of a wall to an adjoining room.

pineapple: a procurer; one who inveigles others into criminal deeds.

pitchman: a peddler who sells novelties, gimcrack goods, balloons, small mechanical toys, and so on, from a small *pitch*, or collapsible stand.

prattman: a member of a pickpocket mob, but one of lesser ability. The function of the prattman is to bustle a chump in a crowd in such fashion as to expose the chump's *pratt*, i.e., rear trousers pocket, to the meticulous ministrations of the *claw*.

pool-selling: a method of gambling on horseraces. It has been almost entirely superseded by bookmaking and the pari-mutuel machines.

push: a crowd of people. To *gather a push* is to collect a crowd of people. In carnival lingo, a *push* is also the process by which a chump is bustled up close to a game or pitch.

shark: a professional card-player or dice-thrower, competent, shrewd, and talented.

shill, shillaber: an assistant in the ballyhoo of a sideshow attraction or concession, who at an appointed moment moves to "buy" a ticket as a method of prodding others to buy; also, an assistant to a swindler.

slum: the next-to-worthless junk offered as prizes at carnival concessions. In a *gaffed* game, the public wins only *slum*. They are attracted by, and attempt to win, the *flash*, but never do.

till-tapper: a petty thief; especially one who, working as part of a team distracts a shop-owner so that a confederate may dip his hand in the till and escape with the loose cash.

tinhorn: an adjective usually applied to a small-time gambler.

tip: a crowd of people; a *push*. To *turn a tip* is to persuade a group of people to buy tickets for a carnival attraction.

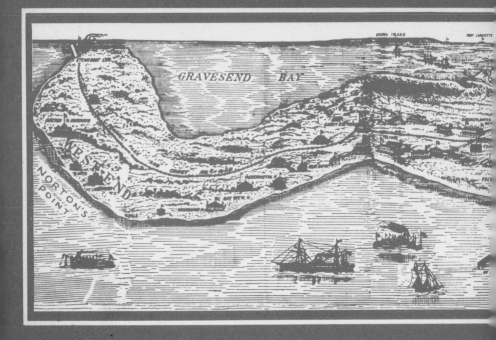

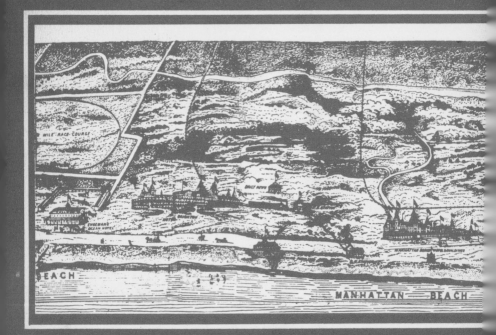